The Roots of the Periphery

The Roots of the Periphery

A History of the Gonds of Deccan India

BHANGYA BHUKYA

OXFORD
UNIVERSITY PRESS

OXFORD
UNIVERSITY PRESS

Oxford University Press is a department of the University of Oxford.
It furthers the University's objective of excellence in research, scholarship,
and education by publishing worldwide. Oxford is a registered trademark of
Oxford University Press in the UK and in certain other countries.

Published in India by
Oxford University Press
YMCA Library Building, 1 Jai Singh Road, New Delhi 110 001, India

ISBN-13: 978-0-19-946808-9
ISBN-10: 0-19-946808-7

Typeset in Adobe Garamond Pro 10.5/13.5
by The Graphics Solution, New Delhi 110 092
Printed and bound in India at Repro India Ltd., Mumbai

To
David Hardiman
in honour of his classic studies
on the Adivasis of India

CONTENTS

FIGURES

TABLES

ABBREVIATIONS

APSA	Andhra Pradesh State Archives
Comm.	Commissioner
CP	Central Provinces
CPI(ML)	Communist Party of India (Marxist–Leninist)
CrPC	Criminal Procedure Code
GSS	Gondwana Sangarshana Samiti
HD	Home Department
ITDA	Integrated Tribal Development Agency
LTR	Land Transfer Regulation
PM	Political and Military
PWG	People's War Group
RD	Revenue Department
RGSU	Raj Gond Students' Union
RSU	Radical Students Union
SS	Survey and Settlement

PREFACE

THE POPULAR IMAGE OF THE *adivasis* (indigenous peoples or aboriginals) of India as isolated, primitive, barbaric, and uncivilized is what led me to write this book. The crucial question is why certain social groups continue to lead a rugged and wild life, or, as James Scott says, why did civilization not reach the hills and forests? Importantly, why did adivasis evade the state and choose to live in the peripheries of empire, which are now referred to as Scheduled Areas? These are the main concerns of this book, which aims to explore the meaning of such state-evading politics while studying the process of the making of peripheries in India. A periphery is produced mainly by state-making processes or encounters between the mainland state and self-governing communities. Although periphery-making is today a universal phenomenon, there are continental and regional varieties of the periphery. The advent of the Aryans and their subsequent state and empire formations laid the foundation for the creation of the periphery in India. This process acquired momentum during the Sultanate and Mughal regimes, and became more aggressive under British colonialism. The British colonial state is the main focus of this book. However, this study is not about the making of the state or governance in India, but about the effects of state power on subaltern communities such as the Gonds of Deccan India who are the subject of this work.

State-making in India involved war, destruction, violence, taxation, subjugation, and caste suppression. In the process, many self-governing communities were driven into non-state spaces—in this case, the hills and forests. The hill and forest communities had historically maintained differences from those in the mainland/plains. The colonial rulers dubiously created an administrative divide between the plains and the hills, and typified hill and forest communities as isolated, primitive, barbaric, and uncivilized. Forest communities and caste-Hindu society were presented as polar opposites—uncivilized and civilized respectively. There had indeed been a historically embedded difference between the plains and hills, but this was more political, a difference between a statist society and a self-governing society. This book primarily argues that the difference imagined and articulated by the adivasi communities was deeply rooted in self-rule and self-determinism. In this sense, the historically embedded difference between the plains and hills goes beyond the colonial divide. One aim of this book is to study the effects of this colonial divide on the Gonds, while constructing their social history.

This book developed from postdoctoral research on the Gond community of Deccan India undertaken over six years. The idea for this study emerged during a field trip to Adilabad district of Telangana during my doctoral work on the Lambadas of this region. I was astonished to find many ruined forts of the Gond rajas in the area. Local people recounted heroic stories associated with these forts. This made me realize that the Gond community has a strong history of politics. The immediate question that struck me was: how had a ruling community been reduced to such a (materially) vulnerable position? After I completed my work on the Lambadas, I began thinking more seriously about the Gonds. I made many visits to Adilabad district to understand Gond life before I consulted any archival data. Every visit led to me reformulating my research question. Initially, I wanted to document only the history of the Gond rajas. But as my investigations progressed, I learnt from the Gonds that all the present-day non-adivasi towns had at one point of time been Gond *gudam*s (hamlets). My respondents could actually cite dates that marked the arrival of non-adivasi families in their gudams, and repeatedly spoke about how these gudams were being converted into caste-Hindu villages.

That was the point at which I completely reformulated my study, and decided to trace the history of the marginalization of the Gonds and their retreat into the hills and forests. I must emphasize that I learned much about their history and culture from them, rather than from the written literature. Although I have used archival data extensively in this book, many of the arguments were shaped through my interactions with the Gonds. It is difficult to thank all the Gond friends who educated me on their history and culture, but I must at least acknowledge my gratitude to those who gave me long interviews: Dr Thodasam Chandu, Mesram Manohar, Mesram Somji, Gondraje Atram Bir Shah, Atram Laxmana Rao, and Purkaraju Jangu.

I turned my observations and interactions with the Gonds into research questions and submitted a proposal for postdoctoral studies to the Department of History at the School of Oriental and African Studies (SOAS), University of London. The SOAS history department was happy to accept my proposal and invited me for the January 2010 semester to undertake the study. I was fortunate to have Dr Shubnum Tejani as my mentor at SOAS during this period. I must thank her for her warm friendship and the academic insights which shaped my preliminary thoughts on this study. Considerable research was done at the India Office Library, London, and I sincerely thank its staff for assistance provided. I am grateful to my friend Shamrao I. Koreti for making available to me his own collection of material on the Gonds of Chandrapur and helping me to explore data at the Vidarbha Archives, Nagpur. My thanks are also due to the staff of the Andhra Pradesh State Archives, Hyderabad.

I have presented some aspects of this study at the Centre for South Asian Studies Seminar, SOAS; at the International Workshop on 'Space, Capital, and Social History in South Asia' organized by the Department of History, University of Göttingen, Germany; the International Seminar on 'Social Exclusion: Meaning and Perspectives' organized by the Centre for the Study of Social Exclusion and Inclusive Policy, University of Hyderabad; a national seminar on 'Governance, Socio-Economic Disparity and Social Unrest in the Scheduled Areas of India' at the Tata Institute of Social Sciences, Guwahati campus, India; a national seminar on 'Understanding Emancipation Today: Theory,

Philosophy, Politics', Department of Cultural Studies, English and Foreign Languages University, Hyderabad; and the Presidential Address for 'Section III: Modern Andhra History' at the 38th session of the Andhra Pradesh History Congress, Tirupati, Andhra Pradesh. I have benefited a lot from the discussions that followed these presentations. I am especially grateful to Ravi Ahuja, Virginius Xaxa, Gaddam Krishna Reddy, K. Satyanarayana, and Madhava Prasad for their invitations and critical comments and suggestions. Earlier versions of Chapters 2 and 3 of this book were published in *Modern Asian Studies* and *Indian Historical Review* respectively. I thank the editorial board of these journals for considering my articles for publication.

While carrying out this study, I received enormous support and encouragement from many of my old teachers and friends. I wish to start by acknowledging David Hardiman, who has been the source of my inspiration throughout this study. I am grateful to David for reading most of the chapters of this book and offering those wonderful insights and comments which altered many of my preliminary arguments. The other source of inspiration has been my old friend Gita Ramaswamy, who has in many respects been involved in this study from the beginning. I must say it is impossible to thank her for all her unceasing support and encouragement throughout this study. I must also place on record my heartfelt gratitude to Susie Tharu for readily agreeing to read the entire manuscript and offering comments that shaped many of my preliminary ideas into more effective statements. I am also thankful to G. Aloysius, Kalpana Kannabiran, and Murali Manohar for their discussions and sharp insights. I must thank Bodhi s.r. for the wonderful discussions on André Béteille. I am grateful to my new colleagues at the University of Hyderabad for their support; thanks especially to my young colleagues Varghese and Eshwar Rao who were always helpful. I am also thankful to the anonymous reviewers at Oxford University Press for their wonderful comments and suggestions, which resulted in a complete restructuring of the introduction and epilogue of this book.

I could have not completed this study without the financial support of the British Academy. A major part of this study was completed as a British Academy Visiting Fellow at SOAS. I must also acknowledge partial financial support from the SAP Program, Department of History, University of Hyderabad.

Finally, my family which bore the pains of this study: I do not even know how to thank my wife, Sujatha, who has been a source of continuous support and encouragement throughout this time by taking on the major burden of looking after our family. My son, Kanishka, still hates me for spending my life in my study. When I moved to London, my daughter, Swetcha, was six months old, and I missed her early smiles, but later, when I was working on the manuscript, her continuous interruptions, her warm touch, and her flipping in and out of my study helped me cope with the frustrations and stresses of this work.

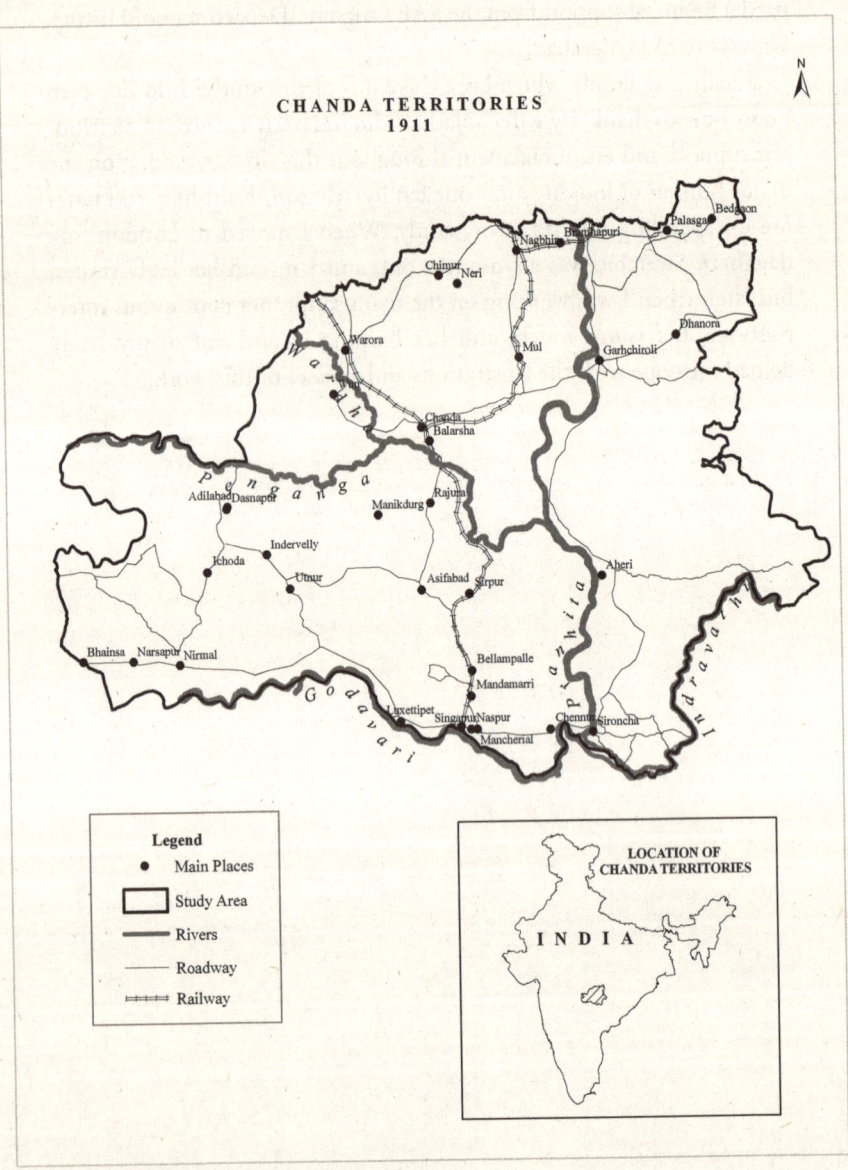

Map showing Chanda territories in 1911

Source: Redrawn based on V.W. Grigson's *The Aboriginal Problem in the Central Provinces and Berar* (Nagpur: Government Printing, C.P. and Berar, 1944).

Note: Map not to scale.

INTRODUCTION

ADIVASI HABITATS, POPULARLY TERMED *JANGLI* (wild), Agency, or Scheduled Areas (as classified by the administration or various agencies) have historically been perceived and constructed as the peripheries of India's mainland. A majority of adivasis live either on the borders of the forest or in the forests. Although historically embedded differences exist, the boundary between the mainland/plains and the hills/forests was administratively developed principally under British colonial rule. The border has now become a zone of contestation, as both adivasis and non-adivasis live here, simultaneously in harmony and in tension with each other. This has happened also partly because forests and hills are spread not only along the fringes or borders of India, but are present in the centre too. The whole of central India and the Deccan abound in forests, and these regions formed the peripheries of empires in Indian history. They also sheltered millions who escaped or migrated from the plains or were driven from the plains to the forests.[1] This is to say that the divide is a by-product of the historical encounter between dominant and subordinate groups of the mainland plains.

Therefore, one needs to see the formation of the periphery as a political act, and not simply as the drawing of administrative or geographical boundaries. Only then can the categories of 'mainland' and 'periphery' be seen as the political and cultural divides that they are. However, these categories have for long been essentialized in terms of the binaries of civilized–primitive, tamed–wild, modern–backward, governed–ungoverned. Such essentialist constructions subvert the political meaning of the periphery. Importantly, the victorious and dominant groups have produced and reproduced these divides through history in order to subjugate the subordinated in perpetuity.[2] This book traces the history and politics of this divide, narrating the case of the Gonds of Deccan India, an adivasi community.

The dichotomy between the mainland and periphery in India is generally perceived in terms of caste and tribe, and the study of caste and tribe has generally been regarded as part of the empire of sociology and anthropology, rather than of history or any other human science. The legacy of colonial anthropology has been carried forward by Indian anthropologists and sociologists even after independence, though from a different standpoint that often goes by the name of national integration or the creation of a universal class. In other words, when it comes to adivasis, the epistemological constructions of Indian scholars have been centred either on the idea of national integration or on the concept of class.[3]

In the first decades of independent India, André Béteille, one of the most prominent sociologists in India, produced influential studies problematizing the formation of class, caste, and 'tribe' in India and investigating their relations.[4] In one important study, he endeavoured to show that there is no difference between tribe and peasantry in India.[5] Subsequently, in a bid to liberate Indian sociological studies from the meta-narrative of evolutionism, Béteille preached the use of the concept of 'coexistence' to study the relations between caste-Hindu society and adivasi society.[6] He took the concept of coexistence from D.D. Kosambi's study of early India,[7] which shows the side-by-side existence of adivasis and caste-Hindus. Béteille developed the concept of coexistence in a historical approach which allows us to study a society in a particular space and time, saying:

> Despite changes in the fortunes of individual tribes and despite incursions into tribal territories by Hindu kings and Hindu ascetics, the tribal identity never became fully effaced in any of the major regions of the country. It is remarkable how close to such renowned ancient and medieval centres of

civilization as Gaya, Ujjain and Madurai tribes could still be found living in their natural setting, so to say, well into the present century. The Hindu kingdom—and to a large extent its Muslim successor—did not seek to eliminate tribes but allowed or even encouraged them to live on its margins.[8]

As is evident from these lines, Béteille suggests that the category of 'tribe' is a historical necessity, and that it grew in the lap of civilization—in other words, in caste-Hindu society or statist society. By invoking the concept of 'coexistence', he romanticizes the relationship between adivasis and non-adivasis. By saying this I do not mean to imply that adivasi politics and society were isolated or closed. For many centuries, as we will see shortly, a complex relationship existed between plains and hill people. Responding to a more recent debate on indigenous people, Béteille argues that it is difficult to apply the concept of 'indigeneity' in South Asia as castes and tribes have fused so intimately and no population can be described as settlers.[9] What is missing in Béteille's argument is a discussion of the historically developed tensions between India's 'mainland' plains and its forests and hills. This book points to the historically embedded tensions that existed between the two societies despite their interdependency. Importantly, the term 'coexistence' expunges the history of wars, struggles, resistances, contestations, and insurgencies by the adivasis against India's mainland plains people; further, it obscures adivasi marginalization in the history written by plains people. In other words, the term ignores the contested history of the making of the periphery in India, which is the main concern of this book.

A similar argument has also been propounded by Nandini Sundar. For Sundar, British colonialism was a significant watershed in the history of the adivasis, which produced state effects in the hills and forests of India. She argues that the frontier areas were not isolated from the larger economy in pre-colonial India; on the contrary, they were crucial in shaping the regional economies. Colonial intervention destroyed these local economies and constructed the adivasi areas as isolated regions. Sundar critiques colonialism for creating a divide between tribe and caste. She also worries that the adivasi areas have not yet been absorbed fully into the capitalist economy.[10] In a similar vein, challenging the general assumption that the adivasi people have always lived in forests and practised shifting cultivation from time immemorial, Archana Prasad argues that the adivasis of central India practised settled agriculture till the advent of the Marathas. It was the subsequent marginalization of adivasis by caste-Hindu immigrants that forced them to adopt shifting cultivation.[11] On these grounds, she questions the theory of 'original inhabitants' and contests the labelling of adivasis as *swadeshis* (aboriginals). This position reminds us of that of G. S. Ghurye, the renowned sociologist of India, who described adivasis as backward Hindus. Indeed, Prasad charges anthropologists—particularly Verrier Elwin and the environmentalists—with ecological romanticism and criticizes them for stigmatizing the adivasis by attributing an aboriginal identity to them.[12] Prasad is probably the strongest critic of the colonial construction of adivasi society as primitive and as practising *bewar* (shifting cultivation). She also observes that such constructions not only prevented the adivasis from transforming into a labouring class, but also blocked their region from being integrated into the capitalist economy.[13]

Although both Sundar and Prasad have significantly contributed to our knowledge of adivasi society, their studies have some limitations in that they romanticize the coexistence of adivasis and caste-Hindus in pre-colonial India. One has to see this so-called coexistence as a political strategy by the adivasis to maintain their sovereignty and control over their territories. Sundar and Prasad read colonial rule in opposition to pre-colonial formations. This approach does not allow them to explore the historically built contentious relations between caste-Hindus and adivasis in pre-colonial India. These authors have essentially looked at the adivasi question from a modernist perspective that strongly believes in a universal class society. Their advocacy of the integration of adivasi economy in the regional economy of pre-colonial India obscures and indeed expunges the divide and dichotomy between castes and adivasis. The main danger with their anachronistic argument is that it posits a singular peasant or labouring class, brushing aside the dichotomy between mainland India and its periphery.[14] Taking their overall argument forward from this standpoint, both Sundar and Prasad seem to share the position of integrationists/assimilationists who not only advocate complete absorption of adivasis into caste-Hindu society, but also their integration into the capitalist economy in independent India. A series of volumes have been produced by the Indian Institute of Advanced

Studies, Shimla, advocating this philosophy of assimilation.[15] Thus, these studies (based both on modernist and integrationist approaches) have failed to give an ideological integrity to adivasi society.

Such modernist and integrationist constructions place adivasis in a disadvantageous position. In such interpretations, adivasis lose all ability (and the rights) to negotiate with the modern state. Yet for the adivasis, their premodern identity has been an important means of negotiating with the modern expansionist state. As Ajay Skaria puts it, 'wildness', or being jangli, was in itself a political claim that was interpreted in different ways by both the forest-based adivasi societies as well as those located outside of the forests.[16] In recent times, the notions of wildness or 'jangli' and tribe or adivasi have been reconfigured by the adivasis in a more positive sense and to their advantage. Indeed, it sets the ground for their new politics aimed at keeping the state obliged to protect and realize their rights. Against the background of such politics, it is important to read 'mainland' and 'periphery' as continuously engaged with each other. Only a reading such as this shows the adivasis as agents in carving out a space for themselves in the modern state establishment. It is important to write the history of the periphery from the vantage point of the present.

In his recent study of the Zomia, a remote hill people living in the India–Bangladesh–Myanmar border areas, James Scott develops a history of the periphery in which he underlines the distinction between the 'civilized' society of the plains regions in Asia and the 'wild' societies of the mountain and forest tracts, where each exists in a continuing dialogue or a relationship of dependence and tension.[17] Scott's main argument is that lowland and upland are both products of *state-making processes* in history:

> [The] pattern of state-making and state-unmaking produced, over time, a periphery that was composed as much of refugees as of peoples who had never been state subjects. Much of the periphery of states became a zone of refuge or 'shatter zone', where the human shards of state formation and rivalry accumulated willy nilly, creating regions of bewildering ethnic and linguistic complexity. State expansion and collapse often had a ratchet effect as well, with fleeing subjects driving other peoples ahead of them seeking safety and new territory.[18]

Scott foregrounds an unending conflict between the upland and the lowland, which in turn produced complexities in the relationship between the two. He says the distinctive features of hill societies, their agriculture, religion, social system, and their physical dispersal, are consciously designed to escape from the effects of the state. For him, primitivism does not precede civilization, it is the continuing antithesis of civilization. Further, Scott argues that the rude character of the hill societies should not be seen as a result of them being left behind, as generally held by evolutionists, but instead as 'barbarism by design', which he calls 'secondary primitivism'. He argues that the upland people voluntarily and purposefully adopted barbarism and primitivism not only to evade the state but also to minimize the likelihood that a state-like concentration of power will arise among them.[19]

However, Scott has been criticized for his overgeneralizations on the relationship between the lowland and upland.[20] One important danger in Scott's argument is that it romanticizes primitivism, although the broader framework of his study is useful for understanding the trajectories of the formation of the periphery and its relation with the mainland across the world. The Indian reality, in particular, given the presence of caste, is different from that of Southeast Asia. The phenomenon of tribes becoming castes and castes becoming tribes was present in Indian history till the advent of British rule. Many historical processes in India were ruptured and deflected by caste practices. It is therefore difficult to see the resonance of universal phenomena in the way they occurred in other parts of the world. One has to read every historical phenomenon in India against the backdrop of caste. Scott's description of the periphery as egalitarian and heterogeneous reminds us of Rousseau's state of nature.[21] The periphery in India was also stratified, and this stratification was largely sourced from the philosophy of caste. The relations between social groups were full of tension.[22] However, these differences within the periphery were counterbalanced through cultural bonds and celebrations, and a difference held in common against mainland India was maintained throughout their history by the people of the periphery.[23] This book essentially studies the history of this difference that was mainly rooted in self-rule and self-determination.

IN DEFENCE OF THE PERIPHERY

The history of the creation of the periphery in India may be traced back to the advent of the Aryans. The Aryans conquered the indigenous Naga people and settled first in the Punjab and then in the Gangetic basin and coastal strip of the peninsula.[24] As they advanced eastwards from the sixth century BCE onwards, the Aryans burned down the forests. Burning the forests was their method of clearing land for cultivation. This is confirmed by various adjectives for *agni* (fire) in the Rgveda. Agni is described as the swallower of the forest, or as the 'axe'. The burning of the forest is represented not just as a method of land clearing, but also as an action to satisfy the Aryan god of fire, Agni. The popular Mahabharata story of the burning of the Khandava forest (on the Jamuna river) to satisfy Agni is a well-known story of holocaust in which all living creatures were burned alive.[25] The expansion of the Aryans into the Gangetic basin and coastal strip of the Indian peninsula involved ruthless destruction of the Nagas. Kosambi explains, 'The Aryans trampled down so many isolated primitive groups and their beliefs, to create the pre-conditions for the formation of a new type of society from the remains.'[26] This process thus forced the Nagas towards central India and north-east India, both described as the peripheries of Aryavarta in the Hindu epics.[27] It is interesting to note here that the Gonds of central India are identified with the early Nagas.[28] Importantly, the Gangetic valley that came to be known as Aryavarta was established as the mainland of India and the regions beyond it as its fringes. Thus, the early settlements of the Aryans created for the first time a boundary between the mainland and forests in India, which was further constructed culturally in Hindu religious texts.[29] In fact, both Brahmanic Hindu texts and Buddhist/Jaina texts constructed Aryans as civilized and *mleccha/milakkha* (indigenous tribes) as barbarians from the sixth century BCE onwards.[30]

The encounter between the Aryan and the non-Aryan became more vigorous with the intensification of the state-making process in India, which pushed innumerable non-Aryan communities towards non-state spaces or forests and hills.[31] Vyaghraraja and Simharaja (the tiger and lion kings of the great forest) who ruled the whole central Indian forest in the early Christian era were conquered by the Aryan emperors. The tiger and lion are both tribal totemistic names, and they were royal symbols of the Gond kingdoms of the medieval period.[32] The fact is that Aryan groups successfully sedentarized many non-Aryan communities and made them state subjects. However, like escaping slaves in other parts of the world, those who were lovers of freedom evaded the state by running away to non-state spaces. It is these people who are now branded as the tribes of India.[33] This is to say that the adivasis of India are those who evaded empire building in history and believed strongly in self-rule and self-governance.[34] As will be evident from this study, this has been a continuous process in Indian history right up to the twentieth century.

State-making processes, which involved land enclosures, sedentarization, migration, wars, and destruction, produced peripheries across the world. Warfare by bigger empires that began in India with the advent of the Sultans continued till the final war of the British with the Marathas in 1818. If an army passed through a village, that village would be destroyed. On coming to know about the army's impending arrival, villagers in the plains would abandon their villages and run away into the forests. Evasion of land tax by escaping to the forest was a common phenomenon in medieval India. Many communities also embraced the forests and hills in order to escape from caste practices on the mainland plains.[35] Importantly, in India, state expansion into the forests and hills was largely achieved through land grants. This process began with the Vakataka (150 BCE) period and continued throughout history. Lands were granted to Buddhist temples in the beginning and later to Hindu temples and Brahmans. Land grants reached their peak under the Guptas, during whose rule vast forest areas were brought under the state, both directly and indirectly.[36]

Clearing the forest for agriculture has been a continuous process in history. This practice was vigorous when state-making processes were pursued aggressively under the big empires. In India, the process picked up momentum under Mughal rule. The development of agriculture was crucial to the Mughal rulers for enhancing state revenue. To realize their objective, they adopted two strategies: the extension of the area under cultivation, and increase in the cultivation of cash crops. As vast areas lay untilled, these were given for cultivation under multiple tenures. Peasants were encouraged to bring new land under cultivation through offers of revenue concessions. The land which was brought under cultivation for the first time was taxed half or less than half in the first year, and the rate was thereafter raised annually till the fifth year, when the full amount was reached.[37] These concessions led to the formation of new villages near the forests and hills. It is recorded that the number of villages in Mughal north India was almost double the number of villages in the last decades of the nineteenth century. The reason cited for such a drastic decrease is that many villages in the eighteenth century became deserted or were merged with other, bigger villages for better defence.[38] Interestingly, much before the Mughals, small kingdoms in the south played an equal role in expanding the state-making process into the forests and hills by bringing waste and forest lands under cultivation.

From the thirteenth century, vast forest areas were cleared in the Deccan and deeper south by the Kakatiyas, Vijayanagaras, and Qutb Shahis. Until the reign of the Kakatiyas, the whole of the central Deccan region was largely covered by dense forests and sparsely inhabited by pastoral groups and adivasi communities.[39] The Kakatiyas evolved a specific system called the Nayaka system to expand agriculture into the forests, in which *nayaka*s acted as village chiefs. The nayakas were brought from the coastal Andhra region and assigned huge tracts of forest land to be brought under cultivation. The nayakas formed new villages in the forests and wastelands and developed agriculture by building tank irrigation. Kakatiya rulers are famous for their tank-irrigation systems.[40] It is estimated that about 5,000 tanks were built by the nayakas under the Kakatiyas. This system had indeed laid the foundation of feudal practices in the region. However, this tank irrigation established a new economy which gradually transformed former herders or local cultivators into a predominantly agrarian society.[41] Similar trends were continued by the Vijayanagaras and Qutb Shahis. Tank irrigation was encouraged with revenue concessions by the Vijayanagaras, and this brought vast forest lands under cultivation.[42] The Qutb Shahis adopted a policy of rent-free lands to encourage the expansion of agriculture in the region. Following a tradition started by the Hindu rulers, the Qutb Shahis exempted Brahmans completely from land-revenue assessment, whereas Muslims had to pay half the assessment.[43] This process drove many social groups to the forests and hills. However, the process was full of tension. Empire building in the forest was often resisted by local people. The popular legend about the heroic fight of Sammakka and Sarakka against the expansion of the Kakatiyas in the Warangal forests is still celebrated by the Koya adivasis of Telangana.[44] Another popular legend, that of Sarvayi Papadu's fight against Mughal expansion in Telangana, is also well remembered by the people of Telangana.[45]

Thus, the expansion of agriculture was crucial in forming the periphery in India. And the process was full of tension between new groups and historically settled early groups. However, these tensions were mediated through negotiation, dialoguing, and sharing powers. Indeed, Mughal rulers realized the diversity of the Indian subcontinent and confined their rule to an overarching political suzerainty, exploiting peasant subjects through intermediaries and chiefs. Thus, multiple local sovereign powers were recognized and given a free hand in administering their territories. Even Gond chiefs acted as Mughal intermediaries. Many Kolis, Bhils, Gonds, Bhattis, and other adivasis worked with the Mughal army. This is not to claim that there was a complete surrender of the adivasis to the plains mainland, or adivasi assimilation into the dominant culture. But there were socio-economic and cultural exchanges between the mainland and the periphery. Forest produce and wood were crucial to agricultural development on the mainland. Some Gond rajas also married Rajput women. But the tension between the empire and its fringes continued. One should not forget the continuous attacks by the Mughals on Gond kingdoms.[46] As we will see shortly, the Gonds' relation with the mainland and its empires was tactical.

Interestingly, the chiefs of forest groups or Gonds who were pushed to the fringes of the empire emerged as dominant political powers from the middle of the thirteenth century in central India. They formed their own independent states and ruled vast territories. The agency for such assertions came from the subalternity of these communities. That is, subalternity itself acts as a catalyst in the self-emergence of any subordinated community. The Gond rajas kept regimes such as those of the Bahmanis, the Qutb Shahis, the Mughals, and the Marathas at a distance, and retained a great measure of autonomy. Their system of administration relied on independent traditions of the community that were crucial in the governance of land and in the shaping of political, social, and cultural institutions—traditions that had been historically built up. The Gond rajas also adopted the policy of expanding agriculture by inviting Maratha peasants to the region and providing tank irrigation. However, by the middle of the eighteenth century, these Gond dynasties lost their power to the Mughals and Marathas, who later transferred these territories to the British colonial rulers.[47]

Although Gond rule had ended, the rajas/*mokhasis* (Gond chiefs) who served as the traditional heads of groups of villages and as revenue collectors continued to enjoy their traditional powers under the rule of the Marathas and the Nizams. However, a large part of the Gondwana region was opened up to the Marathas and Brahmans under Maratha rule, and this forced the Gonds to settle deeper in the forests. The Gonds also asserted their traditional rights when the region was transferred to the British. However, the British colonial state did not tolerate this and began levelling them, adopting both coercive and legal methods. Similar methods were also adopted by the princely state of Hyderabad. The lands and forests ruled by the Gonds were enclosed for commercial purposes, and the land they cultivated made subject to taxation.[48]

Indeed, colonial rule witnessed the last incident of land enclosure in India. The colonial state promoted ownership of land, commercialization of agriculture, and a market-based economy in the hill tracts. This led to a process of migration of plains people into forest tracts and the marginalization of hill and subordinate communities in those areas. A large number of Gonds were evicted from their lands through moneylending and by force. This process forced the Gonds and their rajas either to earn their livelihood as agricultural labourers, often bound to a particular master for life, or to migrate into the remaining forest tracts. Under British colonial rule, the creation of the periphery was a phenomenon. The British conquered the hill and forest tracts, and initially sought to integrate the Gonds into the wider caste-Hindu society as property-owning peasant farmers by offering *zamindari* (the land or estate given to a landlord) rights to some Gond rajas, as well as by encouraging caste-Hindus to migrate into the hill tracts so as to spread modern agriculture among the adivasis.[49] This policy largely failed for a variety of reasons, which will be examined in this study.

During the early twentieth century, the strategy shifted from settling Gonds as agriculturists to one of protectionism, with the reservation of tracts, land, and positions for the Gonds. This was, in itself, controversial. The wider process of settling these communities continued right into the twentieth century, and in some cases was never fully carried through. Many Gond rajas evaded colonial state control through tax evasion. They also rebelled against colonial police stations and courts by settling civil and criminal disputes in their own village panchayats. A large number of adivasis fled the colonial and princely states. They tried to retain their independence by migrating to the remaining forest tracts which the British and princely rulers now classed as reserved and intended for the sole use of the state. This led the colonial state to view hill society as a separate space compared to the more 'civilized' society of the plains typified by the caste system.[50] Colonial anthropology also advanced such arguments. This reconfigured the notion of the periphery, with adivasis generally seen as being the least 'civilized' members of Indian society, or on the fringes of Indian society. This was not the case in pre-colonial India, where the periphery was always seen by emperors as a political zone, a zone of autonomous or non-state people. This is not to say that the adivasis had no relationship to statecraft, but rather that they had their own state and systems of governance that operated on the basis of a completely different apparatus rooted in the philosophy of autonomy and self-rule.

Colonial rulers described this autonomous lifestyle as 'primitive' and represented the adivasis as 'primitive tribes'. This construction has been heavily criticized by many recent studies.[51] The construction of the notion of 'tribe' with all its implications can largely be attributed to the colonial state and its anthropology. This is not to suggest that the notion is purely a colonial invention, for the derogatory descriptions of adivasis in the Hindu *shastras* (religious texts) also played an equal role in its creation. As mentioned earlier, the Hindu shastras postulated the forest communities as outside the grand *chaturvarna* (four varnas) scheme, designated them as *vanavasis* (forest dwellers), and sentenced them to living in pits and eating creatures from holes.[52] There are many such derogatory descriptions of adivasis in the Hindu Puranas and epics, particularly in the Mahabharata and Ramayana. These descriptions became the basis and pretext for the colonial state and its anthropological investigations to set up a separate category of the 'tribe' as the other of, and opposite to, caste-Hindu society. This project of knowledge production was undoubtedly a collaborative one.[53]

Thus, the British colonial Indian state, in collaboration with anthropologists, missionaries, and influential native informers, produced a large body of knowledge concerning various aspects of the lives of its subject peoples. Such a production of knowledge necessarily involved classifying, categorizing, naming, and also ordering what the British must have found to be a bewildering variety of formations and groups. In this obviously complex process, those communities and groups which lived for the most part in the more inaccessible hill and forest tracts, and survived largely from hunting-gathering or rudimentary and swidden agriculture, were separated from the others and categorized as 'aboriginals' or 'early tribes'. They were distinguished by their 'clan-based' systems of kinship and 'animistic' religious beliefs. Sometimes, they were also defined in terms of their habitat, as 'jungle tribes'. Those amongst them who were constrained to 'raid'—even occasionally—were branded as 'criminal tribes'. In this way, putting together different related aspects, a category of 'tribe' was created, and a body of knowledge about it developed. This knowledge was preserved and reproduced in the form of anthropological and ethnological notes, gazetteers, and census reports. Needless to say, it was this knowledge that became the framework as well as provided the guidelines for administrative practices. As a sub-process, these scattered communities in different places also came to acquire an internal unity they had not hitherto possessed.[54] In this book, we use the term 'adivasi' to describe forest and hill communities not only to avoid using derogatory colonial terms but also because of the new political meaning attached to the term 'adivasi'.[55]

Under colonial rule, therefore, the mainland and periphery were represented oppositionally, and the periphery was never understood as comprising a strategic political zone. It should be pointed out that pre-colonial empires treated their peripheries as resulting from political acts. Even raids by the forest and nomadic groups were seen by pre-colonial empires as political acts through which they realized their right to collect tax. Colonial rulers represented adivasis and their habitat in a derogatory manner mainly to deny their right to raid, right to self-rule, right to forest resources, and right to land. In this sense, the colonial notion of periphery was different from the pre-colonial one. Under colonial rule, pre-colonial peripheries which were political zones were converted into cultural and sociological zones—zones of poor, backward, archaic, primitive, and marginalized people. Ironically, the postcolonial Indian state is not fundamentally different from the colonial state in this respect, although the position of adivasis has changed from being colonial subjects to citizens of the Republic of India. It is because of this attitude of the state that the adivasi areas have been in unrest from the time of independence. In fact, adivasi areas have become more violent in recent times with globalization, as the state and multinational companies eye these areas for their rich natural resources.

Colonial rule thus stereotyped the historically embedded difference between the mainland plains and periphery in order to deny self-rule to adivasis. I argue that the divide created by colonial rule was dubious and driven by purely administrative concerns. The historically embedded differences went beyond the colonial divide. Importantly, these differences that moulded modern adivasi identity have become crucial in the adivasis' negotiations with the postcolonial state.

STRUCTURE OF THE BOOK

This book aims to trace the genealogy of this divide—the contrasting perceptions of hill and plains people—showing how the 'isolation' of Gonds in the forest was a result of their marginalization caused by empire-building in Indian history. Although the book traces the history of the creation of the periphery from the pre-colonial period, the main focus will be on the colonial period. The study is mainly based on archival sources, but oral sources have come to the rescue where there is a dearth of archival sources. The oral evidence is mainly drawn from my own ethnographic notes, long interviews with the Gonds, and colonial documentation. This interdisciplinary approach not only makes the Gonds themselves and their ideas a part of the study, but also gives a different understanding of adivasi history.

The book is divided into five chapters, in addition to the introduction, the postscript, and an epilogue. It begins by tracing the history of the

Gond community and its land and politics. This discussion is basically centred on the political history of the Chanda state, which falls in the present-day Chandrapur district of Maharashtra and Adilabad district of Telangana state. Bringing an oral narrative of Gond sovereignty into the study, an attempt is made to reconstruct the history of Chanda in the first chapter. The chapter sets out to explain the encounter between the Gond rajas and imperial powers in pre-colonial India, and shows how the Gond rulers negotiated different levels of sovereignty at different times. Even as subordinate rulers, the Gond rajas and chiefs had maintained considerable sovereignty over their territories by adopting different strategies. The chapter shows how pre-colonial India witnessed the existence of multiple sovereignties, and how this past in which they ruled is articulated and rearticulated by the Gonds to challenge the colonial and postcolonial states.

The second chapter deals with the ways in which the colonial state subordinated the sovereign rajas through treaties, agreements, and by force. After successful negotiations with the Gond rajas, the British used several techniques to level them and bring them under the aegis of colonial modernity. Although their rights over their tiny territories were respected, they were controlled and monitored systematically by the British agent. The rajas and their politics were represented as different from the British in every way. The deployment of colonial political rationality subordinated them and their peoples. Indeed, the British endeavoured to bring the adivasis into colonial modernity through the rajas. This process subordinated the rajas and their people in perpetuity. Thus, this project sought to civilize and empower the rajas and hill people, but in practice the dice was loaded against them. Interestingly, the civilization project led to the emergence of a new consciousness among the rajas that challenged colonial domination in their daily affairs. One aim of this chapter is to examine the early encounters of the Gond rajas with British colonial rulers and how this politics impacted the Gond community in subsequent times.

The third chapter explores the history of land enclosure under British rule in India, a process which was crucial to colonial state-making in the forests and hills. The colonial state established its power over inaccessible forest and hill areas and their people through the rule of property and forest regulations. A variety of agricultural revenue tenures were designed to produce the effects of colonial state power. The colonial state was equally concerned about civilizing agricultural production practices and enhancing yields. The colonial project of civilizing agriculture, indeed, furthered the expansion of agriculture, as it created a great demand for land with the introduction of settled agriculture, commercial crops, high-yielding seeds, and modern agricultural technology. The colonial forest policy was crucial in opening up forest areas to the plains. The British colonial state adopted the practice of grabbing forests from adivasi chiefs on lease or sale. The wood in these forests was exploited soon after, and the land parcelled out to plains peasants to bring it under cultivation.

I then move on, in the fourth chapter, to discussing how the enclosing of adivasi spaces led to the creation of the periphery in India. Colonial revenue and agriculture policies brought heavy pressure to bear on land, both in the plains and in the hills. Under British colonial rule, adivasis lost their lands mainly through forced surrender and moneylending. The colonial state did not have a good opinion of the adivasi mode of cultivation and wanted to hand over the rich lands of the adivasis to peasants of the dominant caste, as it felt that the latter would not only produce high yields using modern methods but would also pay their rents on time. In fact, the adivasis relinquished their lands in protest against colonial revenue and agricultural policies. It was this development that evicted a large number of Gonds from their lands and drove them deeper into the forest, leading to revolts and resistance in this region. In response, the colonial state adopted a policy of protectionism which created an administrative boundary between the mainland plains and the hills. This new boundary was, indeed, an artificial one that served to exoticize and stigmatize a minority of adivasis. They were judged to be 'primitives' who did not deserve self-rule. Here, I shall discuss the ways in which the adivasis were marginalized, and how this marginality constituted the periphery under colonial rule.

The fifth chapter narrates how the notion of adivasi autonomy was reconfigured in newer ways during the last decades of colonial rule through Kumaram Bhimu's revolt against the Hyderabad state. It also examines how the failure of protectionism and development initiatives often resulted in an insurgency demanding self-rule. In this sense,

Bhimu's revolt was political in that it built on the intellectual history of the Gonds that was preserved in the form of ballads, myths, and rumours. The state once again responded to adivasi insurgencies with a programme of developmentalism. This programme was advanced by anthropologists who constructed the adivasi question as poverty-related but not political, and therefore to be addressed through developmental initiatives. I argue that adivasi developmental projects, which I call anthropological developmentalism, are based on an anthropological understanding of adivasi society that makes the adivasis perpetually dependent, and often result in violent insurgencies in independent India.

A discussion on what has been happening to the Gonds in independent India constitutes the postscript. Even after India's independence, adivasis continue to embrace insurgency. This is partly because the independent Indian state inherited colonial mentalities and policies with respect to adivasis and did not recognize the latter's political rights. As a result, open plunder of the adivasis has continued. Interestingly, the accumulated grievances of adivasis has been capitalized on by the Naxalite parties, and adivasis were roped into the movement. Importantly, the political language of the Naxalite parties attracted the adivasis as their questions are also political in nature. However, adivasis were subjected to the wrath of the police. The genocide of Gonds at Indravelli village of Adilabad district of Andhra Pradesh (now part of Telangana state), the old seat of the Gond rajas, reminds us of colonial brutality against the adivasis. The sovereign past and the insurgent consciousness of Bhimu were crucial in organizing the Gond community both within and outside the Naxalite movement. This chapter discusses how the postcolonial state is detrimental to adivasis even though their colonial-subject position has changed to one of modern citizenship.

Let us now move on to the early history of the Gonds.

NOTES

1. Chetan Singh has illustrated this phenomenon in medieval India, where peasant communities ran away to the forests from the mainland plains in a bid to evade taxation. See his 'Forests, Pastoralists and Agrarian Society in Mughal India', in *Nature, Culture, Imperialism: Essays on the Environmental*

History of South Asia, edited by David Arnold and Ramachandra Guha (New Delhi: Oxford University Press, 1995), p. 37.

2. Biswamoy Pati underlines how the construction of adivasis was a reality of Indian history much before colonial rule. See his 'Introduction', in *Adivasis in Colonial India: Survival, Resistance and Negotiation*, edited by Biswamoy Pati (New Delhi: Orient BlackSwan, 2011), pp. 1–27.

3. Alpa Shah, 'The Dark Side of Indigeneity: Indigenous People, Rights and Development in India', *History Compass* 5, no. 6 (2007): 1806–32.

4. For example, see André Béteille, *Caste, Class and Power: Changing Patterns of Stratification in a Tanjore Village* (New Delhi: Oxford University Press, 1971).

5. André Béteille, 'Tribe and Peasantry', in *Six Essays in Comparative Sociology* (New Delhi: Oxford University Press, 1974), pp. 60–81.

6. Béteille first used the concept of 'coexistence' in his article 'On the Concept of the Tribe', *International Social Science Journal* 34, no. 41 (1980): 825–45. This essay was later reproduced in a couple of places: see André Béteille, 'The Concept of Tribe with Special Reference to India', *European Journal of Sociology* 27, no. 2 (1986): 297–318; and André Béteille, 'The Concept of Tribe with Special Reference to India', in *Indian Tribes and the Mainstream*, edited by Sukant K. Chaudhury and S. M. Patnaik (Lucknow: Rawat Publications, 2008).

7. D. D. Kosambi, *An Introduction to the Study of Indian History* (Bombay: Popular Prakashan, 1956), pp. 26–34.

8. Béteille, 'The Concept of Tribe with Special Reference to India', p. 309.

9. André Béteille, 'The Idea of Indigenous People', *Current Anthropology*, vol. 39, no. 2, April 1988: 187–92.

10. Nandini Sundar, *Subalterns and Sovereigns: An Anthropological History of Bastar, 1854–1996* (New Delhi: Oxford University Press, 1997), pp. 4–6.

11. Archana Prasad, *Against Ecological Romanticism: Verrier Elwin and the Making of an Anti-modern Tribal Identity* (New Delhi: Three Essays Collective, 2003), p. xx.

12. Prasad, *Against Ecological Romanticism*, pp. 35–68. She says that the use of the term 'swadeshi' by Verrier Elwin in the 1940s had a little less potent and different import in the central Indian context. The term 'swadeshi' was not used in a Gandhian sense, but it denoted the moral right of the 'indigenous' people to rule over their land according to their own values. It was used to identify the original inhabitants of the Indian subcontinent, and was reflective of an idealistic sense of the past.

13. Prasad, *Against Ecological Romanticism*, pp. 53–5.

14. Shereen Ratnagar argues that the category of 'adivasi peasantry' does not match that of the caste-Hindu peasantry. See her *Being Tribal* (Delhi: Primus Books, 2010), p. 2.

15. For example, see K. Suresh Singh (ed.), *The Tribal Situation in India* (Shimla: Indian Institute of Advanced Study, 1972); Mrinal Miri, *Continuity and Change in Tribal Society* (Shimla: Indian Institute of Advanced Study, 1993); Dev Nathan (ed.), *From Tribe to Caste* (Shimla: Indian Institute of Advanced Study, 1997).

16. Ajay Skaria, *Hybrid Histories: Forests, Frontiers and Wildness in Western India* (New Delhi: Oxford University Press, 1999), pp. 59–62.

17. James C. Scott, *The Art of Not Being Governed: An Anarchist History of Upland Southeast Asia* (New Haven: Yale University Press, 2009), pp. 1–39.

18. Scott, *The Art of Not Being Governed*, p. 7.

19. Scott, *The Art of Not Being Governed*, pp. 8–9.

20. For a more detailed criticism of Scott on this issue, see Michael R. Dove, Hjorleifur Jonsson, and Michael Aung-Thwin, 'Debate: The Art of Not Being Governed: An Anarchist History of Upland Southeast Asia by James C. Scott', *Bijdragen tot de taal- Land- en Volkenkunde [Journal of the Humanities and Social Sciences of Southeast Asia]* 167, no. 1 (2011): 86–99; also see Sanjay Subrahmanyam, 'The View from the Top', *London Review of Books* 32, no. 23 (2 December 2010): 25–6.

21. Scott, *The Art of Not Being Governed*, pp. 274–8.

22. Shashank Kela brings out well the conflictual relations between ruling and non-ruling adivasis in central India. See his *A Rogue and Peasant Slave: Adivasi Resistance 1800–2000* (New Delhi: Navayana Publishing, 2012).

23. David Hardiman has shown how this process works in adivasi society. See his *The Coming of the Devi: Adivasi Assertion in Western India* (New Delhi: Oxford University Press, 1987).

24. In early India, all the non-Aryans were grouped under the generic name 'Nagas'. 'Naga', also denominated as 'Takshaka', means carpenter, or superior craftsman. The Naga cult of snake worship is popular in many parts of India even today. See D. D. Kosambi, *An Introduction to the Study of Indian History* (Bombay: Popular Prakashan, 1956), pp. 128–30.

25. Kosambi, *An Introduction to the Study of Indian History*, pp. 123–4.

26. Kosambi, *An Introduction to the Study of Indian History*, p. 84.

27. Kosambi, *An Introduction to the Study of Indian History*, p. 128.

28. The Gonds of Adilabad have erected a temple for the snake god Nagoba at Kesalapur, 25 miles from Utnur town, and worship him every year on the night of the full moon in the Telugu month of Pushya (February). The

Nagoba *jatara* (celebration) is very popular among the adivasis of the whole of the Deccan region. See Christoph von Furer-Haimendorf, *Life among Indian Tribes: The Autobiography of an Anthropologist* (New Delhi: Oxford University Press, 1990), pp. 72–3.

29. Eyre Chatterton, *The Story of Gondwana* (London: Sir Isaac Pitman & Sons, 1916), p. 7.

30. Aloka Parasher says that the construction of Arya and mleccha/milakkha as different civilizations was linguistic rather than religious—a difference between the Indo-Aryan speakers and non-Indo-Aryan speakers. For a detailed analysis, see her *Mlecchas in Early India* (Delhi: Munshiram Manoharlal, 1991), p. i.

31. Romila Thapar has illustrated this process in detail. See her *From Lineage to State: Social Formations in the Mid-first Millennium B.C. in the Ganga Valley* (New Delhi: Oxford University Press, 1984).

32. Suranjit K. Saha, 'Early State Formation in Tribal Areas of East-Central India', *Economic and Political Weekly* 31, no. 13 (1996): 824–34, see pp. 828–9.

33. Michael J. Casimir and Aparna Rao, 'The Historical Framework of Nomadism in South Asia: A Brief Overview', in *Nomadism in South Asia*, edited by Aparna Rao and Michael J. Casimir (New Delhi: Oxford University Press, 2003), pp. 43–72.

34. During my recent field trip, I observed the continuation of this process in the adivasi areas of Adilabad district. Even now if non-adivasis come and settle in the Kolam adivasi hamlet, adivasis would leave that hamlet and settle in a new place, generally deeper in the forest. Field notes, 25 January 2015.

35. A number of examples of this process are provided by Mahomed Kasim Perishta, *History of the Rise of the Mahomedan Power in India*, edited by John Briggs, 4 vols (New Delhi: Oriental Books Reprint Corporation, 1981 [1829]). For such processes in the early British period, see Francis Buchanan, *A Journey from Madras through the Countries of Mysore, Canara and Malabar*, 3 vols (London: Printed by Fort Cadell and W. Davies, and Black Parry and Kingsbury, 1807).

36. Kosambi illustrates how land grants to religious institutions and Brahmans were important to the state-making process in the forests and hills in early India. See Kosambi, *An Introduction to the Study of Indian History*, pp. 312–41.

37. Irfan Habib, *The Agrarian System of Mughal India 1556–1707* (New Delhi: Oxford University Press, 1999), pp. 292–7.

38. Habib, *The Agrarian System of Mughal India*, pp. 23–4.

39. Richard M. Eaton, *A Social History of the Deccan, 1300–1761: Eight Indian Lives, The New Cambridge History of India* (New York: Cambridge University Press, 2005), p. 14.

40. P. V. Parabrahma Sastry, *The Kakatiyas of Warangal* (Hyderabad: Government of Andhra Pradesh, 1978), pp. 197–9.

41. Eaton, *A Social History of the Deccan*, p. 14.

42. Satyanarayana Kambhampati, *A Study of the History and Culture of the Andhras*, vol. 2 (New Delhi: People's Publishing House, 1983), pp. 333–49.

43. Kambhampati, *History and Culture of the Andhras*, vol. 2, p. 500.

44. A narration of this legend was documented by Anjana Devi Diviti (in Telugu), *Sammakka Saralamma Jatara Sahitya Samskritika Amshalu* (Karimnagar: Anilasai Prachuranlu, 2006).

45. Eaton, *A Social History of the Deccan*, pp. 155–76.

46. Singh, 'Forests, Pastoralists and Agrarian Society', pp. 26–33.

47. Chatterton, *The Story of Gondwana*, pp. 10–12; C. B. Lucie Smith, *Report on Land Revenue Settlement of the Chanda District, Central Provinces* (Nagpur: Chief Commissioner's Press, 1870), pp. 60–76.

48. Richard Jenkins, *Report on the Territories of the Rajah of Nagpur* (1827; reprint, Nagpur: Government Press, 1925), pp. 74–6; Smith, *Land Revenue Settlement of the Chanda District*, pp. 179–85.

49. W. V. Grigson, *The Aboriginal Problem in the Central Provinces and Berar* (Nagpur: Government Printing, 1944), pp. 15–122.

50. Grigson, *The Aboriginal Problem*, pp. 79–97.

51. For example, see Bhangya Bhukya, 'The Mapping of the Adivasi Social: Colonial Anthropology and Adivasis', *Economic and Political Weekly* 43, no. 39 (2008): 103–9; Virginius Xaxa, *State, Society and Tribes: Issues in Post Colonial India* (Delhi: Pearson Longman, 2008), pp. 13–27.

52. Lieutenant General Briggs, 'Two Lectures on the Aboriginal Race of India, as Distinguished from the Sanskritic or Hindu Race', *Journal of the Royal Asiatic Society of Great Britain and Ireland* 13 (1857): 275–309; also see Wendy Doniger and Bardwell Smith (eds), *Laws of Manu* (New Delhi: Penguin Books, 1991), p. 39.

53. Edward W. Said, *Orientalism: Western Conceptions of the Orient* (London: Penguin, 1995), p. 36; Ronald Inden, *Imagining India* (Oxford: Blackwell, 1992); Nicholas B. Dirks, *Caste of Mind: Colonialism and the Making of Modern India* (New Delhi: Permanent Black, 2002).

54. Bhukya, 'The Mapping of the Adivasi Social', pp. 103–9; Vinita Damodaran, 'Colonial Constructions of the "Tribes" in India: The Case of Chotanagpur', in *Adivasis in Colonial India: Survival, Resistance and*

Negotiation, edited by Biswamoy Pati (New Delhi: Orient BlackSwan, 2011), pp. 55–87; Meena Radhakrishna, 'Of Apes and Ancestors: Evolutionary Science and Colonial Ethnography', in *Adivasis in Colonial India: Survival, Resistance and Negotiation*, edited by Biswamoy Pati (New Delhi: Orient BlackSwan, 2011), pp. 31–54.

55. Although the term 'adivasi' has been in use from the late 1930s, it has gained a wider currency in recent times with the emergency of identity politics among the forest groups. I have given an explanation justifying the use of the term 'adivasi' in my recent book. See Bhangya Bhukya, *Subjugated Nomads: The Lambadas under the Rule of the Nizams* (New Delhi: Orient BlackSwan, 2010), p. 13.

1

REMEMBERING RAJAS, REMEMBERING SOVEREIGNTY
THE GOND COMMUNITY AND ITS POLITICS

THE REPRESENTATION OF A GRIFFIN destroying an elephant, carved upon a wooden wall-hanging in a Gond house in Utnur town of Adilabad district, Telangana state, caught my eye during my visit to the town. As I walked through the town, I found paintings of this scene on the front walls of many Gond houses. I asked a Pardhan (Gond storyteller), Mesram Somji, what this painting meant to the Gonds. He said that it was the crest of the Chanda rajas: 'We have them as a memory of our rajas and our sovereign rule over Gond territory.' He also said that the crest was still to be found on the gateway and tower of the Chanda fort, the capital of the Gond rajas.[1] Such remnants of the sovereign past of the Gonds are very apparent across the Gond habitat. These are crucial to constructing the history of the Gonds.

Historically, the country that lies between the Narmada and the Godavari rivers, and which later constituted part of the British Central Provinces, was ruled by four powerful Gond dynasties for 500 years from the middle of the thirteenth century to the middle of the eighteenth century. The region was also popularly called Gondwana, as it was largely inhabited by Gond communities. In this land, four independent Gond kingdoms arose, more or less simultaneously: in the north, Garha; in the centre, Deogarh and Kherla; and in the south, Chanda.[2] We shall confine our discussion in this study to the Chanda dynasty.

The sources of information about these dynasties are scanty. However, their history is preserved in the oral literature of the Gonds. Although the oral traditions tend to exaggerate the power of the Gond rajas, they narrate the major historical developments and processes. Although British colonial administrators and anthropologists depended largely on these oral sources to reconstruct the history of the Gonds they, however, valorized the Gond community and their history in many respects. The construction of textual knowledge about Indian communities became a major genre in the colonial milieu, forming part of the project of colonial knowledge creation as a means of extension of colonial power. This resulted in the production of massive literature on almost all communities, which was used as a source for legal and general administration.[3] The initial construction of knowledge about the adivasis took place in the context of their violent resistance to colonial expansion into the forest world, which began with the revolt of the Pahariya Sirdars of Bihar in 1778.[4] As we will see in the next chapter, the Gonds of central India strongly resisted the expansion of the British empire into the hills. This forced the British rulers to study the history of Gondwana, which resulted in the production of many volumes on the history of the Gonds. The main task of this chapter is to examine these contested genealogies of the Gond community and the parallel history that runs through the Gonds' oral literature, and how the latter acts as a catalyst in negotiations with the present-day establishment. Attempts will be also made to explore the political history of the Gonds. Before we take up these questions, it is important to provide a brief ethnographic account of the Gonds.

A BRIEF ETHNOGRAPHY OF THE GONDS

There has been debate since the colonial period about who the Gonds are. In recent studies, the Pulindas mentioned in the Hindu Puranas are identified as Gonds. It is said that Visvamitra cursed the progeny of fifty of his sons to living on the borders of Aryan settlements; his sons are also called Dasyus in history. The Pulindas are one of these communities, and they lived in the Vindhya and Satpura hills.[5] However, the Gonds trace their mythological origins to Mahadeo (Shiva) and Parvati, which relates them to the Naga or Dravidian or south Indian cultural tradition.[6] It is difficult to establish the Gonds' association with Buddhism, but historical evidence shows that Buddhist influence on the Chanda territory was very strong from the Satavahana period down to the seventh and eighth centuries CE. Hiuen Tsang, a Chinese Buddhist pilgrim who in 639 CE visited the city of Kosala located close to Chanda town, said that 'one hundred monasteries are here and ten thousand Buddhist priests are among the inhabitants.'[7] However, as in other parts of India, Buddhism disappeared after this period in the Chanda region.

The adivasis inhabiting the area between the Godavari and Narmada rivers are described by the generic word 'Gond'. However, they are not racially, culturally, or linguistically a homogeneous population. There are great differences in customs and material circumstances between many of these widely scattered adivasi groups.[8] Also, the derivation of the word 'Gond' is uncertain. It is said that the name was given to these communities by the Hindus or Muslims, while they describe themselves as Koitur or Koi. There was also serious debate among colonial administrators and ethnologists about the original homeland and racial origin of the Gonds. General Alexander Cunningham believed that the Gonds came from eastern India (the Gauda kingdom), whereas R. V. Russell argued that they came from south and central India.[9] Fürer-Haimendorf, who studied the Gonds extensively, ascertained that the Gonds of the Deccan were a pre-Aryan, Dravidian race, based on their linguistic association with the Dravidian languages. The Gondi language, along with its many local dialects, is a Dravidian language, and is closer to Tamil and Kannada than to Telugu.[10] Recent studies by Gond scholars also link the Gondi language and culture with the Indus Valley Civilization. Further, these studies argue that the Gonds are descendents of the Indus people.[11] However, Gond history has witnessed many interfaces. The present-day Gonds came under the influence of local languages, abandoned Gondi, and picked up the local Hindi and Telugu languages. Strictly speaking, only Gondi speakers are called Gonds, otherwise they are called 'Koitur', which is a universal word to describe all of the Deccan adivasis. According to Fürer-Haimendorf, the Gonds of Adilabad district of Hyderabad state and the Yeotmal and Chandrapur districts of the Central Provinces are close kin groups.[12]

The Gonds of Chanda and Adilabad, who form the subject of this book, divide themselves into four endogamous tribes: the Raj Gonds, the Maria or Madia Gonds, the Dhurve Gonds, and the Khatulwar Gonds. There are also other minor sub-adivasi groups, such as the Koyas, Gaitas, Pardhans, Nayakpods, and Kolams, who do not class themselves with any of the above adivasi communities and are few in number. These sub-adivasi groups all speak dialects of the Gondi language.[13] The Gonds of Adilabad, except for a few Dhurve Gonds who came from Chanda, describe themselves as Raj Gonds. In the beginning, the 'Raj Gond' title was attached only to ruling Gond chiefs, but it was later used by all Gonds. However, the title is no longer fashionable. The Raj Gonds maintained some degree of difference from their subjects by adopting Brahmanic/Rajput or ruling-group values when they were in power, but the gap was expunged as they lost their dominance.[14] Further, each endogamous group is divided into four kin groups (phratries or clans[15]): the Seven-Pen (seven-god worshippers), the Six-Pen (six-god worshippers), the Five-Pen (five-god worshippers) and the Four-Pen (four-god worshippers). Each group worships these junior gods besides the Persa Pen (Great God).[16] Each group contains ten to fifteen septs which are named after trees and animals, such as *markam* (mango tree), *tekam* (teak tree), *netam* (dog), *irpachi* (mahua tree), *tumrachi* (tendu tree), *warkara* (wild cat), and so on. Members of the same kin group (or worshippers of the same number of gods) are considered brethren, and marriages take place between kin groups. The local Gond chiefs play a crucial role in maintaining this order. Indeed, they settle all civil and criminal disputes at the village level.[17] Let us now move on to the contested political history of the Gonds.

CONTESTED GENEALOGIES OF THE GOND RAJAS

The early history of the Gond rajas of Chanda is uncertain, but their sovereign past is still fresh in the memory of the Gond people. They articulate these histories in a variety of ways, preserving them in the form of oral legends and stories in the community. They also speak abundantly of their rule in the region. When the British started collecting the histories of Gondwana, they were surprised by the accounts of great achievement that were preserved in the stories and legends of the Gond rajas. Although British administrator-scholars stressed the use of archival and archaeological evidence, the oral tradition of the Gonds was always crucial in the construction of their histories. However, there were differences of opinion among these officials regarding the history of Gond rule in this region. As mentioned previously, the oral articulations of the Gonds go beyond the comprehension of written documents or histories; they speak of great empires, a large number of rajas, and big *gaddis* (thrones).[18] Thanks to the efforts of colonial officials to document Gond oral traditions, orality has now become an authentic source of Gond history.

The main contestation regarding the Chanda kingdom pertains to when it was founded. C. B. Lucie Smith broadly established that a Gond chief, Bhim Ballal Singh, organized the Gonds and established his rule in Sirpur (in the eastern part of Adilabad district in Telangana) in 870 CE.[19] As shown in Table 1.1, he also names about nineteen Gond rulers along with the years of their rule. In all, these nineteen reigns cover a period of 881 years, or an average of about forty-six years for each reign. It is assumed that some names were omitted. In most cases, the kingdom was represented as descending from father to son, and in some cases to an adopted son.[20] However, the supposed date of establishment of the dynasty fixed by Smith does not match the historical evidence. There was a serious debate on the period of rule the Gond rajas among colonial administrators. Babji Ballal Shah, who is said to have ruled from 1442, is mentioned in the *Ain-i-Akbari* as ruler of Chanda. Based on Mughal records and archaeological evidence, it may be presumed that Babji Ballal Shah was a contemporary of Akbar and ruled from 1572 to 1597. On this computation, the reign of Khandkia Ballal Shah, the founder of the present city of Chanda, would fall between 1437 and 1462. After examining all the available sources, it is generally accepted that the Chanda dynasty must have been established by Bhim Ballal Singh in Sirpur in 1240.[21] However, for oral histories, the years of rule are not the main concern, but rather the regimes of the rajas, their sovereign

Table 1.1 Rulers of the Chanda kingdom as recorded by C. B. Lucie Smith

Ruler	Beginning of Reign (AD)
Bhim Ballal Singh	870
Khurja Ballal Singh	895
Heer Sing	935
Andia Ballal Singh	970
Tulwar Singh	995
Keshur Singh	1027
Dinkur Singh	1072
Ram Singh	1142
Surja Bullal Singh (Sher Shah Ballal Shah)	1207
Khandkia Ballal Shah	1242
Heer Shah	1282
Bhooma and Lokba, two brothers who ruled jointly	1342
Kundia Shah, also known as Kurn Shah	1402
Babji Ballal Shah	1442
Dhoondia Ram Shah	1522
Krishna Shah	1597
Beer Shah	1647
Ram Shah	1672
Nilkanth Shah	1735–51

Source: Smith, *Land Revenue Settlement of the Chanda District*.

rule, their freedom in the hills and forests. In this sense, the regimes of the Gond rajas are not measured in terms of years but in the language of sovereignty and freedom.

Indeed, interesting Gond legends relating to every incident of Gond history were recorded by colonial administrators. According to these legends, the Deccan forest tract was inhabited by Gowaree, Gond, and Mana communities, and there were ferocious fights for supremacy over the region and its resources. The Manas first rose to power and established strong forts at Surjagarh, Manikgarh, Wyragarh, Gurboree, and Rajgarh (Rajura). In the course of these struggles, there arose among the Gonds a man called Kol Bheel. He was both wise and strong. He gathered the scattered Gonds into one nation, taught them how to extract iron from ore, and led them against the Manas. The Manas fell to the Gonds after a troubled supremacy of two hundred years. Then Bhim Ballal Singh, a Gond of the Atram house, subdued his fellow chief and ruled over a wide dominion, the first of the Gond kings of the Chanda line. Bhim Ballal Singh established his capital at Sirpur, on the right bank of the Wardha, but the Manas' fort of Manikgarh in the high ranges of the hills remained his stronghold.[22] From there, the kings shifted their capital to Ballarshah and then to Chanda during the reign of Khandkia Ballal Shah. The Gonds have a romantic story which explains these shifts, as narrated below.

Khandkia Ballal Shah suffered from ill health. His wife was the dominant partner. She worried about her husband's health and suggested that he abandon the home of his ancestors at Sirpur and seek a healthier and more secure capital on the opposite side of River Wardha. He built a fort there, and it was named Ballarshah after him. But Khandkia still suffered from disease; he spent much of his time hunting in the surroundings of the fort. Riding one day some 10 miles from Ballarshah, he became extremely thirsty. He found a small pool of water nearby. He drank the water and washed his face and hands. That night, on his return to Ballarshah, he slept as he had not slept for years. In the morning when he awoke, his queen noticed that the swellings and tumours which had disfigured his handsome face and body for some years had almost vanished. The delighted queen enquired about the pool. She took Khandkia to the pool and found five deep footprints of the sacred cow on the solid rock, each filled with an unfailing supply of water. She realized that these spots were the marks of the great god Achaleshwar. Continued bathing in the pools' sacred waters soon restored the king to complete health.

The god then appeared in Khandkia's dream, and his wife understood that the god wanted them to build a temple for him over the pool. While the construction of the temple was in process, Khandkia was in the habit of visiting it regularly. On his rides, he was invariably accompanied by his favourite dog. One day, when he was returning from the temple, a hare darted out of a bush and began to chase his dog. The dog fled in wild terror with the hare in close pursuit. Astonished at the sight, the king followed the chase as closely as he could. At last the dog killed the hare after an intense struggle. After its death, the king approached the hare and observed a strange white mark or *teeka* on its forehead. He told his wife, and she had a vision of the place as one that was powerful and unconquerable. She suggested that the king build a fort where the hare had chased the dog, and named the fort 'Chanda' after the moon-shaped mark on the hare's forehead. Chanda served from then onwards as the capital of the Gonds till the fall of the last Gond raja.[23]

The story tells us that the Gond rulers of Chanda expanded their power from the south northward as the strong northern political powers were weakening. It also explains how the Gond rajas came to patronize the Shiva cult, as Achaleshwar represents Shiva. Importantly, the legend exhibits the power of Gond rationality in choosing the right place for a fort. Chanda remained a strong fort throughout its history. Even the last Bhonsle king took shelter there when he was attacked by the British army in the last Maratha war.

The growing power of this dynasty has to be understood in the context of the wider historical developments of that time. Before the Gonds, the region had been ruled by the Satavahanas, Vakatakas, Kalcuris, Rastrakutas, the Chalukyas of Kalyani, and the Yadavas of Devagiri. The fall of the Yadavas of Devagiri and the Kakatiyas of Warangal at the hands of Ala-ud-din Khilji marks a turning point in the history of the Deccan and the peninsular south, leading to the rise of many local powers. After the fall of the Yadavas and Kakatiyas, the Gonds of Chanda seem to have risen as a political power.[24] This was also partly due to the subjugation of the great Rajput clans of central India by the Delhi Sultans during the fourteenth century. When the Delhi Empire began to break up during the fifteenth century, new rulers—such as the Gond rajas—were able to assert their power in Chanda territory.[25] The northern boundary of their rule, it is said, reached the Wardha basin, and the southern boundary reached the northern bank of the Godavari River.[26]

The most debated issue during colonial rule and even in postcolonial times is: Were the Gond rajas sovereign rulers? If so, at what point of time were they sovereign? When were they reduced to the status of feudatories? What was their relation with the Sultans and Mughals? These questions are still contentious. Gond legends assert the sovereign rule of the Gond rajas of Chanda. It is said that Surja Ballal Singh visited the ruler of Delhi and fought for him in a war against the Rajput chief of Kaibur. Impressed by his achievements, the Delhi ruler granted him rights over a huge territory, and conferred on him the title of Sher Shah, after which he was known as Sher Shah Ballal Shah. His successors used the title 'Shah' as a suffix in their names.[27] Fürer-Haimendorf dismisses this genealogy on the ground that it has no historical evidence to substantiate it.[28] However, this legend underlines the Sultans' influence on the Gond rajas of Chanda. The defeat of the northern Gondwana kingdoms by the Delhi emperors gradually weakened the Chanda raja's sovereignty.

Mahomed Kasim Ferishta records that Sultan Feroz Shah was the first to attack the Gondwana kingdoms. In 1399, an invasion was launched on Kherla, the western kingdom of Gondwana. Nursing Ray, the Gond raja of Kherla, ruled the territory and possessed great wealth and power. When the sultan sent him a message commanding him to accept his authority, Nursing Ray refused and tried to wage a war, asking for help from the Malwa and Kandesh rajas, but they wanted him defeated and did not extend help. Still, he went ahead with the war and was at last defeated in battle. But after the war, Nursing negotiated with the sultan and got his territory back by paying him a huge war compensation and an annual tribute, and sending one of his daughters to the sultan's harem.[29] In order to escape the sultans' supremacy, however, the Gond raja of Kherla joined hands with Nusseer Khan, ruler of Kandesh, when he invaded Berar in 1437.[30]

A major blow for Gondwana was Akbar's attack on Gurha, another strong northern Gondwana kingdom. Hearing about the riches of the Gurha territory ruled by Rani Durgawatty, Asuf Khan (*mansabdar* [a military rank] of Kurra Manikpoor) obtained Emperor Akbar's permission to subdue the country. In 1564, Asuf Khan attacked Gurha with a huge army. The rani put up a tough fight, but stabbed herself to death when Asuf Khan's army apprehended her. Asuf Khan occupied Gurha and looted its jewels and other valuables, including no fewer than a hundred jars of gold coins from the reign of Ala-ud-din Khilji. Of all this booty, Asuf Khan presented to the king only a small part, along with a thousand elephants, and kept the remaining loot for himself. Learning about this, Akbar expelled him from Gurha in 1566 and took over the country.[31] After learning that all the Deccan kings had refused to acknowledge his supremacy, Akbar instructed Mirza Khan and Khan Khanan to march on the Deccan. They conquered all the forts in the Deccan including Kherla, and formed these territories into the province of Berar in 1599. Akbar himself came to the Deccan and led the invasion after his son Murad Murza was killed in battle.[32]

It appears that the southern kingdoms of Deogarh and Chanda largely escaped Mughal attack until the reign of Aurangzeb. It also seems that the Chanda rulers did not pay tribute to the Mughals.[33] It is recorded in the *Ain-i-Akbari* that Babji Ballal Shah paid no tribute to Delhi, and possessed an army of 10,000 cavalry and 40,000 infantry.[34] However, Aurangzeb brought Deogarh and Chanda under his suzerainty. By 1666, his commander Raja Jaising had brought most of central India under the control of the Mughals. In 1635, Deogarh was attacked by the Mughal army, and its ruler Raja Kukia surrendered to the Mughals. The fort was restored to him when he promised to pay an annual tribute. But the tribute fell into arrears, and in 1655 a Mughal army marched into Deogarh and forced the raja (Kesari Singh) into abject submission. Later rulers including Bakht Buland, Dindar, and Chand Sultan, although they adopted Islam, continued to evade Mughal power till Deogarh was completely taken over by the Marathas in 1739.[35]

It was in 1667 that Aurangzeb's commander Dilir Khan first went to the kingdom of Chanda; Manji Mallar, the raja, received the Khan, gave him five lakh (500,000) rupees, and agreed to pay one crore (10,000,000) rupees as fine to the imperial government and two lakhs of rupees as his permanent annual tribute.[36] After this incident, the Gond rajas of Chanda accepted Mughal suzerainty, but the relationship was full of tension, though it endured. In September 1674, Kumar Kishan Singh, the son of Raja Ram Singh of Chanda, was appointed mansabdar of a *hazari* (a unit of 4,000 troops) and received presents from the emperor.[37] After his death in 1682 due to wounds received in a brawl, his son Bishan Singh took his place as the mansab of a hazari.[38]

Raja Ram Singh of Chanda also visited the emperor in Delhi in 1681 and presented him with four elephants and nine horses; in return, he was sent home with a special robe, a horse with gold *saz* (ornaments), an elephant, and an emerald *sarpech* (an ornament worn at the front of a turban).[39] However, these relations changed suddenly when the zamindari of Chanda was transferred from Ram Singh to Kishan Singh (the latter's relationship with Ram Singh is not ascertained) in 1683.[40] When Ram Singh opposed this move, he was defeated by the Mughal army in 1684. He fled to the hills with 200 troopers, leaving his family behind; and Itiqad Khan, Hamza Khan (both commanders in the Mughal army), and Kishan Singh entered Chanda. On 19 November 1684, Ram Singh came to Chanda with three men and attempted to enter his mansion. Murad Beg, a servant of Kishan Singh who was guarding the door, rose to prevent him from entering. Ram Singh stabbed him with a *jamdhar* (a type of dagger), but was himself attacked and slain. Murad Beg died the next day. After this incident, the emperor sent a robe, a *farman* (a government order or decree), and an elephant to Kishan Singh.[41] Kishan Singh was succeeded by his elder son, Bir Singh, in July 1696. He too refused to pay tribute to the Mughals and was summoned by the emperor's camp in 1700. He went to the army camp personally and paid the tribute arrears into the Berar treasury.[42]

After the death of Aurangzeb in 1707, it appears that the Chanda kingdom enjoyed considerable freedom from imperial power until it was brought under the control of the Marathas in 1743. The Bhonsle Marathas first established control in Berar, expanded their power towards the east, and finally made Nagpur their capital. Raghoji Bhonsle successfully subjugated the Gonds of the Deogarh and Chanda territories and created Nagpur state as a distinct entity.[43] With the death of Chand Sultan, raja of Deogarh, in 1738, the Bhonsles began establishing their sway in southern Gondwana. Upon the death of Chand Sultan, one of his illegitimate brothers, Wali Shah, usurped the throne. Chand Sultan's widow, Ram Ratan Kaur, thereupon invited Raghoji Bhonsle to help his sons Burhan Shah and Akbar Shah. Raghoji put Wali Shah to death, placed the legitimate son Burhan Shah on the throne, and received huge rewards along with an assignment on the revenues of several districts. Bhonsle's help was again sought when dissension broke out between the two brothers in 1743. Bhonsle supported Burhan Shah and forced Akbar Shah to flee to Hyderabad state. Bhonsle became the protector of Burhan Shah and gradually established himself at Nagpur.[44]

It appears that Kanhoji Bhonsle was the first Maratha to invade Chanda, though it is not certain when this happened. The invasion, meant to collect the dues of *cauth* (a tax collected from foreign territories by Maratha rulers), was unsuccessful. In 1730, Raghoji Bhonsle marched on Chanda. But it is said that Bhonsle was so impressed by Raja Ram Shah's saintly disposition that he honoured him with the gift of a robe, collected the tribute, and left the Chanda territories unravaged. This relationship between Chanda and the Bhonsles, however, changed during the reign of Nilkanth Shah, who succeeded Ram Shah in 1735.

Nilkanth Shah tried to overthrow the Bhonsles' sway over Gondwana with the help of the *dewan* (prime minister) of Deogarh, Raghunath Singh, while Raghoji Bhonsle was busy with a Bengal expedition. Learning about this, Bhonsle invaded and annexed Deogarh in 1748, killing the dewan. He next proceeded against Nilkanth Shah and defeated him, engaging in treachery with Nilkanth Shah's dewan. After this defeat by Raghoji Bhonsle, Nilkanth Shah had to enter into a treaty in 1749, requiring him to surrender to Bhonsle two-thirds of the revenue of his kingdom. Bhonsle even retained the Chanda fort and the ancient Wyragarh fort. Nilkanth Shah was forced to live in the Ballarshah fort. Bhonsle appointed Sivajipant Talkute as the keeper of the Chanda fort. In 1751, Nilkanth Shah took back possession of the Chanda fort by driving Talkute out. Bhonsle immediately swooped down upon Nilkanth, defeated him easily, and imprisoned him permanently in the Ballarshah fort. Thus, Gond rule in Chanda ended in 1751.[45]

Despite the continuous conflict with the Bahmanis, Imad Shahis, Nizam Shahis, Qutb Shahis, and the Mughals, with the western and southern boundaries of the dynasty often shifting, the Chanda rulers had been largely independent till their defeat at the hands of the Bhonsles of Nagpur.[46] Their crest depicting a griffin destroying an elephant, carved upon the gateway and tower of Chanda fort, may also be seen as a symbol of their sovereign power over the region. They used titles such as 'Rajadi Raja' (king of kings) and 'Sri Bhupatiraj' (lord of the earth). However, the dynasty's official seal came from Delhi. Their coinage too bore the name of the Delhi emperor. As mentioned earlier, when Asuf Khan invaded Chanda, he found gold coins of the reign of Ala-ud-din Khilji in the Chanda treasury. This suggests that despite the imperial suzerainty over them, the Chanda rulers enjoyed a considerable degree of sovereignty.[47]

The region also witnessed considerable prosperity under the rule of the Gond rajas. The rajas rewarded their Gond *tarvels* (warriors) with large tracts of forest land, making them subordinate rajas or zamindars of those tracts. They, in turn, encouraged cultivators to settle on the land and bring it under cultivation. In this way, large areas were developed. These subordinate rajas' territories were marked by boundaries and were properly documented. They were encouraged to build tanks and irrigate their lands.[48] We shall take up this point in the next chapter. Despite their achievements, however, the colonial rulers branded the Gond rajas' regimes as careless and feudal.[49]

The subordinate local Gond chiefs/rajas constructed their own forts, generally on hilltops, and administered their respective territories almost autonomously. They were not only responsible for the civil administration of their estates, but also had to send soldiers to the Chanda rajas on demand. All the service castes (blacksmiths, pot makers, leather workers, and so on) lived with the Gond community, but maintained their differences in cultural and other spheres. Merchants from the plains visited the courts of the tutelary rajas regularly. Even during the Bhonsles' rule, these rajas enjoyed power, albeit in a reduced degree.[50] Although Nilkanth Shah was, as mentioned earlier, besieged by the Bhonsle rulers in the Ballarshah fort, the tutelary Gond rajas continued to assert their power in their respective territories, including Manikgarh and Sirpur, the ancient seat of the Ballal Shah dynasty that passed into the hands of the Nizam in 1803 under the treaty of Deogaon with Raghoji II.[51] The Anglo-Maratha wars of the late eighteenth century and early nineteenth century were advantageous to the Gond rajas. We shall take up this point again in the next chapter. The power of the Bhonsles was destroyed in the last Anglo-Maratha war, and Nagpur state—including Chanda—was brought under British control as a protectorate in 1818. Although the country was handed over to the Bhonsles in 1830, the British supervised the administration very closely, and in 1853 they annexed the state.[52]

The Gond rajas thus ruled the whole of central India at one point of time. It appears that the local Gond chiefs had control over their people and resources from the early medieval period, and whenever there was a weakening of imperial power they asserted their dominance in their respective territories. The Chanda rulers established their own dynasty sometime in the middle of the thirteenth century. Although there is uncertainty about the period of their reign, they ruled Chanda for some time as independent rulers and at other times as subordinate rajas. Many a time they evaded imperial power because of the inaccessibility of the region. Even after the Marathas established their dominion, the local rajas continued to control their respective territories. This arrangement persisted in an attenuated form under British rule. Importantly, this history of sovereignty is told and retold among the Gond community in all their social gatherings. There are many legends which recount the heroic acts of the Gond rajas, and this past has endured as a metaphor in Gond society. It is against this claim that they demand their right to land and forests in modern times. Their sovereign past behaves as a catalyst in their mobilization against the modern state.

METAPHOR OF A SOVEREIGN PAST: AN ETHNOHISTORY OF THE GOND FORTS

As mentioned earlier, although there is uncertainty about the period of Gond rule due to scanty evidence, the history of their past sovereignty is still alive in the memory of the Gond people. The Gonds have a long tradition of preserving their history. The Pardhans, traditional storytellers of the Gond community, have been instrumental in this task. These histories and legends were largely documented during the colonial period as well as in the postcolonial period.[53] Apart from these legends, the magnificent ruined forts of Sirpur, Manikgarh, Utnur, Nirmal, Rajura, Wyagarh, Partabgarh, Ballarshah, and Chanda all speak of the extent and power of Gond rule in the region.[54] These ruins tell us about Gond politics and society.[55] Indeed, they are the manifestations of the sovereign past of the Gonds. Dassera, a major Hindu festival, provides an occasion to recast the ruined Gond forts so as to challenge the present. When we say the 'present', we refer to the current subjection of the Gonds under the postcolonial regimes.

Dassera is celebrated in India in the lunar month Asvina (September–October) to commemorate the victory of good over evil; the festival is also called Vijaya Dasami. There are many mythological explanations for the festival. The most popular accounts involve the victory of Rama over Ravana, the protagonists of the epic Ramayana, and also of the goddess Durga's victory over Mahishasura, the buffalo demon. However, these explanations vary from region to region, and from community to community too. For the Gonds, Dassera is the time to celebrate Persa Pen (the Great God of the Gonds). Importantly, it is a royal festival. The Gond rajas and village heads once celebrated it with elaborate rituals to demonstrate their power to their subaltern subjects.[56]

Nandini Sundar illuminates how the Dassera celebration not only encapsulates the process of state-making, but also illustrates the establishment of royal hegemony in the Bastar polity.[57] There are analogies of such histories in Chanda politics. The Chanda Gond rulers had a tradition of celebrating Dassera as a way of establishing their royal hegemony. During the festival, the subalterns paid Gondi dues and *man* (gifts to their rajas) as both a right and an obligation. In turn, the raja gave them a feast at the palace.[58] In other words, as Sundar says, Dassera was an expression of public loyalty, simultaneously depending on the king's proper behaviour and acknowledgement of the role of his subjects. In this sense, the establishment of hegemony is not a one-time accomplishment, but something which is ceaselessly contested and constantly re-established. Dassera celebrations thus were instrumental in shaping the dialectics of power throughout Gond history.[59]

The dialectics of Dassera, however, changed drastically after the rajas lost power to the Marathas. Indeed, these power dynamics took quite a different shape under the rule of the British, and even more so under the postcolonial Indian state. Dassera was no longer an occasion for the Gond rajas to expand their power or to legitimize their rule over subaltern Gonds, but a space for negotiating power-sharing within existing power structures. Similarly, Dassera celebrations today are an occasion for Gonds to forge a community within the language of modern identity politics by remembering and celebrating their sovereign past.[60] We shall discuss how these politics materialized in subsequent chapters.

After the death of the last sovereign raja Nilkanth Shah, the royal family continued the tradition of declaring someone from the family as a successor. Raja Yadav Shah, who belonged to the seventh generation of descendants of Nilkanth Shah, and who passed away recently, was the last raja who maintained this tradition. On the day of Dassera, the ex-raja and his ex-zamindars bring life to their ruined fort by decorating it with lights and flowers (see Figures 1.1, 1.2, and 1.3). The royal flag

PATHANPURA GATE, CHANDA

Figure 1.1   Chanda Fort main entrance gate
Source: Chatterton, *The Story of Gondwana*, p. 57.

Figure 1.2   Utnur Fort
Source: From the author's personal collection.

Figure 1.3   Sirpur Fort (Sirpur was the first capital of the Chanda dynasty)
Source: From the author's personal collection.

is hoisted to mark their sovereign rule in the fort. The raja gives a public appearance (darbar) dressed in traditional royal clothes, seated on the gaddi. After sacrificing goats to Persa Pen, the subaltern Gonds are given a feast by the raja. The last raja, Yadav Shah, emphasized the reassertion of Gond culture, and sacrificed a cow to Persa Pen, as traditionally done, instead of goats. He strongly believed that Gondi dharma was different from Hindu dharma. A similar celebration is held by almost every ex-zamindar of the erstwhile Chanda kingdom, in a condensed form, of course, as they have lost their lands and positions to outsiders, but those who are economically and politically established celebrate the festival in a big way.[61] Gondraje Dr Birshah Atram, cousin of Yadav Shah, told me that he performed the Dassera celebration at his hometown of Warora in Chandrapur district, but was able to give return gifts (saris) to only a few people because of his poor economic position.[62]

My study of Utnur fort provides a thicker illustration of the trajec-tories of the Gond Dassera celebrations. Utnur is located at the heart of the Adilabad Agency, 144 kilometres from the Chanda fort to the south. On my visit on 14 June 2014, I found that the fort was completely ruined; only some walls were still standing. A *firangi* (cannon) stood in front of the ruins. Mesram Somji told me that there were actually two such cannons, but one had been taken to Adilabad town. Somji further narrated the genealogy of the fort. He said that he could trace the genealogy of the Utnur rajas back over five generations. Sitagondi Atram Chin Bapu Raja was the first to come to Utnur from Jennaram. He was a pious man and a priest of the goddess. He was succeeded by his son Hanmanth Rao, and after him by Hanmanth Rao's son Jalpath Rao. Chin Bapu and Hanmanth Rao both died at the fort and their tombs are still located here. Jalpath Rao was the last raja, as his *jagir* (estate) was taken over by the Nizam's government. But he continued to live at the fort even after he lost his jagir. He later moved out of the fort and built a house in the common Gond locality, as his children had died and this ill-fortune was attributed to the fort. It is said that there is a big snake inhabiting the fort as a result of which people are afraid to enter it.

Christoph von Fürer-Haimendorf provides an elaborate account of the Utnur fort. He says that Jalpath Rao informed him that his fam-ily had genealogical links with the raja of Chanda. They had come to

Utnur approximately fifteen generations previously, and built the fort of Wodur Wakri on the Nirmal–Adilabad road. Jalpath Rao's ancestors had held *maqta* (land-cultivation rights with a fixed rent) rights over the *pargana*s (a pargana is a territorial division, above the village) of Utnur (its *haveli* or surroundings), Sirpur, and Indraveli, paying an annual revenue of Rs 600. The rights over these parganas were confiscated by the Nizam's government in 1227 Fasli (1817–18). Raja Isru Jangu was the last to hold these parganas. Jalpath Rao's father Hanmanth Rao was given just five villages as compensation for the confiscation of maqta rights.[63] He held only one village (Lakkaram) as maqta, and exercised *watan* (revenue-collection rights) rights in Jannaram village.[64]

Mesram Somji says that Jalpath Rao used to correspond with the sixth Nizam, Osman Ali Khan. The raja stood by his people and got some *patta* lands (lands with paper deeds) for them. He was succeeded by his son Dev Shah, who was the last to be declared a successor of the royal family. Dev Shah was elected president of Utnur tahsil for seven years, and was a member of the legislative assembly for eleven years during the Indira Gandhi regime. He was defeated when he contested for the third time, and died in 2005. His sons chose not to enter public life and remained agriculturists.[65]

Until the time of Dev Shah, says Somji, Dassera was celebrated with elaborate rituals. On the day of Vijaya Dasami, the raja would dress in royal clothes, carry weapons, and ride in a palanquin to the fort (see Figure 1.4). Some in the procession would act as soldiers bearing weapons and follow the raja on horses.[66] Music and dance troupes performed at the front of the procession. The fort was about a kilometre from the raja's house. The procession would pass through the village streets on its way to the fort. After reaching the fort, the raja would hoist the royal flag. A Gond priest would perform a puja to the *jammi* tree (*Prosopis cineraria*), and then to Persa Pen and to the ancestors of the raja. A goat would then be sacrificed to Persa Pen. Till 1970, a cow had been sacrificed, but because of Brahmanization the cow was replaced thereafter by a goat. Gond people offered goats, fowl, and foodgrains to the raja. The raja would host a feast for his people. After the feast there was dancing and singing till late in the night. People returned home with gifts of 'gold' (jammi tree leaves).[67]

Figure 1.4   Raja Jalpath Rao of Utnur
Source: From the author's personal collection.

In fact, cultural programmes (dancing, singing, and stick play) continue for nine days every evening. On these occasions, the Pardhans tell legendary and mythological stories in which the ancestors of the raja's family are remembered. Of all these legends, Ankum Raja's love legend is still popular in Adilabad district, and it is performed accompanied by stick-play during Dassera. The legend goes as follows: Ankum Raja was the son of Babji (the raja of Chanda who is known in historical accounts as Babji Ballal Shah). He disliked his father's reign and came down to Jangoam (present-day Asifabad). Now, there happened to be two sisters, Virubai and Gangubai, of whom the former was married to Ankum and the latter to Ramji, the raja of Rajgarh, about 30 miles to the east of Chandrapur. When Virubai delivered a baby, Gangubai came to see her. Ankum, attracted by Gangubai's beauty, wanted to have extramarital relations with her. When his overtures bore no fruit, he hatched a plot to capture and rape Gangubai. He succeeded in securing the consent of his wife, who had initially been unwilling. Gangubai was childless, and Virubai suggested that she pray to the deity Baleshvar, who was known to fulfil the wishes of his devotees. When Gangubai entered the temple of Baleshvar, Ankum, who was hiding there, raped her. A helpless Gangubai came home and told her husband Ramji. Ramji planned revenge on Ankum. He had it declared that Ramji was dead and his wife, pretending to be a widow, secretly invited Ankum to her place. On the appointed day, Ankum came to Gangubai's house. As plotted, Ramji went to the bedroom wearing Gangubai's dress. When Ankum came in, he seized and blinded him, saying that the problem was not with the person but with his eyes. Ankum, according to this legend, repented all his life for the crime he had committed.

Raja Ankum was a very popular ruler among his people. Having agreed to pay a heavy tribute to the Delhi rulers, Babji had started imposing heavy taxes on his people. The people pleaded with Ankum to save them from the heavy taxes. Ankum took up the matter with Babji and remonstrated with him. When Babji did not heed his pleas, he headed back to Jangoam. But his minister poisoned the raja's ear, saying that Ankum might approach the Delhi emperor, which would not be a good thing. A party was then sent to kill Ankum. As he was escorted by just two soldiers, Ankum was killed easily on his way to Jangoam. Hearing this, Virubai decided to die along with her husband and jumped onto her husband's funeral pyre. Both Ankum and Virubai are still remembered by the people of Asifabad.[68]

Another popular legend sung during Dassera relates to Raja Beer Shah's heroic victory at Deogarh. According to the legend, Beer Shah gave his daughter in marriage to Durgapal, son of the king of Deogarh. After some time, he came to know that Durgapal had insulted his daughter. Beer Shah was disturbed by this and decided to wage war against Durgapal. He vowed to Goddess Mahakali that if he won the war, he would offer Durgapal's head to the goddess. Beer Shah himself led his army against Durgapal, defeated him, and cut off Durgapal's head with his family's sacred sword, crying 'Victory to Mahakali!' Taking the head he returned to Chanda and offered it to Mahakali.[69]

Many such legends are sung during Dassera and on other social occasions. Many of the names mentioned in these legends are recorded in historical documents. Myths, rumours, gods, and goddesses inhabit these legends.[70] But what is important for our purpose is how the sovereign past of the community is remembered, and how it endures as a metaphor around which a new politics is articulated, the politics of difference.

The Gond community thus is conscious of the forms of power associated with history. History produces dominance and subordination, establishing divides between written and oral cultures, civilized and uncivilized, political and apolitical, and so on. The source of such divides is rooted in European Enlightenment philosophy.[71] However, in the case of the Gonds, their marginality is reimagined by reproducing their sovereign past. Their identity as a ruling community not only distinguishes the Gonds from caste-Hindu subjects but also helps them to contest state power. When the Gonds were starving under colonial rule, their sovereign past served as a weapon. Remembering the rajas was remembering their sovereignty and their freedom in the hills and forests. In particular, the telling and retelling of these stories helped to legitimize their practice of carrying out raids in the adjoining areas. Such raids were indeed central to the negotiations of the Gonds with the British. We shall now move on to examine this history.

NOTES

1. Mesram Somji, aged seventy, is a Pardhan who acts as storyteller for the Gonds. He worked for the last Utnur raja, and retired as the warden of the Tribal Welfare Hostel, Marlavai (Adilabad district). Interview, Utnur, 14 June 2013.

2. Eyre Chatterton, *The Story of Gondwana* (London: Sir Isaac Pitman & Sons, 1916), pp. 1–11.

3. Edward W. Said, *Orientalism: Western Conceptions of the Orient* (London: Penguin, 1995), p. 36.

4. V. R. Raghavaiah, 'Background of Tribal Struggles in India', in *Peasant Struggle in India*, edited by A. R Desai (New Delhi: Oxford University Press, 1979), pp. 12–27; also see K. S. Singh (ed.), *Tribal Movements in India*, vols I–II (New Delhi: Manohar, 1982–3).

5. K. S. Singh (ed.), *The Mahabharata in the Tribal and Folk Traditions of India* (Shimla: Indian Institute of Advanced Studies, 1993), p. 7. Also see Satyanarayana Kambhampati, *A Study of the History and Culture of the Andhras* (Hyderabad: Visalandhra Publishing House, 1999), vol. 1, p. 102; B. N. Sastri, *Andhra Desa Charitra Samskruti from 1518 to 1990* [History and culture of the Andhra country from 1518 to 1990] (Telugu) (Hyderabad: Musee Publication, 1990), p. 313.

6. Stephen Hislop first documented this mythology, popularly called 'Gondi Puranam' [The Story of Lingo], which explains the origin of the Gonds from the Shiva tradition. According to the legend, the Gonds were created by Parvati but Shiva shut them up in a cave, holding them responsible for a foul smell in the forest. But they were later liberated from the cave by a divine hero, Lingo. It is a very long story sung by Pardhans on all Gond social occasions. For the full story, see R. V. Russell and Hiralal, *The Tribes and Castes of the Central Provinces of India*, 4 vols (1916; reprint, New Delhi: Asian Educational Services, 1993), vol. 3, pp. 47–62.

7. Chatterton, *The Story of Gondwana*, p. 54; also see *Maharashtra State Gazetteers: Chandrapur District* (hereafter *Chandrapur District Gazetteer* 1973) (Bombay: Government of Maharashtra, 1973), p. 61.

8. Christoph von Fürer-Haimendorf (in collaboration with Elizabeth von Fürer-Haimendorf), *The Gonds of Andhra Pradesh: Tradition and Change in an Indian Tribe* (New Delhi: Vikas, 1979), p. 1.

9. Russell, *The Tribes and Castes of the Central Provinces*, pp. 42–3.

10. Fürer-Haimendorf, *The Gonds of Andhra Pradesh*, pp. 1–3.

11. Lhendup G. Bhutia, 'The Eternal Harappan Script Tease', *Open*, 8 December 2014, pp. 40–5; M. C. Kangali, *Decipherment of Indus Script in Gondi* (Hindi) (Nagpur, 2002).

12. Fürer-Haimendorf, *The Gonds of Andhra Pradesh*, pp. 1–3.

13. *Central Provinces District Gazetteers: Chanda District* (hereafter *Chanda District Gazetteer* 1909) (Allahabad: Pioneer Press, 1909), pp. 97–8.

14. Shashank Kela argues that in adivasi society, the relation between 'ruler' and 'ruled' may vary widely among different social formations. The existence of chieftains does not indicate the hierarchy that we see in the mainland, but shows the particular nature of subservience of the subjects. This relationship was transformed drastically under colonial rule, whereby the ruling chiefs were reduced to the position of peasants or agricultural labour. See Shashank Kela, *A Rogue and Peasant Slave: Adivasi Resistance 1800–2000* (New Delhi: Navayana, 2012), pp. 96–7 and Chapter 9.

15. In general, the Gond community is divided into twelve phratries, but only four are found in Chanda territory.

16. According to Gond mythology, these divisions were said to have been created by Lingo at Poropatar Dhanegon in order to maintain the code of conduct in the Gond community. Poropatar Dhanegon is considered by the Gonds as their ancestral home and the birthplace of their gods, and is identified with modern-day Kachhargadh, Salekasa taluka of Gondia district in Maharashtra. It is located on the borders of Maharashtra, Madhya Pradesh, and Chhattisgarh. The Gonds of central India assemble there every year in February on the full moon to celebrate the birthplace of their gods.

17. Christoph von Fürer-Haimendorf, *The Raj Gonds of Adilabad: A Peasant Culture of the Deccan* (London: Macmillan, 1948), pp. 184–5; Russell, *The Tribes and Castes of the Central Provinces*, pp. 66–7.

18. These stories were collected by British officials in the early nineteenth century. If the interviewee was between sixty and seventy years old at the time, legends from the middle of the eighteenth century, when the Gonds were still ruling Chanda, would have been fresh in their minds.

19. Richard Jenkins was the first to study the Nagpur territories in the 1820s, but it was Smith who systematically documented the history of the Gonds of Chanda. See Smith, *Land Revenue Settlement of the Chanda District*, p. 61.

20. Smith, *Land Revenue Settlement of the Chanda District*, p. 69.

21. *Chanda District Gazetteer*, 1909, pp. 37–8.

22. Smith, *Land Revenue Settlement of the Chanda District*, p. 61.

23. Chatterton, *The Story of Gondwana*, pp. 60–3.

24. *Chandrapur District Gazetteer*, 1973, pp. 60–71.
25. On this, see C. U. Wills, *The Raj-Gond Maharajas of the Satpura Hills, the Central Provinces* (Nagpur: Government Press, 1923), pp. 6–7; and Setumadhava Rao Pagdi, *Among the Gonds of Adilabad* (Bombay: Popular Book Depot, 1949), pp. 15–16.
26. Irfan Habib, *An Atlas of the Mughal Empire* (New Delhi: Oxford University Press, 1982), sheet 9A; Smith, *Land Revenue Settlement of the Chanda District*, pp. 61–6.
27. Smith, *Land Revenue Settlement of the Chanda District*, pp. 63–4.
28. Fürer-Haimendorf, *The Gonds of Andhra Pradesh*, p. 7; also see *Chandrapur District Gazetteer*, 1973, p. 78.
29. Mahomed Kasim Ferishta, *History of the Rise of the Mahomedan Power in India till the Year A.D. 1612*, translated by John Briggs (1829; reprint, New Delhi: Oriental Book Reprint Corporation, 1981), vol. 2, pp. 232–3.
30. Ferishta, *History of the Rise of the Mahomedan Power*, p. 263.
31. Ferishta, *History of the Rise of the Mahomedan Power*, pp. 133–4.
32. Ferishta, *History of the Rise of the Mahomedan Power*, pp. 168–71.
33. Habib, *An Atlas of the Mughal Empire*, p. 66.
34. Allami Abul Faz, *The Ain-i-Akbari*, translated by H. S. Jarrett (Calcutta: Baptist Mission Press, 1891), vol. 2, p. 230.
35. Jadunath Sarkar, *A Short History of Aurangzib* (1930; reprint, Calcutta: Orient Longman, 1979), pp. 360–3.
36. Saqi Mustad Khan, *Maasir-i-Alamgiri: A History of the Emperor Aurangzib-Alamgir (Reign 1658–1707)*, translated by Jadunath Sarkar (1947; reprint, New Delhi: Oriental Books Reprint Corporation, 1986), p. 39.
37. Khan, *Maasir-i-Alamgiri*, p. 84.
38. Khan, *Maasir-i-Alamgiri*, p. 134.
39. Khan, *Maasir-i-Alamgiri*, p. 133.
40. Khan, *Maasir-i-Alamgiri*, p. 146.
41. Khan, *Maasir-i-Alamgiri*, p. 153.
42. Sarkar, *A Short History of Aurangzib*, p. 361.
43. Govind Sakharam Sardesai, *New History of the Marathas: The Expansion of the Maratha Power 1707–1772* (Bombay: Phoenix Publications, 1946–8; reprint, New Delhi: Munshiram Manoharlal, 1986), vol. 2, pp. 341–2.
44. Wills, *The Raj-Gond Maharajas of the Satpura Hills*, pp. 170–4.
45. Smith, *Land Revenue Settlement of the Chanda District*, pp. 69–71; *Chandrapur District Gazetteer*, 1973, pp. 88–93.
46. Pagdi, *Among the Gonds*, pp. 26–7; *Gazetteer of the Central Provinces of India*, 1870, p. 143.

47. Smith, *Land Revenue Settlement of the Chanda District*, p. 70.
48. *Stephen Hislop's Papers Relating to the Aboriginal Tribes of the Central Provinces*, IOR/F/4/755/20541, India Office Records, British Library, London, p. v.
49. *Report on the Administration of the Central Provinces for the Year 1901–1902* (Nagpur: Secretariat Press, 1902), p. 9.
50. Pagdi, *Among the Gonds*, p. 28; Kidar Nath Thusu, *Gond Kingdom of Chanda, with Particular Reference to Its Political Structure* (Calcutta: Anthropological Survey of India, 1980), p. 247.
51. *Chanda District Gazetteer*, 1909, p. 54.
52. Thusu, *Gond Kingdom of Chanda*, pp. 227–8.
53. For example, see Chatterton, *The Story of Gondwana*; J. Forsyth, *The Highlands of Central India* (1871; reprint, Dehra Dun: Natraj, 1994); Smith, *Land Revenue Settlement of the Chanda District*; Verrier Elwin, *Folk-Songs of Chhattisgarh* (Madras: Oxford University Press, 1946); Fürer-Haimendorf, *The Raj Gonds of Adilabad*; Madhadi Narayana Reddy, *Ankama Raju Katha: Kolata Patalu* [Story of Ankama Raju: Stick play songs] (Telugu) (Hanmakonda: Rainbow Printers, 2001). I will be using these texts here besides my own ethnographic notes from the field.
54. *Stephen Hislop's Papers*, p. iv; also Pagdi, *Among the Gonds*, pp. 15–20.
55. Apart from these forts, I identified about twelve Gond forts in Adilabad district during my field trips in 2015. They are: Siddeshwar, Wankdi, Devadurjari, Gandarla, Jangoam, Mauwad, Sitagondi, Kawala, Buttapur, Badankurthi, Thiryani, and Meshelakar Madow. Of these forts, Siddeshwar and Wankdi have been converted into Hindu temples, while the rest lie in ruins with only some walls and stones still standing.
56. Fürer-Haimendorf, *The Gonds of Andhra Pradesh*, pp. 526–7.
57. According to Sundar, all regimes from the Kakatiyas down to the postcolonial state, including the Gond rajas, used the Dassera celebration and darbar to expand and legitimize their power over the subaltern people of Bastar. See Nandini Sundar, *Subalterns and Sovereigns: An Anthropological History of Bastar, 1854–1996* (New Delhi: Oxford University Press, 1997), pp. 57–9.
58. Thusu, *Gond Kingdom of Chanda*, p. 263.
59. Sundar, *Subalterns and Sovereigns*, p. 58.
60. Interview with Atram Laxmana Rao, Modi (Adilabad), 25 January 2015.
61. Thusu, *Gond Kingdom of Chanda*, pp. 251–67.
62. Interview with Dr Birshah, Hyderabad, 22 February 2015.
63. The five villages were Lakkaram, Gangapet, Koinur, Pamalawada, and Jannaram.

64. Christoph von Fürer-Haimendorf, *Tribal Hyderabad: Four Reports* (Hyderabad: Revenue Department, Government of H.E.H. the Nizam, 1945), pp. 63–5.

65. Dev Shah is survived by three sons and seven daughters. Among the three sons, the eldest, Pursotham Rao, is employed with the Food Corporation of India, and the other two, Gangadhar Rao and Sudhakar Rao, are both agriculturists. Sudhakar Rao now looks after family matters, and is considered the successor of the royal family by the Gond community. He receives gifts from the community on Dassera.

66. Mesram Manohar says that every Gond family used to have weapons—guns, arrows, or *dol* (a defence weapon used by soldiers)—but these were taken away by the Rajakars (volunteers of the Majlis-I-Ittehad-ul-Mussulmeen party) and the Indian military during the armed struggle for Telangana state. Interview, Utnur town, 18 November 2014.

67. Kidar Nath Thusu offers an elaborate ethnography of Dassera celebration under the present Ahiri raja, and shows how important it is to the community to recast its sovereign past in the context of modern politics. See his *Gond Kingdom of Chanda*, pp. 153–73.

68. Narrated by Atram Laxmana Rao of Modi (Adilabad), 25 January 2015. Laxmana Rao took me to visit Ankum Raja's tomb located in the centre of Asifabad town, and to the Baleshvar temple on the outskirts of the town. Madhadi Narayana Reddy has documented elaborately how the full legend is sung during Dassera, with descriptions of Ankum Raja's contributions in agriculture, irrigation, culture, and the protection of the region's interests in general. For the full story, see his *Ankama Raju Katha*, pp. 6–14. The same story is told differently in Chanda district. For details, see *Chandrapur District Gazetteer*, 1973, pp. 81–2.

69. Narrated by a Pardhan, Manohar Rao, Utnur, 15 June 2014. This legend is also recorded in Smith, *Land Revenue Settlement of the Chanda District*, pp. 67–8.

70. Elwin recorded a heroic legend which narrates the greatness of the Chanda kings and describes their wars with the Wyragarh (Chhattisgarh) rajas. See his *Folk-Songs of Chhattisgarh*, pp. 279–86.

71. Shail Mayaram, *Against History, Against State: Counterperspectives from the Margins* (New Delhi: Permanent Black, 2004), pp. 234–5.

2

SUBORDINATING THE SOVEREIGNS
THE COLONIAL PROJECT OF TAMING THE
GOND RAJAS*

WHEN THE BRITISH ARMY BEGAN marching towards the forests and hills of the Nagpur territories after the last Maratha war, the Gond rajas responded through a programme of raids. As discussed earlier, the Gond rajas largely maintained their sovereign power in their forests and hill tracts until the mid-eighteenth century, keeping outside rulers at bay. Even after they were conquered by the Marathas, they negotiated with the paramount imperial powers and continued to hold their positions.[1] Indeed, India had a tradition of the existence of multiple sovereignties even during times of strong imperial rule.[2] Pre-colonial imperial powers enjoyed symbolic sovereignty, particularly over forests and hill areas, while local powers had undisputed sovereignty over their territories' resources and people.[3] Under British colonial rule, however, sovereign rulers and their peoples were brought under close control. This was in part carried out by force, agreements, and treaties, and in part by a use of a colonial political rationality that was

---

* This chapter was originally published as 'The Subordination of the Sovereigns: Colonialism and the Gond Rajas in Central India, 1818–1948', *Modern Asian Studies* 47, no. 1 (2013): 288–317 © Cambridge University Press. Reproduced with permission from Cambridge University Press.

rooted in the canon of Western state power.[4] However, the process was full of tensions. It also brought about enormous change in the external and internal relations of the rajas, their relationship with the paramount power, with other adivasis, and with non-adivasis.

The British, in the beginning, held that the forests and hills were purely the lands of wild and troublesome people, and it would not only be difficult to administer these tracts but also uneconomic to the government, as the whole of the vast area was barren and uncultivable land. This led the British to allow the traditional local rajas to keep these territories, subject to payment of a tribute to the colonial state, which adopted a paternalistic approach towards them. This is not to suggest that the British adopted a policy of taming the Gond rajas out of their indolence, but a policy essentially to deal with the Gonds' politics of raids and ruggedness. This policy thus not only brought financial and commercial benefits to the colonial state, but also avoided resistance and raids both from the local chiefs and their people. The rajas were also seen as a potential mediating agency between the colonial state and the hill people, and it was sought through them to normalize and civilize the hill land and its people.[5] In other words, the colonial state endeavoured to govern the 'troublesome' and 'uneconomic territories' through an alliance with the local traditional powers—a system of indirect rule. Although the British were dependent on the local rajas in building and continuing colonial rule in India, they soon reduced the rajas to being their dependants. The power of the rajas was effectively frozen, leaving them with what Nicholas Dirks has called 'hollow crowns', or rajas with very limited powers.[6] Their financial position also became increasingly precarious.[7] However, the process of taming the rajas resulted in the emergence of a new consciousness particularly among educated rajas, which turned them against colonial domination.

Recent studies have explored many of these developments for western and central India. However, they have tended to focus on violent suppression, subordination, and exploitation of the adivasis, and on the importance of an adivasi articulation of primordial loyalties in revolt against the colonial state.[8] They say less about the process of inculcating a new culture and way of life among the adivasi rajas and their people. This chapter focuses more on this latter aspect, bringing out the way in which the colonial state-making process subordinated, marginalized, and sought to hegemonize the Gond rajas.

RESISTING THE EMPIRE

From the time that the British took charge of Nagpur state as a protectorate up until 1860, the Gond rajas continued to carry out raids on the
territories of both the British and the Nizam of Hyderabad. In this, they
were carrying on a long tradition. Importantly, the source of such politics
was the reproduction of their sovereign past. As seen in Chapter 1, oral
traditions tended to exaggerate the power of the Gond rajas. The rajas
were supposed to have had huge armies, conquered and ruled vast tracts,
and to have sat on great gaddis. The Gonds recalled these legends and
stories time and again at their social gatherings—reinforcing their self-
image of enjoying the freedom of the forests and hills.[9] They deployed
these accounts to both assert their rights over land and forest, and to
raid neighbouring countries. In this sense, the adivasi construction of
sovereignty differed from that of the rulers of the plains regions. Orality
articulated the past in multiple ways, with each articulation relating to
present aspirations.[10] In particular, the telling and retelling of these stories helped to legitimize their practice of carrying out raids on adjoining
areas. Such raids were indeed central to the negotiations of the Gonds
with the British. The British saw the raids as criminal activities, but for
the Gonds it was an act of realizing their right to collect dues. Tracing
the history of the raids, Jenkins says:

> [T]hese *zamindarees* [Gond subordinate chiefs] have been always in a kind
> of feudal subjection, first to the Gond Rajahs, and since to the Marathas.
> The unproductiveness of the hills and forest, and the natural strength of the
> country preserved these chiefs from entire subjection to the Marathas, who,
> however, possessed themselves of the most accessible parts; and whose policy
> it generally was to support one of the most powerful of them to keep the rest
> in check, and to be responsible for the depredations they were always in the
> habit of committing on the neighbouring plains.[11]

Such raids grew out of the politics of the time. In this way, the Gond
rajas collected a tax from the neighbouring countries and imposed their
authority over them.[12] For Gond sovereignty, raids were very important
to reiterate their control over natural resources and the social life of
the communities. These raids continued while the British East India
Company was expanding its power in the Maratha region during the
last quarter of the eighteenth century. The depredation of the Gonds was

rampant in the region.[13] Indeed, the Bhonsle rulers themselves encour-aged the Gond rajas to assert their power in their respective territories by raiding the territories conquered by the British. In 1789, Venkojee Bhonsle (commonly called Nana Sahib) released Bhillal Shah who was being held captive in Nagpur, granting him a yearly pension of Rs 600.[14] This was at a time when the Bhonsles were fighting the British, and Bhillal Shah was released so as to harass the British. The period from 1798 to 1817 saw a wave of raids by the Gond rajas and chiefs on the Narmada territories that were under British control. These raids mainly targeted agricultural crops, and had a marked impact on British land revenues.[15] Similar polities of raids were also adopted by many nomadic groups of central India, and these were suppressed brutally by the colo-nial state.[16]

Appa Sahib, the last raja of Nagpur state, deployed the Gonds in his final struggle with the British. He looked to Chanda city as a strategic place to carry on his resistance, as it was located in a hilly region that was surrounded by dense forests. He ordered the Chanda *killadar* (keeper of the fort) to recruit Gonds and keep a large garrison there. He himself planned to escape from Nagpur and lead his resistance from Chanda, but was captured and imprisoned by the British resident before he could do so. Despite this, some of his leading adherents rallied in Chanda—people such as Bhujang Rao, the Gond zamindar of Ahiri, and his brother Kondu Bapu, Gond zamindar of Arpalli. They allied with the Gonds to defend the city. After defeating Peshwa Baji Rao's army at Pandarkaura, west of Wardha, the British army marched on Chanda. A message was sent to the killadar to ask the garrison to surrender, but the messenger was killed by the Gonds. Despite a heroic fight by the Gonds, led by Bhujang Rao, Chanda fell to the British army on 2 May 1818.[17]

Even after this defeat, raids by the Gond rajas and chiefs continued. It was hard for the British to suppress the Gonds in this respect, as the lat-ter sheltered in highly inaccessible areas and carried out guerrilla warfare against the British patrols. Frustrated by their lack of success, the British appointed a special commissioner to negotiate settlements with the Gonds.[18] Captain Crawford managed, with considerable difficulty, to persuade each Gond raja and chief to execute a written bond that stated that they would agree not to protect thieves, to make good to travellers

any loss they may sustain from robberies in their zamindaris, and to fur-
nish men, ranging from three to twenty, depending on the chief, when
called on by government. In return, the British government promised to
respect their proprietary rights over their zamindaris. The rajas agreed
to pay a nominal *takoli* (tribute) to the British government as a mark of
British suzerainty—a traditional practice in Gond politics.[19]

The British thus endeavoured to bring the Gond rajas under their
paramount power through treaties and agreements. In return, the British
agreed to honour and respect the powers of the Gond rajas. However,
these agreements did not last long. Many Gond rajas breached their
agreements and began raiding British territories once again. The *Land
Revenue Settlement Report* of Chanda recorded that 'plundering revived
in spite of military parties posted thickly over the district, and as late
as 1852, A.D., a government treasure escort was attacked and robbed
by Gonds on the Mool road, not sixteen miles from Chanda'.[20] Such
raids were widespread not only in Chanda but also all over the Central
Provinces. The situation was aggravated by the rise of the Bundelas in
the Narmada region.[21]

Although such raids were ongoing throughout the 1850s, the British
came to see them as a part of the 'Mutiny' only from March 1858
onwards. During this month, Babu Rao, a Gond raja of Mollampalli in
the Ahiri zamindari, commenced plundering in the Rajgarh pargana. He
was soon joined by Venkat Rao, Gond zamindar of Arpalli and Ghot.
These two leaders then openly declared that they were in revolt, and
recruited a mixed force of Rohillas and Gonds.[22] On 29 April 1858, they
carried out an attack on Chunchgondi in which two British telegraph
employees, Gartland and Hall, were killed. Chunchgondi is one of the
largest villages in the Ahiri zamindari and within a distance of 1 mile
from Ahiri town.[23] It was then rumoured that Lakshmi Bai, the zamindar of Ahiri, had joined hands with Babu Rao and Venkat Rao. The two
leaders became very popular in a short period, with stories spreading
amongst the Gonds about their prowess. Other Gond zamindars joined
the revolt, and many village *patels* (village heads) and mokhasis (village
heads from Gond community) extended financial support to them. The
support for the revolt came mainly from the smaller chiefs. The larger
zamindars, for the most part, remained aloof.[24]

The activities of these two ringleaders were not confined only to Chanda district but also spread into the Wardha region of the province and the northern territories of Hyderabad State. Many zamindars, Rohillas, and Arabs of these regions responded positively to their appeal and openly supported their activities.[25] Rohillas and Arabs were recruited by them in large numbers on payment and sent to Sirpur and Rajura *taluk*s (administrative division of a district) of Hyderabad State, as the Nizam was allied with the British. The celebrated Rohilla leader Turre Baaz Khan, who attacked the Hyderabad Residency, was paid twenty rupees a month, and his hundred or so followers ten rupees a month each.[26] A force of about a thousand Gonds and Rohillas under the leadership of Ramji Gond created havoc in Adilabad district of Hyderabad State throughout 1860.[27] The British put pressure on the Nizam's government to suppress this revolt.[28] They did this with considerable difficulty. Eventually the rebels were rounded up, but Ramji Gond managed to escape.[29] He was caught and later hanged at Nirmal in 1860.

In Chanda itself, Deputy Commissioner Captain Crichton led a 1,700-strong force against the rebels in 1858. Advancing into the hills, they were attacked by Gonds who shot arrows, threw stones, and blocked the roads by felling trees. Unaccustomed to operating in such jungle and mountain areas, the force failed to make any dent on their opponents and had to retreat.[30] It was widely believed that after this, Captain Crichton no longer dared to set foot in the hill tracts of the district.[31] Back in Chanda, he announced rewards of Rs 1,000 and Rs 500 for apprehending Venkat Rao and Babu Rao respectively. Later on, Babu Rao's head was also priced at Rs 1,000. Nothing, however, came of this.[32] Pressure was then brought to bear on the superior zamindars to help the British in their suppression of the revolt. They were warned that if they were seen to be complicit with the rebels in any way, they would be held accountable. Most important in this respect was the zamindarin of Ahiri, Lakshmi Bai. Both Babu Rao and Venkat Rao held zamindari rights in some of the villages in her territory and Venkat Rao was also related to her.[33] Under the threat of having her rights revoked, she agreed to help the British.[34] She visited Crichton and provided an agreement in writing that she would hand over Venkat Rao in a few days and Babu

Rao in less than two months, or sooner, and would assist in every way in seizing any rebels that she apprehended in her zamindari. The disruption had caused severe food scarcities in her territory, and in return for her help Crichton agreed to supply cattle fodder, *chenna* (pulses), and wheat to her zamindari.[35]

After returning to Ahiri, Lakshmi Bai caught and imprisoned Venkat Rao. She wrote to Crichton, stating that she would hand him over to the British on condition that he was imprisoned for life, but not hanged. His zamindaris (Arpalli and Ghot) should be given to her, and she would pay the Rs 1,000 tribute that Venkat Rao had paid to her directly to the British government. She also said that she had already spent Rs 1,200 in trying to catch Babu Rao, and that she needed a further Rs 4,000 to complete this task. The British refused to compromise, demanding that she deliver Venkat Rao unconditionally or be taken into custody herself, with her estate being forfeited.[36]

Despite this threat, Lakshmi Bai did not hand over Venkat Rao. It was believed by government officials that Lakshmi Bai had, in fact, formed a confederacy with Venkat Rao and Babu Rao to commit dacoity in British territories.[37] This rumour was strengthened further when Venkat Rao escaped from Lakshmi Bai's prison. Crichton believed that Lakshmi Bai herself had set him free, while the commissioner of Nagpur believed that Babu Rao had kidnapped Lakshmi Bai and forced her to do this.[38] Lakshmi Bai herself informed Crichton that she was completely ignorant of the incident as she had been busy with her daughter's wedding. By now, the monsoon had set in and the military could not carry out any operations in the hills. Taking advantage of this situation, Babu Rao along with about two hundred followers increased his attacks on military outposts.[39] Under threat of punishment, Lakshmi Bai and her relatives once again met Crichton and promised, both orally and in writing, that she would recapture Venkat Rao and Babu Rao and hand them over.[40]

Soon after this, Babu Rao was rounded up by Lakshmi Bai's *kamdar*s (servants) and handed over to Crichton. He was hanged at Chanda on 21 October 1858. Venkat Rao escaped to Bastar and continued his raids on British territories till he was captured by the raja of Bastar in April 1860 and handed over to the British. He was sentenced to transportation.

Lakshmi Bai was rewarded with sixty-seven villages of the confiscated Ghot and Arpalli zamindaris.[41] After this incident the region was, by and large, free from raids until Kumaram Bhimu revolted against the Nizam in 1940.

The long-standing tradition of raids that effectively came to an end in 1860 played an important part in the politics of the Gond rajas. It helped the rajas to unite people under their leadership, as many common people took a direct part in the raids and the booty was distributed to all. Stories of triumphant raids created a climate in which people looked forward to the next one. Such stories also created an aura of power and masculinity around the Gonds and their rulers. Outside rulers were wary of taking them on, and left them largely in control of their hills and forests. The British were not, however, prepared to accept this state of affairs, as it posed a challenge to their imperial sovereignty. For British imperial sovereignty, producing the effects of state power was crucial—in other words, making people feel that state power was central in British imperial sovereignty. The British believed that the politics of raids represented a continuing threat to law and order and an affront to their 'civilizing mission'. Instead, they sought to tame and 'civilize' the Gond rulers, making them an instrument of their governance. It is to this process that we shall now turn.

POLITICS OF TAMING THE RAJAS

From the beginning, the rajas and zamindars were central to British power in the plains of India because they were not only the source of Maratha power, but also had considerable control over the people. The dwindling power of the rajas/zamindars was thus important to British colonial rulers so as to root out Maratha power and impose British suzerainty over the people.[42] It was this understanding that led the colonial rulers to adopt a policy of taming the Gond rajas. Ajay Skaria has pointed out how the British viewed the forest communities as essentially 'wild', treating them in a different way from the settled peoples of the plains.[43] The colonial state was concerned first and foremost with maintaining law and order in the hill tracts, and second, to gradually weaning the inhabitants away from their former occupations and turning them into settled peasants. The 'civilizing mission' thus operated in different ways in the two regions. The way in which tribal rulers were treated, however, had certain parallels with the treatment of the princes of the plains regions.[44] After treaties and agreements had been made with these rulers, they were honoured with pensions, allowed to conduct darbars (public appearances of the king or raja), provided gifts, turbans, colonial titles and army salutes, and exposed to caste-Hindu society and English education. In this way, the colonial state sought to tame and subordinate the adivasi rajas and chiefs.

Nonetheless, as so-called 'aboriginal rulers', it was recognized that the 'civilizing' of these chiefs would be a long and slow process. The *District Gazetteer* of Chanda noted:

> [T]o secure comparative law and order it was necessary to use a light hand with natural chieftains of the aborigines, whose subjugation would have been of very little profit, while their enmity would have been a source of continual annoyance. Both Gonds and Marathas were, therefore, content to recognise the petty chiefs who were the ancestors of the present Zamindars, and by this policy of moderation to glean a certain amount of revenue in the shape of the Zamindar's tribute or *takoli*, leaving the management of the internal concerns of the zamindaris in their hands.[45]

In a similar way, Lucie Smith, who was an officer of the land revenue settlement of 1869, stated:

> [I]t is true that much is done by the Zemindars which is gravely wrong but it must be remembered that until recently they were left wholly to themselves, and it is not strange that, so left, they failed to be all we wish; and now I trust a day of better thing has dawned. Six Zemindars, or the near relatives of Zemindars, are studying at the High School and an English officer, it is hoped, will soon be available for the special charge of the zemindari country. With firmness, patience, and kindness there is scarcely a limit to the degree in which the Zemindars, who have much of the old-world loyalty, may not be influenced for good; and I can hardly imagine a more interesting or a nobler work than to raise and improve these chiefs, and through them their people.[46]

Thus, the apparent target of the colonial state was to rule the Gond rajas and chiefs with a light hand while gradually 'civilizing' them through education. Also, the main aim of the civilizing or taming of Gond rajas was to avoid violent responses and resistances by the Gonds.

The British were able to exert control over the Gond rulers through a politics of recognition of rights that was put into place in the 1860s, after the revolt of 1857–8 had been suppressed. Separate agreements and treaties had already been negotiated with particular rulers and chiefs during the early nineteenth century. The process was continued with the granting of pension rights to certain rulers. In 1867, the British granted a political pension of Rs 1,490 per annum to the royal family of the Chanda dynasty, and Yadav Shah was recognized as the successor of the last Gond king, Nilkanth Shah.[47] Apart from the pension, he was also allowed to receive customary dues from the Gonds whom they had once ruled. Each Gond family used to pay them an annual tribute of Re 1 and a contribution of Rs 1–4 was made on the occasion of a marriage between Gonds.[48] In 1903, seeing that the family of the raja was in reduced circumstances, the British increased their pension to Rs 500 per month. All such pensions were given to an individual recognized by the government, who would then distribute it among his recognized relatives.[49]

There were always problems in recognizing the successor of the royal family for sanctioning the pension. The eldest son of the family or the person approved by their family was generally considered as the legal pensioner. The government prepared a genealogical chart of the rajas from the time of Nilkanth Shah to avoid confusion.[50] The first person who received a pension from the British was Yadav Shah. He was succeeded by Ram Shah who died in 1905 leaving no issue; then Deo Shah, his uncle, was recognized as head of the family. Deo Shah died in 1906. He also had no issue. Govind Shah, brother of Ram Shah, had intemperate habits and waived his claim in favour of his son Dinker Shah. Dinker Shah died in 1918 and his son Yadav Shah was the last holder of the pension. His pension was continued after independence in 1947 by the government of independent India.[51]

The tutelary rajas (zamindars) who hitherto had symbolic rights in land were given proprietary rights to their estates in the settlement of 1869. In this way, twenty zamindaris were created in Chanda district, among which seventeen zamindars were Gonds, two were Hindus, and one was a Muslim, all of whom were said to have been granted zamindari rights by Gond kings.[52] However, no paper evidence for these has survived, and they were handed out largely on consideration of their long-standing customary rights. Importantly, the British revenue system had successfully converted the relatively independent rajas into dependent zamindars.[53]

A different system was put in place for the Gond rajas and chiefs of Adilabad district of Hyderabad State, an erstwhile territory of the Chanda dynasty. In this region, the former Maratha rulers had replaced many of the traditional Gond chiefs with non-adivasi Deshmukhs and Deshpandes (traditional revenue collectors at the village level and also landlords). They acted as heads of groups of villages, usually ten to fifteen in number. The Gond chiefs were designated as mokhasis and were assigned duties of maintaining peace in their respective areas. Although this position gave them a highly respected social status, they lost their hold over the land.[54] When, from 1864 onwards, the *ryotwari* system (a form of land tenure under the British) was implemented in Hyderabad State by its prime minister Salar Jung I (1853–83), the Gond rajas and chiefs all lost their jagirs and *watans* (revenue collection rights).[55] Only the raja of Sirpur was honoured with a jagirdari right and the raja of Utnur with a maqta right over five villages.[56] A small number of mokhasis were honoured with village patelships, but most were converted into mere cultivators.[57] However, they did not lose the mokhasi titles and played a crucial role in settling civil and criminal disputes within their community. It was recorded that there were thirty-seven mokhasis in the Adilabad district at the end of the Nizam's rule.[58]

The Gond zamindaris of Chanda district differed from the zamindaris of the plains regions. They were spread mainly in the eastern and southern part of Sironcha and Gadchiroli tahsils of the district, over an area of 4,900 square miles, which is about 50 per cent of the district.[59] The Ahiri zamindari was the largest among the twenty zamindaris of the district, spread over an area of 2,672 square miles. The area of the other zamindaris varied between 17 and 370 square miles. At the beginning of the twentieth century, the occupied area formed only 8 per cent of the total zamindari area and the remaining 92 per cent was mostly forest and hill.[60]

According to the rules of the settlements of 1869, these zamindaris were indivisible, non-transferable, and hereditary holdings, which would be transferred to the zamindar's eldest son or nearest male heir approved by the chief commissioner. The zamindari right was subject to loyalty to the British government, the execution of good police administration, and the improvement of cultivation within the estate. If the zamindar failed to fulfil these conditions, the British government might intervene to either force the holder to remedy the situation or depose him.[61] The zamindars, as proprietors of the land, were allowed initially to enjoy the revenue from land, forest, excise, *pandhri*, ferries, and ponds, but in time the latter four sources of income were resumed by government with due compensation being made to the zamindars. They were not permitted to levy transit duties, so as to ensure the free flow of goods between the zamindari and British territories. The forest was considered to be the property of the zamindars, but they were not allowed to sell wood without consulting the deputy commissioner. Zamindars subtitled land to mokhasis and *maqtadar* (estate head), and patels, who were given power to make agreements with tenants or actual cultivators.[62]

The zamindars and their territories were thus subjected to close supervision and control by colonial officials. As a rule, each zamindari was administered by a qualified manager who would be selected by the deputy commissioner of the district, but was appointed by the zamindar.[63] The manager had to send reports every six months on the overall conditions of the zamindari. The deputy commissioner would also visit the zamindaris regularly and make suggestions to the zamindars on how to improve the administration of their estates.[64] In cases where the zamindar was disqualified from managing his estate, a Court of Wards system was established under the Central Provinces Court of Wards Act of 1899 to manage the estate. Under Section 7 of the Act, the commissioner of the division was able, as Court of Ward, to take over the administration of an estate during the minority of a zamindar, if there was a female heir, or if a zamindar was found to be mentally or physically unfit to rule, or had been convicted of a non-bailable offence.[65]

We may examine the way that this system operated in the case of the Ahiri zamindari. This estate was brought under the management of the Court of Wards on 29 January 1902 owing to the maladministration of the then zamindar Bhujang Rao. Even after his death, the Court of Wards continued to manage the zamindari, as his son Dharam Rao, born on 21 March 1907, was a minor. The zamindari was handed over to him only on 20 March 1928, when he reached the age of twenty-one.[66] During these years of Court of Wards management, the zamindari witnessed many changes. As mentioned earlier, this was a huge estate having an area that greatly exceeded that of all the other zamindaris combined. In 1909, it possessed 451 villages in Sironcha tahsil on *malguzari* (a revenue tenure in which the village was the unit of assessment), zamindari, and ryotwari tenure, and 77 malguzari villages in Gadchiroli tahsil. Traditionally, this zamindari was, from the beginning, held by a member of the Chanda ruling family. But its history is evident only from the time of Koksha, who held the zamindari from 1703 to 1769 and who was a relative of the Gond king Ram Shah. Bhujang Rao assumed the zamindari in 1893. He was considered to be a most brilliant man, but was addicted to alcohol and gradually mired the zamindari deep in debt. The colonial administration held that the forest contractor had taken advantage of the zamindar's alcoholism to exploit the forests at a cheap rate. Arguing that the administration of the zamindari had sunk into a deplorable state, the Central Provinces government brought the zamindari under the management of the Court of Wards. Believing that this was a ruse to confiscate his zamindari in perpetuity, Bhujang Rao mobilized his followers and revolted violently against the government. Treasurers and officials were beaten up and warned not to enter the estate. The district superintendent of police marched into Ahiri and forced Bhujang Rao to come to Chanda. There, he was told by the deputy commissioner that the government had no intention of taking over the zamindari for perpetuity, and that the Court of Wards would merely manage the estate until its financial and administrative problems were rectified.[67]

During the management of the Court of Wards, the Ahiri zamindari achieved considerable prosperity. After streamlining the administration, the manager focused on the expansion of agriculture and scientific exploitation of forests. Between 1906 and 1923, the total occupied area was increased to 42 per cent and the cropped area by 7 per cent. The colonial model of development was introduced in the zamindari during this time. The development of roads and communications attracted many caste-Hindu peasants from the plains areas, particularly Telugu peasants from adjoining areas of Hyderabad State who developed extensive rice cultivation in the tract. The zamindari had a huge forest area covering about 2,607 square miles.[68] It was managed by a deputy ranger, and brought a good income to the treasury of the estate. During the financial year 1926–7, for example, the overall profit from the forest was Rs 17,000.[69] When the Court of Wards took over the zamindari, the accumulated debts of the zamindari was over one lakh rupees (1 lakh = 100,000).[70] At the time of handing back the zamindari in 1928, there was a surplus of Rs 186,500 that was invested in government securities. Besides the management of the zamindari, the manager also supervised the education of Dharam Rao, the heir apparent. In this way, the Court of Wards played a parental role in rearing the children of zamindars till they achieved their majority and took over the zamindari.[71]

Indeed, the education of the zamindars and their sons was a major concern of the colonial government. English education was held to provide one of the most important means through which these territories might be transformed.[72] To achieve this, the government of the Central Provinces established the Raj Kumar College in Raipur in the 1882. The medium of instruction was English, though local languages were also taught. The zamindars were expected to send their sons to this college, exposing them to Western values, institutions, and political principles, as well as ideas about modern forms of cultivation and forestry.[73] Eyre Chatterton, a Christian missionary, noted of this institution that it ensured that there was a 'happy contrast between what we see of the younger chiefs, and what we hear of their ancestors, [and that it] justifies us in hoping for steady improvement in these small Gond States'.[74] Dharam Rao was sent to the college during his minority, and after graduating he was then trained as a *naib* (deputy) tahsildar in order to familiarize him with colonial forms of administration.[75]

The educated zamindars were gradually brought into the colonial political system by offering them places on the local boards, district councils, and the provincial legislative assembly.[76] In the 1939 election, fifty-six adivasi members were both elected and nominated/selected to the local boards of the province, of whom two were from Chanda district. Fourteen adivasi members were also either elected or nominated to the district councils of the province. There was, however, only one adivasi member in the Chanda District Council.[77] In the 1937 provincial assembly elections, one seat was reserved for the Scheduled Tribes.

However, Dharam Rao of Ahiri and another Gond raja, the raja of Jabalpur, were elected from the non-reserved constituencies Gadchiroli-Sironcha and Dindori-Niwas respectively. Although under-represented in terms of the overall adivasi population, the fact that any adivasis were elected at all was a political breakthrough.[78] Dharam Rao's rise to ministership in the provincial government exemplified this achievement. In this way, he became a role model for other Gond chiefs.[79]

The colonial state also encouraged education among the adivasi community, offering them special scholarships. It was mainly the petty chiefs and Gaitas and Bhumias (traditional Gond village heads) who took advantage of this facility, which enabled them to gain official posts. In 1901, there were 288 schools in the feudatory states and zamindaris of the province, in which 13,404 pupils were studying.[80] The number steadily increased in subsequent years. By 1941 there were 69,164 literate adivasis in the Partially Excluded Areas of the province.[81] Educated adivasis were in a favourable position to gain appointments as teachers and village patels. In the Partially Excluded Areas, the position of patel was largely held by adivasis, and indeed many Gaitas and Bhumias had been granted patelships in the 1897–1906 land revenue settlements.[82] In 1941, there were 165 aboriginal teachers, both trained and non-trained, in the province, of whom 35 were from Chanda district.[83]

Alongside this process of Westernization through education, there was a parallel process of Hinduization and Rajputization in the hill tracts. Not only Gond chiefs, but their people too began imitating caste-Hindu practices and often claimed Rajput and thus Kshatriya status within the varna hierarchy. The colonial state also encouraged such claims, for it held that caste society was more civilized than adivasi society. The interaction between the two societies would make the latter more civilized and sober. It would then be easy for the colonial state to control them.[84] We shall take this up further in the next chapter.

Thus, although the 'civilizing mission' among the Gonds succeeded to some extent on its own terms, the project in turn gave rise to a new self-consciousness and spirit of self-assertion among the Gonds. This assertion could at times turn against British colonial rule, as we shall see in the next section.

RAJAS BESIEGED

British rule—in contrast to Maratha rule—gradually reduced the Gond chiefs to being little more than proprietary peasants. Although they had been subordinate rulers under the Marathas, they had been considered 'rajas' with full power over their territories. As Jenkins stated: '[T]heir submission to the authority of the Peshwas rests on extorted compliance, and the basis of treaties, as between independent rulers. In support of these pretensions they had frequent wars with the Peshwas.'[85] After the conquest, the British removed their title of 'raja' and converted them into 'zamindars'.[86] Many found it hard to make ends meet (the Ahiri zamindar was an exception in this respect). They even lost the respect of their community as they became powerless to protect them from land-grabbing caste-Hindu peasants and unscrupulous moneylenders.[87]

The British adopted an ambivalent attitude towards the Gond chiefs. On the one hand, they sought paternalistically to protect them in their positions, believing that this would bring greater stability to the forests and hill tracts. They encouraged them to display their power on certain celebrations, as at Dassera or in the *tilak* ceremony, which was held on the succession of a new zamindar. There was also a ceremony where the Gond zamindars anointed a new Bhonsle prince with a teeka on his succession to the throne. The zamindars would appear at these ceremonies dressed in British coats and with royal Indian turbans on their heads. These were lavish occasions attended by colonial officials, neighbouring zamindars, and subordinate chiefs and people.[88] A confidential report of the 1940s stated that 'it is important not to diminish the zamindar's personal authority and the respect in which his *ryots* [peasants] and the public generally apart from some disgruntled contractors and others at Chanda hold him'.[89]

On the other hand, as Gonds, the chiefs were still judged by the British to be relatively low in the overall scale of civilization. Unlike in the 'civilized' tracts of British India, administration was deemed to be rudimentary, with an inefficient system of land-revenue collection, lack of any proper accounting, a failure to collect a range of taxes such as grazing fees, and with corrupt kamdars, indiscriminate exploitation of the forest, and wasteful expenditures by the chiefs on social and religious ceremonies and on hunting.[90] The British always maintained the threat of taking over a zamindari if things became too bad in these respects.

Zamindars who reformed their ways along the lines advocated by the British could still find themselves in conflict with the paramount power. This was seen in the case of the British-educated zamindar of Ahiri, Dharam Rao. After he took over his estate in 1928, he demanded that he be accorded a higher status than 'zamindar'. To this end, he used an old forest sale agreement.[91] The British colonial state had a practice of grabbing forests from adivasi chiefs on lease or sale to use for their own commercial purposes.[92] In this way the colonial state had purchased large tracts of forest from the Ahiri zamindari in 1873 and 1883, totalling in all 80,775 acres, for which a combined sum of Rs 160,000 was paid.[93] The second part was registered under the Registration Act, but the first part remained unregistered. Dharam Rao then argued with the colonial administration that the deal for the first part of the sale of the forest was illegal, and that it should be formally acquired under the Land Acquisition Act and monetary compensation paid to him; or he should be compensated in some other way. A further inquiry found that he wanted to be recognized as a feudatory chief. However, the colonial state dismissed the zamindar's aspiration and forced him to enter into an agreement on the first part of the sale of the forest under the Land Acquisition Act without any compensation.[94]

Dharam Rao also had serious problems with his manager, who had been appointed by the colonial government. Such managers often had effective power in the estates. In some cases, they were retired colonial administrators, and also corrupt.[95] The colonial administration informally held that 'the manager should have the real power and not be liable to be overruled by the zamindar.'[96] Being a well-educated man, Dharam Rao well understood all this, and demanded strongly that he be given the right to appoint his own manager. Seeking clarification on the appointment of the manager, he wrote to the deputy commissioner of Chanda:

> [I]n one important respect, I find that the letter of Government is not quite explicit. Is the Manager to be appointed by me as Zamindar, or by Government? Is it proposed that the Manager should be selected by Government and should merely be formally appointed by me as Zamindar? In this

connection, I would only urge that if the appointment is to be made by me the selection of the manager must also both in law and in equity rest with me.[97]

He went so far as to advertise the post in a local newspaper without informing the deputy commissioner. Alarmed by this, the commissioner called for an investigation of the zamindari by Deputy Commissioner K. N. Subramanian. The resulting report sought to show the zamindar in the worst possible light. It accused him of consuming intemperate quantities of alcohol and keeping numerous wives and concubines.[98] Dharam Rao was then sent a letter from the colonial administration stating that the management of the estate should be taken over by an officer appointed by government, and that he had to accept a government nominee as manager.[99]

Many zamindars suffered from severe indebtedness, having fallen into the clutches of usurers. Even the raja of Chanda owed Rs 4,000 to local moneylenders at the beginning of the twentieth century.[100] The colonial rulers claimed that the chiefs were reducing themselves to poverty because of their drunkenness and heavy expenditure on social and religious ceremonies.[101] Many zamindaris' revenue and expenditure were almost equal, and the zamindars were left with no income to subsist.[102] It was, for example, recorded in the *Chanda District Gazetteer* of the Chandala zamindari that

> the family are Raj-Gond; the present representative is Najuk Rao, a man between 65 and 70 years of age. Assets were taken at Rs 548 at the recent settlement; the *takoli* was fixed at Rs 30 while Rs 16-8-0 are also payable on account of cesses. The income of the estate is something quite insignificant, probably not more than Rs 400 or Rs 500, and is insufficient to meet the expenses of the Zamindar.[103]

The zamindars were no longer able to offset their expenditure with the offerings that they had in the past received from their subjects. The 1869 settlement had stated that the offerings to zamindars at Dassera should be purely voluntary, and that no zamindar was to insist on it. As a result, the Gond peasantry stopped making such payments. As it was, their economic condition was very poor, so they were hardly in a position to do so.[104] This was worsened by the influx of outside settlers, who, encouraged by the British government, were from the late nineteenth century onwards granted *pattas* (paper deeds) free of charge for as much land as they could make arable. It was about this time that many of the old maqtas and jagir estates of Gond rajas and the village headships of Bhumias, Gaitas, and mokhasis were resumed by the government, and the Gonds, who until then had lived on and cultivated the land of their feudal lords, were suddenly forced to fend for themselves and secure land of their own.[105]

Most of the rich and irrigated lands of the Chanda territories had already been grabbed by non-adivasis before the British took over the district. The adivasis were pushed deep into the forest, surviving through *podu* (shifting cultivation). All of the *khalsa* or government villages—which were largely in the plains areas—were owned by non-adivasis. Of the 1,568 khalsa villages, 523, which paid rather more than one-third of the total land revenue of Chanda district, were owned by Brahmins, who constituted 1.82 per cent of the total population. Kumbis, Kolis, and Marathas possessed 296, 133, and 107 villages respectively.[106] The zamindari territories were, as mentioned above, largely covered by forests and hills with a very low agricultural yield. As the caste-Hindu peasants took over the better land, the Gonds were forced to survive increasingly in the forest. At the same time, the forests of the zamindars were being leased or purchased by the British and brought under the colonial forest administration.[107] Attempts by the Gonds to use forest resources led to ongoing clashes with forest officials. We shall take up these processes in detail in the succeeding chapters.

Under such pressures, many Gond chiefs were reduced to being little more than village headmen. We have seen in Chapter 1 how the Gond raja of Utnur (in Adilabad) was reduced from a Paragandar (head of paragana) to a village head. An interview conducted by the anthropologist Christoph von Fürer-Haimendorf with the Sirpur raja, Atram Bhim Rao, also brings this out. Sirpur was the original seat of the Chanda raja. Atram Bhim Rao's ancestors had held zamindari rights over the Sirpur taluka from the seventeenth century. The Marathas and the Nizam had recognized their zamindari rights, though in a reduced form.[108] The raja told Fürer-Haimendorf,

> My grandfather was still a rich man with a big house and hundreds of head of cattle; at the great feasts Gonds and Kolams from the whole Sirpur *patti* [track] assembled and he feasted two and three hundred men at a time. But

I am so poor that I can only just provide a goat and some *jawari*; so only a few people from the nearest villages come to me.[109]

The British colonial state thus sought to transform the hills and their Gond rajas and chiefs through its various programmes, which were both coercive and reformative in their operation. While ostensibly a project that sought to 'civilize' and thus empower the Gonds, in practice, the dice was loaded against them. The whole project had indeed reduced them to the level of ordinary Gond peasants. Though the chiefs were granted a certain degree of self-rule, their main sources of earning were taken from them. Attempts to levy tribute or raid villages in the plains, which were central to Gond sovereignty, were suppressed by force. Their forest resources were denied them in a series of highly disadvantageous treaties and enforced sales. With no adequate source of income, they soon became deeply indebted to usurers who were supported in their operations by colonial law.[110] Caste-Hindu peasants were encouraged to settle in their tracts, and they either purchased or muscled their way into controlling the best lands. Those chiefs who tried to resist were, in the early years, captured, imprisoned, hanged, and deposed, and after 1860 threatened with deposition. Even those who were educated in English schools continued to be treated in a condescending and patronizing manner.

The British colonial intervention in India thus sought to establish an exclusive sovereignty as embodied by the modern states of the West. India had had a long tradition of the existence of multiple sovereignties. The British colonial state disturbed this shared sovereignty by assimilating the local sovereign powers into the state through a programme of colonial modernity, treaties, agreements, and by force. This process produced contested histories. Local powers such as the Gond rajas were, to some extent, reduced to a subordinate position. The reduced power of the Gond rajas allowed the British not only to expand their power in the hills and forests but also to establish control over adivasi land and forest resources. We shall now move on to a discussion of these processes of colonial state-making and resource control.

NOTES

1. Eyre Chatterton, *The Story of Gondwana* (London: Sir Isaac Pitman & Sons, 1916), pp. 60–9.

2. Ajay Skaria, *Hybrid Histories: Forests, Frontiers and Wildness in Western India* (New Delhi: Oxford University Press, 1999), pp. 165–75.

3. Andre Wink, *Land and Sovereignty in India: Agrarian Society and Politics under the Eighteenth-Century Maratha Svarajya* (Cambridge: Cambridge University Press, 1986), pp. 110–12.

4. Richard Jenkins, *Report on the Territories of the Rajah of Nagpur* (1827; reprint, Nagpur: Government Press, 1925), p. 251.

5. Jenkins, *Report of the Territories of the Raja of Nagpur*, p. 139; Nandini Sundar, *Subalterns and Sovereigns: An Anthropological History of Bastar, 1854–1996* (New Delhi: Oxford University Press, 1997), pp. 90–2.

6. Dirks describes how the raja of Pudukkottai in south India was made powerless under the colonial paramount power. See his *The Hollow Crown: Ethnohistory of an Indian Kingdom* (Ann Arbor: University of Michigan Press, 1993), p. 6.

7. Christoph von Fürer-Haimendorf, *Tribal Hyderabad: Four Reports* (Hyderabad: Revenue Department, Government of H.E.H. the Nizam, 1945), p. 67.

8. Sundar, *Subalterns and Sovereigns*; Skaria, *Hybrid Histories*.

9. Verrier Elwin, *Folk-Songs of Chhattisgarh* (Madras: Oxford University Press, 1946), pp. 280–6.

10. Sundar, *Subalterns and Sovereigns*, p. 23.

11. Jenkins, *Report of the Territories of the Rajah of Nagpur*, p. 252.

12. David Hardiman and Ajay Skaria provide a full history of Bhil raids in western India. See David Hardiman, 'Power in the Forest: The Dangs, 1820–1940', in *Subaltern Studies VIII: Essays in Honour of Ranajit Guha*, edited by David Arnold and David Hardiman (New Delhi: Oxford University Press, 1994), pp. 99–100; Skaria, *Hybrid Histories*.

13. *Early European Travellers in the Nagpur Territories: Reprinted from Old Records* (Nagpur: Government Press, 1930), pp. 119–21.

14. C. B. Lucie Smith, *Report on the Land Revenue Settlement of the Chanda District, Central Provinces* (Nagpur: Chief Commissioner's Press, 1870), p. 72.

15. Chatterton, *The Story of Gondwana*, p. 94.

16. Bhangya Bhukya, *Subjugated Nomads: The Lambadas under the Rule of the Nizams* (New Delhi: Orient BlackSwan, 2010), pp. 46–7.

17. *Chanda District Gazetteer*, 1909, p. 55.

18. Board's Collection, IOR/F/4/755/20541, India Office Records (henceforth IOR), British Library, ff. 74, 135–41.

19. Jenkins, *Report of the Territories of the Rajah of Nagpur*, p. 251.

20. Smith, *Land Revenue Settlement of the Chanda District*, p. 75.

21. Chatterton, *The Story of Gondwana*, p. 101.

22. *Chanda District Gazetteer 1909*, pp. 57–8.

23. Letter no. 8 from Commissioner (hereafter Comm.) of Nagpur to Deputy (hereafter Dy.) Commissioner of Chanda, dated 7 May 1858, IOR/L/PS/6/460, ff. 239.

24. Letter no. 49, Comm. of Nagpur to Secretary Government of India, IOR/L/PS/6/460, f. 231.

25. Letter from Comm. of Nagpur to Resident of Hyderabad dated 7 May 1858, IOR/L/PS/6/460, f. 238.

26. Letter no. 23, Comm. of Nagpur to Dy. Comm. of Chanda dated 5 July 1858, IOR/L/PS/6/460, f. 279.

27. *Andhra Pradesh District Gazetteers, Adilabad* (Hyderabad: Government Central Press, 1976), pp. 33–4; *The Freedom Struggle in Hyderabad: A Connected Account, 1857–1885*, vol. 2 (Hyderabad, 1956), pp. 118–20, 156–7.

28. Letter, Comm. of Nagpur to Resident of Hyderabad dated 7 May 1858, IOR/L/PS/6/460, f. 238.

29. *The Freedom Struggle in Hyderabad*, vol. 2, p. 157.

30. Letter no. 53, Dy. Comm. of Chanda to Comm. of Nagpur, dated 8 May 1858, IOR/L/PS/6/460, f. 243.

31. Letter no. 2, Dy. Comm. of Chanda to Comm. of Nagpur, dated 3 May 1857, IOR/L/PS/6/460, f. 233.

32. Letter no. 2, Dy. Comm. of Chanda to Comm. of Nagpur, dated 3 May 1858, IOR/L/PS/6/460, f. 233.

33. Letter no. 63, Comm. of Nagpur to Secretary Govt. of India, dated 28 May 1858, IOR/L/PS/6/460, f. 254.

34. Letter no. 18, Comm. of Nagpur to Dy. Comm. of Chanda, dated 8 June 1858, IOR/L/PS/6/460, f. 265.

35. Letter no. 74, Dy. Comm. Chanda to Comm. of Nagpur, dated 3 June 1858, IOR/L/PS/6/460, ff. 267–8.

36. Letter no. 71, Dy. Comm. of Chanda to Comm. of Nagpur, dated 17 June 1858, IOR/L/PS/6/460, ff. 272–3.

37. Letter no. 87, Comm. of Nagpur to Secretary Govt. of India, IOR/L/PS/6/460, f. 278.

38. Letter no. 23, Comm. of Nagpur to Dy. Comm. of Chanda, dated 5 July 1858, IOR/L/PS/6/460, f. 288; Letter no. 88, Dy. Comm. of Chanda to Comm. of Nagpur, IOR/L/PS/6/460, f. 280.

39. Letter no. 90, Dy. Comm. of Chanda to Comm. of Nagpur, dated 6 July 1858, IOR/L/PS/6/460, f. 282.

40. Letter no. 25, Comm. of Nagpur to Dy. Comm. of Chanda, dated 8 July 1858, IOR/L/PS/6/460, f. 283; Letter no. 87, Dy. Comm. of Chanda to Comm. of Nagpur, dated 20 July 1858, IOR/L/PS/6/460, f. 283.

41. Smith, *Land Revenue Settlement of the Chanda District*, p. 76.

42. Letter no. 7 from Lt. Col. Broughton to N. B. Edmonstone, Secretary to Government, 2 April 1804; *Selection from the Nagpur Residency Records, 1799–1806*, vol. I, compiled by H. N. Sinha (Nagpur: Government Printing, M.P., 1950), pp. 53–6.

43. Skaria, *Hybrid Histories*, pp. 193–4; see also Hardiman, 'Power in the Forest', p. 110.

44. On this, see A. Vadivelu, *The Ruling Chiefs, Nobles and Zamindars of India*, vol. 1 (Madras: Guardian Press, 1915), pp. 74–84; G. R. Aberigh-Mackay, *The Chiefs of Central India*, vol. 1 (Calcutta: Thacker, Spink and Co., 1878), p. xiv.

45. *Chanda District Gazetteer*, 1909, p. 324.

46. Smith, *Land Revenue Settlement of the Chanda District*, p. 184.

47. Letter no. 162, Dy. Secretary Foreign Department to Chief Comm. of Central Provinces (CP), dated 28 May 1867, Vidarbha Archive, Political and Military (PM), S. no. 1477, File no. 5-8/1951, f. 1; Smith, *Land Revenue Settlement of the Chanda District*, p. 70.

48. *Chanda District* Gazetteer, 1909, p. 136.

49. Letter no. 1470, Dy. Secretary Foreign Department to Chief Comm. of CP, dated 19 September 1903, Vidarbha, PM, S. N. 1477, File no. 5–8/1951, f. 3.

50. Letter no. 1470, Dy. Secretary Foreign Department to Chief Comm. of CP, dated 19 September 1903, f. 4.

51. Letter no. 1470, Dy. Secretary Foreign Department to Chief Comm. of CP, dated 19 September 1903, p. 2.

52. Out of the twenty zamindaris, four were transferred to Durg district in 1907; see *Chanda District Gazetteer*, 1909, p. 443.

53. Smith, *Land Revenue Settlement of the Chanda District*, pp. 180, 206.

54. Setumadhava Rao Pagdi, *Among the Gonds of Adilabad* (Bombay: Popular Book Depot, 1949), pp. 29–30.

55. *Report on the Administration of His Highness the Nizam's Dominions for the Year 1294F (1884–1885)* (Bombay: Times of India Press, 1886), p. 258; *Imperial Gazetteer of India, Provincial Series, Hyderabad* (hereafter *Gazetteer of Hyderabad*) (Calcutta: Superintendent of Government Printing, 1909), p. 190.

56. Pagdi, *Among the Gonds*, p. 39.

57. W. V. Grigson, *The Challenge of Backwardness* (Hyderabad-Deccan: Government Press, 1947), p. 41.

58. Pagdi, *Among the Gonds*, pp. 37–50.

59. *Final Report on the Land Revenue Settlement of the Chanda District in the Central Provinces, Effected during the Years 1897–1906*, IOR/W/1429, p. 4.

60. *Final Report on the Land Revenue Settlement of the Chanda District*, p. 75; Smith, *Land Revenue Settlement of the Chanda District*, p. 199.

61. *Final Report on the Land Revenue Settlement of the Chanda District*, pp. 179–83.

62. *Chanda District Gazetteer*, 1909, p. 446.

63. Smith, *Land Revenue Settlement of the Chanda District*, p. 181.

64. Vidarbha, Revenue Department (RD), S. no. 5916, File no. 6/1945, f. 36.

65. *The Central Province Court of Wards Manual* (Nagpur: Secretariat Press, 1902), pp. 2–3.

66. Vidarbha, RD, S. no. 1608, File no. 7-16/1927, f. 1.

67. *Chanda District Gazetteer*, 1909, pp. 448–52.

68. Vidarbha, Survey and Settlement (SS), S. no. 969, File no. 4-39/1923, ff. 11–12.

69. Vidarbha, RD, S. no. 5916, File no. 6/1945, f. 46.

70. *Chanda District Gazetteer*, 1909, p. 451.

71. Vidarbha, RD, S. no. 1608, File no. 7-16/1927, p. 2.

72. W. V. Grigson, *The Aboriginal Problem in the Central Provinces and Berar* (Nagpur: Government Printing, 1944), p. 419.

73. *Rajkumar College Raipur Annual Report, 1936–37* (Calcutta: Catholic Orphan Press), pp. 1–22.

74. Chatterton, *The Story of Gondwana*, p. 109.

75. Vidarbha, RD, S. no. 1608, File no. 7-16/1927, f. 3; Grigson, *The Aboriginal Problem*, p. 419.

76. Grigson, *The Aboriginal Problem*, p. 372.

77. Grigson, *The Aboriginal Problem*, p. 495.

78. Grigson, *The Aboriginal Problem*, pp. 371–2.

79. Vidarbha, RD, S. no. 5916, File no. 6/1945, f. 2.

80. *Report on the Administration of the Central Provinces for the Year 1900–1901* (Nagpur: Secretariat Press, 1901), p. 66.

81. Grigson, *The Aboriginal Problem*, p. 397.

82. Grigson, *The Aboriginal Problem*, p. 497.

83. Grigson, *The Aboriginal Problem*, p. 507.

84. *Report of the Ethnological Committee on Papers Laid before Them and upon Examination of Specimens of Aboriginal Tribes Brought to the Jubblepore Exhibition of 1866–67* (Nagpur: Chief Commissioner's Office Press, 1868), IOR/V/9484, p. 2.

85. Jenkins, *Report of the Territories of the Rajah of Nagpur*, pp. 140–1.

86. In the Nizam's territories, the raja of Sirpur and the raja of Utnur were called by the honorary title of 'Raja'. Even in the British territories, people addressed the zamindars as rajas. See Pagdi, *Among the Gonds*, p. 39.

87. Vidarbha, RD, S. no. 1596, File no. 58-4/1927, ff. 1–8.

88. Vidarbha, RD, S. no. 5916, File no. 6/1945, f. 1; Vidarbha, RD, S. no. 3461, File no. 48-9/1933, f. 2; Sundar, *Subalterns and Sovereigns*, pp. 47–76.

89. Vidarbha, RD, S. no. 5916, File no. 6/1945, f. 2.

90. Vidarbha, RD, S. no. 5916, File no. 6/1945, ff. 36–7.

91. Vidarbha, RD, S. no. 2882, File no. 58-7/1931, f. 2.

92. Hardiman, 'Power in the Forest', pp. 112–16.

93. Vidarbha, RD, S. no. 2882, File no. 58-7/1931, f. 2.

94. Vidarbha, RD, S. no. 2882, File no. 58-7/1931, ff.7–12.

95. Vidarbha, RD, S. no. 5916, File no. 6/1945, ff. 17–19.

96. Vidarbha, RD, S. no. 5916, File no. 6/1945, f. 16.

97. Vidarbha, RD, S. no. 5916, File no. 6/1945, f. 21.

98. It was reported that zamindar consumed 31 bottles of whisky, 482 quarter-bottles of beer, 270 pint bottles of beer, and 8 bottles of brandy between January 1941 and February 1942. See Vidarbha, RD, S. no. 5916, File no. 6/1945, f. 111. For his wives and concubines see Vidarbha, RD, S. no. 5916, File no. 6/1945, f. 112.

99. Vidarbha, RD, S. no. 5916, File no. 6/1945, f. 37.

100. *Chanda District Gazetteer*, 1909, p. 136.

101. Vidarbha, RD, S. no. 5916, File no. 6/1945, f. 112.

102. *Chanda District Gazetteer*, 1909, p. 462.

103. *Chanda District Gazetteer*, 1909, p. 460.

104. Smith, *Land Revenue Settlement of the Chanda District*, p. 183.

105. Fürer-Haimendorf, *Tribal Hyderabad*, p. 67.

106. Smith, *Land Revenue Settlement of the Chanda District*, p. 206.

107. Vidarbha, PM, S. no. 1478, File no. 5-3/1951, f. 2; Vidarbha, RD, S. no. 2882, File no. 58-7/1931, f. 5.

108. Pagdi, *Among the Gonds*, pp. 38–9.

109. Fürer-Haimendorf, *Tribal Hyderabad*, p. 135.

110. On this, see David Hardiman, *Feeding the Baniya: Peasants and Usurers in Western India* (New Delhi: Oxford University Press, 1996), pp. 43–61.

3

ENCLOSING LAND
THE MAKING OF THE COLONIAL STATE
IN THE HILLS*

AFTER VANQUISHING THE FOREST GROUPS' kings, the British enclosed the lands and forests that they had ruled, and the land they cultivated was subjected to tax. This process subordinated and marginalized the hill and forest dwellers who survived largely on hunting, gathering, or rudimentary swidden agriculture. As James C. Scott has argued, the encounter between modern expansionary states and self-governing hill peoples involved a process of internal colonization, land enclosure, migration, and marginalization. This was a feature of the development of modern state systems in many parts of the world.[1] Like any other modern state, the colonial state used a variety of methods to incorporate the areas beyond the reach of earlier state formations into the space of state-making.

The Chanda territories were rich, rice-cultivating lands in central India.[2] As has been discussed, the colonial state, after taking over the

* An earlier version of this chapter appeared as 'Enclosing Land, Enclosing Adivasis: Colonial Agriculture and Adivasis in Central India, 1853–1948' in *Indian Historical Review* 40, no. 1 (2003): 93–116. Reproduced with permission from Indian Council of Historical Research, New Delhi.

Gondwana region, offered zamindari rights and village headship to adivasi chiefs. Some chiefs were pensioned off.[3] On the other hand, the colonial promotion of the ownership of landed property, the ensuing commodification of land, the commercialization of agriculture, and the development of a market-based economy—all these created a growing demand for land in India. This encouraged caste-Hindu peasants to go to forest tracts and bring waste and forest land under cultivation. The colonial state offered them forest land under the *ijara* system (a land tenure system that served to bring forest/wasteland under cultivation) for nominal assessment, sometimes without any assessment. To attract caste-Hindu peasants, the state evolved an internal colonization policy under which irrigation was developed in hill and forest tracts. Indeed, it was designed to stimulate the extension of rice cultivation and the commoditization of agricultural production. New varieties of rice and commercial crops were introduced in forest tracts through various programmes.[4]

On the other hand, the British and princely rulers classed forests as reserved for the sole use of the state. The new forest regulations, ostensibly designed to conserve forests, resulted in clearing 'waste' forest areas and handing it over to non-adivasi peasants. The colonial state essentially regarded the influx of non-adivasi peasants into the hills as crucial in transforming those areas into state territory.[5] This chapter examines the process of British colonial state-making in the hills of India, and how this process pushed the adivasis deep into the forest. I will also show how this process eventually led to the enclosure of adivasis into a social sphere. Before we take up these questions, let us lay out a brief history of the land of the Chanda territories.

A BRIEF HISTORY OF THE GOND LAND

The boundaries of the Chanda dynasty are uncertain since we have only scanty evidence pertaining to them.[6] However, there are some references to these boundaries in records from Akbar's regime. Irfan Habib ascertains that some of the *mahals* (revenue unit of a group of villages) of the *sarkars* (a revenue division in Mughal India) Kalam and Manikdurg mentioned in the *Ain-i-Akbari* were shown as part of the Mughal Empire, but they were completely under the Chanda dynasty. Even Wyragarh was in the possession of a Chanda chief. Also, the forts of Manikdurg, Pauni, Barmapur (Brahmapur), Chimur, Sindehi (Sindewahi), and Partabgarh were principalities of the Chanda raja in 1595–6.[7] A much clearer picture emerges from colonial records. As shown in Table 3.1, Smith identified thirty-three divisions ruled by the Chanda rajas from Maratha documents of 1775, and related them with colonial period divisions of 1869. Since the documents date to only about twenty-five years after the collapse of the Chanda dynasty, this may be taken as a reliable record of the principalities ruled by Gond rajas at the end of their rule.

A large part of the Chanda country was covered with hills and forests, and was thinly populated till the end of the eighteenth century.[8] However, the region enjoyed considerable prosperity under the rule of the Gond rajas. They rewarded their Gond *tarvels* (warriors) with large

Table 3.1 The principalities of the Chanda rajas in 1775

Divisions in 1775 CE	Divisions in 1869 CE
1. Hawelee, 2. Bullalpoor	Chanda (Hawelee Pergunnah)
3. Rajgurh, 4. Barsagurh	Rajgurh Pergunnah
5. Ghatkool	Ghatkool Pergunnah
6. Ambgaon, 7. Gurehiroolee, 8. Konsuree	Ambgaon Pergunnah
9. Burhaumpooree	Burhampooree Pergunnah
10. Gurboree, 11. Phereegurh	Gurboree Pergunnah
12. Wyragurh	Wyragurh Pergunnah
13. Wurora, 14. Segaon	Wurora Pergunnah
15. Bhanduk, 16. Ashta Khatora	Bhanduk Pergunnah
17. Neree, 18. Kursingee, 19. Gondwara	Chimoor Pergunnah
20. Nundoree, 21. Mandgaon, 22. Pohna	
23. Undoree, 24. Deoleo, 25. Nachungaon	
26. Arwee	Wurdah District
27. Woon Sirpoor , 28. Mardee,	Woon District
29. Raleegaon	
30. Manikgurh, 31. Sirpoor, 32. Bejoor	
34. Joongaon	Hyderabad Territories

Source: Smith, *Land Revenue Settlement of the Chanda District*, p. 119.

amounts of forest land, making them subordinate rajas, or zamindars, of those tracts. They encouraged both adivasi and non-adivasi cultivators to settle on the land and bring it under cultivation. The zamindars subtitled the land to the actual cultivator on a lease system and at nominal rents. In this way, large areas were developed.[9] These subordinate rajas' territories were marked by boundaries and properly documented. They were encouraged to build tanks and irrigate the lands. Richard Temple's interesting comment on these tanks was, '[T]he number and size of these tanks is certainly remarkable. In some parts they even cluster thick round the feet of the hills. From the summit of the hill, called "perzagurh" by the Gonds, and "the seven sisters" by the Hindus, no less than thirty-seven tanks were counted as distinctively visible.'[10] In a similar vein, Richard Jenkins writes that it would appear 'from ancient records and traces of old towns, forts, villages and tanks to be met with in the jungles that this country was formerly much more populous than at the present day.'[11]

Like in the plains of India, the village community was instrumental in agricultural production in the hills under Gond rule.[12] All the service castes (blacksmiths, pot makers, leather workers, and so on) lived in the Gond areas. Agricultural practice required the support of all these service castes, and the Gond rajas always encouraged them to settle in forest villages. Merchants from the plain areas visited the courts of the zamindars regularly.[13] It is said that a large amount of caste-Hindu migration from the plains to the hills were witnessed during the reign of Kurn Shah and Ram Shah. Kurn Shah was influenced by Hinduism and granted a considerable amount of land to Hindu migrants. Similarly, Ram Shah granted huge tracts in the western part of the dynasty's territory to Brahmans. Thus, peasant cultivators began occupying land in the Berar region in Chanda territory, as there was pressure on land in the Marathwada region.[14]

The influx of Marathas increased steadily in Chanda after it was conquered by the Bhonsles of Nagpur. The Bhonsles encouraged many peasant castes of the plains to settle in the forest and bring wasteland under cultivation.[15] The relinquished villages were repopulated in the forest and hill areas on the usual establishment of the *barra baluti* system in which twelve service castes would find a place in the village.[16] A village community was generally composed of those who held and cultivated land, established village servants, a priest, blacksmith, carpenter, accountant, washerman, basket maker, potter, watchman, barber, shoemaker, and the *bhumka*, who charmed away tigers from people and cattle.[17] The Bhonsles did not bring about changes in the Gond revenue system, but appointed Brahmans as revenue and finance officers, village patels, and zamindars. All the Gond village patels, in particular, were replaced by Brahman patels in the western part of Chanda.[18] However, this process was violently resisted by the Gonds. The Marathas were confined to rabi crops cultivated areas and did not extend to the hill areas. Indeed, as Mahesh Rangarajan says, they were unable to secure the plains from adivasi attacks.[19]

Chanda territory was exposed mainly to Maratha influx from the British protectorate rule after the last Maratha war (1818). A Brahman revenue officer by the name of Lingo Punt Dikshit, who had helped Captain Crawford in capturing Chanda, became very powerful in the district. As he had access to land records, he parcelled out huge amounts of good, fertile lands to Brahmans. Smith recorded in his settlement report that:

> He [Lingo Punt] amassed a large fortune, and became possessed of many villages; while for his fellow Brahmins he obtained numerous grants of free lands and pensions. His death occurred shortly before Captain Crawford's departure in 1824, A.D., but the system of official intrigue and oppression did not die with him but grew and spread until it reached its culminating point in the latter years of the second Mahratha administration.[20]

The higher-ranked Brahman revenue officials also began extracting heavy revenue from the Gond patels in order to oust them from their patelships. Indeed, there was a nexus between the higher Brahman revenue officials and Brahman local village patels. The harassment of Gond patels was a collective ploy of the Brahman revenue officials and Brahman patels. Many Gond patels gave up their patelships and moved further into the forest towards the east. Most of the Brahman patels soon became absentee landlords who exploited the Gond masses. The latter too followed their patels. New villages were formed at the sites of ruined or abandoned villages with Kumbi peasantry brought in from Marathwada. The immigration resulted in populating Chanda considerably.[21] The population increased from 279,555 to 537,295 between 1820 and 1866, of which 176,840 were adivasis, 39,356 Telugus, 301,873 Marathas, and 19,220 from other communities.[22] The number of villages in Chanda district increased to 2,598 in 1866 as against 1,223 villages in 1825; of these villages, 2,273 were inhabited and 328 uninhabited.[23]

Proprietorship of the mahals and patelship of the villages were mainly grabbed by non-adivasis. Out of the total of 2,598 village patels, 1,344 were non-adivasis and 1,254 were adivasis. Of the 1,344 non-adivasi patels, 523 were Brahmans, 296 were Kumbis, and 525 were from other communities. Of the adivasi patels, 969 were from the zamindaris and 285 from khalsa land. This means that the adivasis had been practically pushed into zamindaris that were largely covered by forests and located in the hills by the time the British completely took over Chanda from the Marathas in 1853.[24] Eyre Chatterton recorded:

> During Raghuji's time a great change passed over the southern portion of the Central Provinces. Large numbers of Kumbhis (the cultivating class of Marathas) and of other Maratha tribes poured into the Nagpur country. Gondi, the old language, ceased to be spoken, and Marathi took its place. And with the change the old Gond population withdrew more and more into the wilder parts of the country.[25]

The Gond rajas thus maintained complete control over their territories and people till they fell to the Marathas. They challenged the imperial powers and negotiated a better deal for themselves. Under their regime, they had accommodated both Hindu peasants and adivasi peasants. There were also close economic contacts between plains Hindu society and the adivasis. This does not mean that there was no tension between adivasis and caste-Hindus, but rather that these groups existed in both tension and harmony. The adivasis have had a tradition of strategically maintaining difference from caste-Hindu society from the earliest times. Tensions between the two communities became aggravated with the marginalization of Gonds after the inception of Bhonsle rule, as the latter brought considerable pressure to bear on the positions and lands of the Gonds. These tensions intensified under British colonial rule. Let us now move on to an examination of the ways in which the British colonial state-making process took place in the hills.

THE MAKING OF COLONIAL STATE SPACES

The British colonial rulers initially sought to integrate the adivasis into the wider society as property-owning peasant subjects. They viewed forest communities and their territories as essentially 'wild', treating them in a different way from the settled peoples of the plains.[26] A number of methods were used to bring hill and forest tracts into the colonial state-making process. The introduction of the rule of property in land that led to land enclosure was crucial in the construction of the edifice of the colonial state in the forests and hills of India. The rule of property not only confined peasant subjects to one place, but also allowed the state to realize land tax from inaccessible forest and hill areas that had been beyond the reach of earlier state-making efforts.[27] In pre-colonial India, no one had proprietary rights in land, including the state, but there were a variety of land occupancy rights.[28] Under the new rules, proprietary rights in land were given to zamindars, village heads, and individual peasants under different agricultural tenures such as zamindari, malguzari, ryotwari, and ijara.[29] However, the state was the sole owner of forest areas. The forest was fenced and brought under state control through forest regulations and forest acts. Forest resources were exploited by the state systematically.[30] Let us now move on to examining how these agriculture tenures were crucial in the making of the colonial state in the hills and forest tracts.

LAND ENCLOSURES

In the Chanda territories, Gond rule had produced a number of Gond zamindars. After a long resistance, the Gond zamindars forced the British to honour their zamindari rights. We have discussed at length in Chapter 2 how these zamindaris functioned under British colonial rule. The agreements and treaties with Gond zamindars gave the colonial state a footing in the hills. The creation of zamindaris, indeed, was a colonial strategy to master the non-state wild tracts. The rest of the Chanda plains region was assessed under the malguzari tenure, under which traditional village patels were given hereditary proprietary rights over village land and converted into *malguzar*s (revenue payers). A malguzar subtitled the village land to the actual cultivators. However, he could not oust an occupier or tenant from his land as long as the latter paid rent. The malguzar had no right to collect more than the fixed rent decided by the government. But where the malguzar granted wasteland to a new *assami* (a peasant paying a light rent) in order to get the land cultivated, then, according to custom, he could fix a suitable rent upon expiry of the term. This system helped to bring large, uncultivable tracts of wasteland under cultivation.[31]

Unlike other parts of India, the ryotwari system was introduced in the Central Provinces to bring forests and wastelands under cultivation.[32] This system was first adopted in the province by the Chanda district administration on the general lines of the Bombay system.[33] As mentioned earlier, under the malguzari system, the government retained the proprietorship of the forest and large areas of uncultivated land.[34] Peasants were given proprietary rights over these government-owned forest and uncultivated lands under the ryotwari tenure system, as per the Waste Lands Sales Rules of 1863 as well as the Clearance Lease Rules of 1866. This system did not last long, as these rules were abrogated in 1870 and 1872 respectively. A clear system and rules for excision, allotment, and management on ryotwari terms of waste and forest lands were framed under the provisions of the Land Revenue Act of 1881. Huge forest areas were given to peasants on nominal assessment in order to convert them into cultivable land.[35] In Chanda district, there were 24 ryotwari villages in 1866.[36] This rose to 533 villages at the beginning of the twentieth century, out of which 213 were settled villages, 168 were summarily settled villages, 131 were patch-cultivation villages, and 21 were formed under rice rules (which were introduced to promote irrigated cultivation, particularly paddy crops). About 255 villages were formed only in Sironcha tahsil, which was the main forest tract in the district. All 131 patch-cultivation villages, which were largely inhabited by Gonds, were found in this tahsil. The occupied area gradually increased as the good land of the tahsil was taken up by cultivators. Between 1886 and 1907, about 4.5 lakh acres of land were brought under cultivation under the ryotwari system.[37]

In 1911, the colonial state evolved a special policy called 'land colonization' in the ryotwari villages under the rice rule in order to bring waste land under rice cultivation in the district. However, this policy

did not make any progress till 1928, when the government re-examined
the importance of colonization of wasteland in ryotwari villages. The
policy was intended to provide water by constructing or repairing tanks
on the colonized land at no cost for four years. From the fifth year, there
would be a progressive increase in the water rate at a fixed maximum
of 3 rupees per acre for a period of nine years. The condition was that
the colonizer should cultivate only rice on such lands. It was reported
that it was because of this condition that this policy did not attract new
colonizers, as rice was not a profitable crop. Although there were 70,000
acres of land for allotment under the policy, only 28,329 acres had been
colonized by peasants by 1932.[38] The government withdrew the condition of compulsory growing of rice on the colonized lands in ryotwari
villages in 1937.[39] This measure accelerated the process of the clearing of
forest land for cultivation. The government itself cleared forest land on
a contractual basis and handed over the land to peasants under the ryotwari system. Monkey jacks were made available to peasants to pull down
trees and even to destroy bigger roots underground. In many cases, peasants were allowed to take the forest wood from their land. These policies
were designed to create a demand for land in forest tracts. Indeed, huge
forest areas were brought under cultivation under this policy.[40]

Ijara or *banjar* tenure was another important system under which
considerable forest land was brought under cultivation, particularly in
Adilabad district. Ryotwari tenure was introduced in the state in 1864,
which was practically a copy of the Bombay ryotwari tenure system.[41]
All *diwani* (government) lands were brought under ryotwari tenure,
through which individual property rights in land were created in the
state. The tenure having covered more than 50 per cent of the state land,
created, with the assertion of land as a commodity, a greater demand for
land.[42] It pushed Hindu caste peasants to move towards the hill tracts
where they could grab land more easily. In addition to this, the state gave
a number of concessions to non-adivasis under the ijara tenure in order
to bring deserted land under cultivation.[43] Under this tenure, land was
assessed at light rates, subject to progressive increases till full assessment
was reached, the period of concession varying from five to thirty and, in
some cases, forty years. After the expiry of the period of concession, land
was treated like government land and fully assessed.[44]

In fact, the Nizam's government issued a circular in 1904 by which *talukdar*s (heads of district divisions) were empowered to hand over forest land from any block for cultivation and to dispose of timber without reference to the Forest Department.[45] Besides the offerings of considerable rent concessions and other privileges, under the ijara system, those who brought one-third of the land under cultivation in the leased village would be given the position of police patel in the village, and were sometimes also made *pattadar*s (owner) of the whole village.[46] Under this tenure system, many influential persons in the state bureaucracy and from the dominant peasant castes grabbed thousands of acres of forest land. Many *watandar*s (erstwhile revenue collectors at the village level) were also compensated with forest land when their watan rights were abolished. It was a common practice for a watandar, if he was given 500 acres according to a *sanad* (government order), to expand it to 5,000 acres; and the government almost always sided with the watandar and most graciously allowed him 5,000 acres instead of 500.[47] Forest land was brought under cultivation to the extent of 231,266 acres in 1909 in Hyderabad State.[48] This rose further to 383,180 acres in 1915.[49] Importantly, the clearing of forests in Adilabad was rampant. Between 1901 and 1914, 1,398.84 square miles of forest were converted into cultivable land.[50] When the district was formed in 1905, there were 1,331 villages, of which 143 were jagir villages. In 1946, this number rose to a total of 2,143 villages, apart from 239 deserted villages. The district had the highest number of deserted villages in the state. These were located mainly at the fringes of the plains, and had been deserted by adivasis as the plains caste-Hindu peasants pushed towards the forests.[51]

The agricultural revenue tenures mentioned above were designed to produce the effects of colonial state power in hills. Colonial state-making in the hills was furthered by the introduction of modern agricultural technology. The colonial state was equally concerned with civilizing agricultural production practices and enhancing yields. The colonial project of civilizing agriculture indeed furthered the expansion of agriculture, as it created a great demand for land with the introduction of settled agriculture, commercial crops, high-yielding seeds, and modern agricultural technology.

CIVILIZING AGRICULTURE

The Chanda territory, as mentioned previously, was regarded as rich agricultural country apart from its splendid forest resources. The river system, soil formation, hills, and forests of Chanda and Adilabad districts attracted the special attention of the colonial rulers. The region was drained by a number of rivers and streams. Through the centre of the Chanda district from north to south flowed the Penganga, meeting the Wardha at Seonee, where their united streams formed a delta. The Pranhita drained the eastern part of the district. The southernmost portions were drained chiefly by the Indravati, a tributary of the Pranhita, flowing from the east, while the northern part lay in the valley of the Mahanadi. Apart from these five main rivers, there were a number of small streams and tanks in the Chanda territory.[52] Adilabad district lay between the Penganga and Godavari rivers, and its southern part was drained mainly by the Godavari, its north-west by the Penganga, and north-east by the Wardha. Apart from these rivers, there were minor streams like the Peddavagu, Kapnavarli, and Amlun, the first an effluent of the Wardha, and the latter two of the Penganga.[53]

The greatest portion of the Chanda district soil was red or sandy, with stretches of yellow, brown, and black loam. Black soil, which retains moisture for a long time, formed a belt in the north-west and along the banks of the Wardha and Penganga.[54] This type of soil is favourable for rice cultivation, and Chanda was known traditionally as a rice-producing country. It was against this background that the British identified this region as a rice-producing region.[55] Whereas Adilabad district was situated partly in a trap and partly in a granitic region, the chief soils being *regar* or black cotton soil and *kharab* (sandy soil), it was also traditionally known for rice production, particularly Rajura, Chinnur, Nirmal, and Lakshetipet taluks, but was converted into a cotton-growing country during colonial rule because of Berar's impact on it.[56]

Gonds traditionally grew rice both in valleys and on hill slopes. Although in the plains, the main method of cultivation was plough cultivation, in the forest areas, a large number of Gonds practised *khamori/dhya/podu* (shifting cultivation). In this system, a level or slightly sloping plot of ground was selected and cleared of jungles at the beginning of summer. When it had been covered with wood to a depth of a few inches, the mass of timber was set alight and allowed to burn. Rice was simply broadcast among the ashes, and grown purely with the rains.[57] Whatever their methods of cultivation, the Gonds were known for producing the best-quality rice in the region. It was reported that, 'in spite of these savage methods of cultivation, it must not be supposed that the crop obtained is of poor quality. On the contrary according to Mr. Lancaster the rice grown by the Maria is of the very finest description and far superior to any kind usually to be met within the *khalsa* [government land].'[58]

It was also reported that immense quantities of foodgrain, mainly rice, had been sent from Chanda to supply the Maratha army.[59] Water resources of the region indeed favoured rice cultivation. As discussed earlier, this region was drained by five major rivers, besides a huge number of tanks and streams. When the British took over Chanda, the region possessed 1,749 tanks, 1,831 *boree*s (check dams), and 767 field wells.[60] In the hill areas, rice was mainly cultivated using the *gata* system. The essential condition for this type of cultivation was a small valley with gently sloping sides, watered by a stream. Substantial timber dams were built across the stream at intervals during the hot weather, and were continued on either wing by embankments of earth until they almost but not quite merged into the rising sides of the valley. The gatas were constructed one below the other. When the rains came, a large shallow basin of water was dammed up above each gata, superfluous water being passed onto those below it by escape passages left at the end of either wing, or else cascading over the top of the dam. Rice was planted in the shallow water thus held up, the irrigated area thus being above, not below, the dam.[61]

Thus, the Gond agricultural methods and practices were scientific and suited to their environment. But the colonial state saw the Gonds' methods of cultivation as primitive, and eventually destroyed them. Importantly, the practice of dhya was considered as economically the least profitable as well as the main threat to forest conservation. Dhya was banned under the new forest regulations.[62] The Gonds were gradually induced to adopt regular cultivation under various schemes, by providing them with *thakkavi* (crop loans) and agricultural instruments.[63] However, dhya cultivation continued in the zamindaris into the twentieth century.[64]

As already mentioned, the expansion of rice cultivation in this region was one of the main concerns of the state, for this would bring demand for land and expand agriculture in the forest and hill areas. Towards these ends, the colonial state adopted a policy of civilizing agriculture under which new varieties of rice, new methods of rice cultivation, and new agricultural implements were introduced in the region. The Nagpur Experimental Farm, which was established in 1883, was crucial in promoting modern methods of cultivation in the province.[65] This farm was attached to the Nagpur Agricultural School, which again trained people in modern agriculture. This school not only offered courses for students but also for government officials, schoolteachers, as well as malguzars and their sons.[66] Many agricultural farms were subsequently established across the province. Raipur Farm and Sindhwai Farm (in Chanda) were mainly formed to promote new methods of cultivation in rice and sugarcane. Sindhwai was a railway station on the Bengal–Nagpur Railway. The large village of Garmosi, irrigated by a fine tank of native construction, was purchased by government and handed over to the Sindhwai Farm.[67]

Rice was largely cultivated in the *kharif* season (June–November). There were several traditional processes of rice cultivation. Among them, the transplantation method was very popular in Chanda, in which rice was first sown carefully in a spot of ground. When it grew to about a foot high, the plant was removed and planted in a bunch in a field that was formed into mud for receiving the plants.[68] Modern agricultural farms ascertained this method and further improved it by substituting single seedling transplantation for transplanting in bunches. The latter method required 100 pounds of seed per acre, while the former required only 25 pounds. This method thus anticipated the reduction of expenditure on seeds.[69] In 1915–16, rice was cultivated using the single seedling transplantation method over about 12,000 acres in Chanda, and it was proved that the output of rice transplanted with single seedlings was higher than that of rice transplanted in bunches. This method of rice transplantation was encouraged so as to overcome the shortage of hybrid seeds produced and supplied by modern agricultural farms.[70]

The introduction and improvement of hybrid seeds in the colony was the main agenda of the colonial state. A number of new varieties of rice which were anticipated to yield high output were introduced in the region. Although there were about fifty traditional varieties of rice in the region, they were broadly distinguished into two types—*halka dhan* (early rice) and *bhari dhan* (late rice). The advantages of halka dhan were that it required little water and ripened six weeks sooner than bhari dhan, but was anticipated to give low output. On the other hand, bhari dhan needed more water and took a longer time to mature, but yielded high produce and had a good flavour.[71] The modern agricultural farms identified about fifteen high-yielding varieties of rice from the local varieties. Among them, Gurmatia, Chinoor, Parewa, Bhondu, Madi Pisso, Eklombi, and Bhata Gurmatia were popularized by the Agricultural Department.[72] Gurmatia was anticipated to yield 425 pounds more than the other local varieties per acre.[73] The department also produced hybrid varieties by crossing two standard local varieties which yielded a high produce. The variety produced by crossing Bhondu and Gurmatia was anticipated to yield 2,980 pounds per acre.[74] The hybridizing method helped to combine a strong straw variety with a high-yielding variety that generally resulted in producing fine-quality, high-yielding rice varieties. The crossing of R10 × R6 (Luchai × Budhaiabako) and R8 × R7 (Luchai × Gurmatia) was intended to improve the strength of straw of high-yielding strains. Whereas the crossing of R10 × R2 (Chhatri × Nungi) and R6 × R10 (Bundhiaibako × Chhatri) was intended to improve the yield of fine and scented varieties and to evolve early scented strains. These new varieties of rice were supplied to cultivators for sowing through government and private agencies.[75] Although there was fluctuation in its area of cultivation due to failure of seasons, rice always occupied the largest area in the total cropped area of Chanda territory. In 1869, rice was cultivated on 235,002 acres of land.[76] The average area between 1896 and 1899 was 304,000 acres.[77] Between 1901 and 1921, the average rice cultivation area was 29 per cent of the total crop area.[78] The statistics show that there was a considerable increase in the area under rice cultivation in the region.

Apart from producing new varieties of rice, the agricultural farms also produced new varieties of commercial crops such as cotton and sugarcane. Indeed, the expansion of commercial crops was the top priority of the colonial state. However, the Chanda region was relatively free from this project of commercial crops. Cotton was cultivated mainly in Adilabad district and sugarcane in some pockets of Chanda district. In 1920, the total cultivated area under cotton in Adilabad was 171,906 acres.[79] This had risen to 267,722 acres by 1940.[80] In Chanda, all three new kinds of irrigated cotton did extremely well on *wardi* soil. Yields of 1,063 pounds per acre were received from the Buri variety, 1,335 pounds from Rosea, and 790 pounds from the Cambodia type.[81] The Khari and Sannabille cane varieties which were known for their high yields and were free from red rot had largely replaced the local Kala and Katai types.[82]

Modern cultivation methods and hybrid seeds were greatly popularized by agricultural associations. District- and tahsil-level associations were formed in Chanda in 1918.[83] These associations propagated modern cultivation at the village level by organizing meetings in various places. The Agricultural Department was closely associated with the activities of these associations. Sometimes, peasants were brought to modern agricultural farms and shown new methods of cultivation. The value of high-yielding seed varieties was explained to them.[84] Although modern agricultural methods were confined to rich peasants and did not influence subaltern peasants, they did help to create a demand for land that led to the expansion of agriculture in forest and hill areas. In 1869, the total occupied area in Chanda was 695,032 acres.[85] In 1920, this had risen to 1,149,945 acres, of which 834,734 acres were in plains tahsils (Chanda, Warora, and Brahmapuri), and 315,211 acres in forest tahsils (Sironcha and Gadchiroli). From the beginning of the twentieth century, there was a conspicuous increase in occupied area in Sironcha and Gadchiroli tahsils, which had been largely covered by forests and had remained under the rule of Gond zamindars. The total occupied area in Sironcha and Gadchiroli tahsils increased from 56,976 to 81,001 and 165,330 to 234,211 acres respectively between 1906 and 1920, or by 44 and 41 per cent respectively.[86] This percentage increased further as non-adivasis grabbed land in forest tracts.

Similarly, in 1878 in Adilabad district, the total occupied land and wasteland were 255,501 and 427,774 acres respectively.[87] Whereas in 1902, the cultivated and cultivable wasteland were 384,837 and 369,694 acres respectively,[88] in 1931 the total cultivable land in the district had increased to 1,449,314 acres.[89] In fact, forest tracts of Adilabad district were opened up substantially only from the beginning of the twentieth century. Rather than benefit the adivasis, the encouragement of modern and commercial farming in fact led to their eventual loss of land.[90] We shall take up this history in the next chapter. Indeed, the traditional practice of dhya, traditional crop varieties, and conventional modes of cultivation were more scientific than the colonial ones and suitable to the environment and ecology of the region. The colonial model of agriculture not only destroyed adivasi agricultural practices that had been refined over time taking into account requirements other than high yields and profit, but also forced the adivasis to relinquish their land and flee further into the forest. But even there, the forest officials continued to push them back as, under the new forest laws, forests were no longer a free zone.

FOREST ENCLOSURE

The colonial state brought hill and forest areas under its control largely through forest regulation. Forests were inhabited mainly by adivasis. Further, forests and adivasis were constructed as the opposites of the plains and caste-Hindus respectively. The levelling and ordering of the forest and of the adivasi were important to the colonial state.[91] The disciplining of the wildness of the forest that had its spiritual roots in the post-Enlightenment Age of Reason was fundamental to the modern state. Enlightenment rationality preached that nature was a quantitative, mechanistic mass and a resource to be exploited.[92] This idea was very much entrenched in the colonial forest policy in India. The forest had been enclosed purely for state utilization under the Indian Forest Act of 1878. Section 3 of this act says, 'Local Government may from time to time, constitute any forest-land or wasteland which is the property of government, or over which government has proprietary rights, or to the whole or any part of the forest-produce of which government is entitled, a reserved forest in the manner hereinafter provided.'[93] Thus, the state became the exclusive owner of forests under colonial rule. In pre-colonial India, the state had controlled these forests very loosely and people used them for multiple purposes—for grazing, gathering edible fruits, hunting, banditry, medicine, timber, firewood, and so on.[94] A similar practice continued in the zamindaris before they were brought under colonial forest regulations. The regulation of forests was undertaken in the name of scientific forestry and conservation, but this policy decreased forests in the region drastically. After the Forest Act came into force, the state fenced off the forest and controlled and exploited it systematically.

The Sahayadri hills which traversed Chanda and Adilabad from the north-west to the south-east formed a huge forest area which contained valuable woods such as teak, ebony, sandalwood, rosewood, and so on.[95] In particular, the Chimur, Mool, Phersagarh, Surjagarh, and Teepagarh hills of Chanda contained valuable wood. The district had over 6,000 square miles of forest area in 1869, which constituted about 60 per cent of its total area.[96] In Adilabad, 56.9 per cent of the total area of the district in 1901 was forested.[97]

Although the colonial state had loosely controlled and exploited forest resources from the protectorate period in the Nagpur territories, a systematic fencing of the forests began with the implementation of the forest rules in 1859. The forests of the provinces were divided into six divisions. The Chanda forests fell in the North Chanda and South Chanda divisions. D. Brandis's report on scientific forestry remained the guiding principle for the governance of the forest in the province. There had indeed been interesting debates among British revenue and forest officials on adopting criteria for the exploitation and conservation of forests.[98] Brandis toured the province in February and March 1863 and submitted a report on the scientific exploitation of forests. The Forest Rules were amended and reframed along the lines of Brandis's suggestions.[99]

According to the new Forest Rules, tracts of forest land or wasteland were reserved as the exclusive property of the state. Such waste or forest land was termed 'government reserved forests'. Unauthorized felling, cutting, marking, killing, or injuring of trees, shrubs, or bamboos, the collection of *mowah*, grass, *raal*, or other forest produce within the limits of the reserved forest, or any acts which violated the rights of the state, were made punishable under the provisions of the Penal Code. Dhya cultivation, the grazing of cattle, and interference of any kind with the ground or its products, without the special permission of the officers in charge of the government reserved forest, were prohibited. The roads passing through the forests could also be closed if the concerned officer felt it to be necessary. On top of all this, the boundaries of each reserved forest were marked off by masonry pillars, and the nearby villagers were informed about these boundaries and warned against trespassing, theft, and mischief. However, some concessions were provided to local peasants to graze cattle and fell non-valuable trees in second-category forests. The forests under the zamindaris that had commercial potential were also brought under the state forest either through sale or lease.[100] Further, the forest was surveyed systematically on these lines and boundaries were set up in the province. By 1902, the survey of the forest had been completed in all except 175 square miles of Chanda district.[101]

A similar exercise was also carried out in Hyderabad State. A Forest Department was created in the state in 1277F (1876).[102] Initially, under this department, there were eight valuable species of trees. The rest of the forest produce and administration remained in the hands of the district revenue officials. But later, through the services of trained European forest officers, the Nizam brought in rigorous reforms in forest policy. J. Ballantine, a British forest officer, brought in radical reforms in forest management during 1887 and 1892 in the Nizam's state through which he showed new avenues to extract forest resources.[103]

For both the colonial state and the Nizam's state, the forest was a major concern because of its economic resources. Mineral resources and forest wood not only enriched the state treasury but were also crucial in building railways and modern industries. Colonial administrators were astonished by the forest resources of the Chanda district. A forest officer, Captain Stewart, remarked upon seeing the Chanda forest that 'I have never seen such noble teak, nor the trees so numerous, and yet the most reckless and wasteful cutting has been going on for two seasons in this very tract.'[104] The most valuable forest was spread mainly in South Chanda, which was largely under the zamindari system, particularly in the Ahiri zamindari. Major Pearson was given the task of exploring the forest resources in this zamindari. He literally travelled by foot and counted the teak trees in the zamindari. He reported that 'there are at least two lakhs of trees, containing about three to four lakhs of timbers standing on a comparatively small area of 40 sq. Miles, within 6 or 8 miles of the Pranhita river, out of the forest at least 50,000 to 60,000 trees are ready for the axe.'[105] This led the colonial state to bring zamindari forests under its control.

The British colonial state had a practice of grabbing forests from adivasi chiefs on lease or sale to use for its own commercial purposes.[106] In this way, the colonial state purchased large tracts of forest from the Ahiri zamindari in 1873 and 1883, totalling 80,775 acres, for which a combined sum of Rs 160,000 was paid.[107] If there was opposition from the zamindars against such a move, the colonial state would take over the forest under the Land Acquisition Act, paying a nominal compensation.[108] After establishing its power over the forest, the colonial state policed it systematically.[109]

The enclosing of forests resulted in a huge decrease in the forest area in the province and in Hyderabad State. The dubious conservation policy did not protect the forest. The state itself opened shops to sell forest resources and wood. The greater part of the wood went into railway-line construction. Railway sleepers were supplied from the Chanda forest to the Bengal–Nagpur Railway and the Great Indian Peninsula Railway.[110] Minor resources and grazing rights were auctioned off to contractors, or sometimes the state collected taxes directly from the cultivators.[111] After the wood was cleared, the forest was given over for cultivation, as discussed earlier. The practice was that the Forest Department would transfer the second category (ruined forests) to the Irrigation Department. The cultivators were then encouraged to form villages on those lands under both the ryotwari and malguzari systems. Thus, huge forests were cleared in a short period.[112] The coming of the railways in the district ruined the forests very rapidly. Till the end of the nineteenth century, the district's communication system had been very poor. The road from Chanda to Sironcha, a distance of 129 miles, opened up the district substantially. The railway lines from Ballarshah to Warangal and from Gondia to Chanda (narrow-gauge line), which were laid down in the first decade of the twentieth century, were crucial in transporting Chanda forest wood and resources to other parts of India.[113] The province's forest revenue from all sources increased from Rs 59,189 to Rs 4,791,425 between the financial years 1863–4 and 1934–5.[114]

Whereas the Chanda district's total forest revenue from all sources for the year 1865–6 was Rs 8,393,[115] this had increased to Rs 144,000 in 1906–7.[116]

The government forest in Chanda district in 1904 occupied 3,354 square miles, of which 1,731 square miles (consisting of 1,307 square miles A-class and 424 square miles B-class forests) were in the North Chanda division and 1,623 square miles (composed of 1,280 square miles A-class and 343 square miles B-class forests) were located in the South Chanda division.[117] By 1931, this had been reduced to 2,491 square miles, of which 1,269 square miles were in North Chanda division and 1,222 square miles in South Chanda division. Of the total forest area in the North Chanda division, 1,121 square miles were A-class and 148 square miles B-class forests. Similarly, of the total forest area in the South Chanda division, 968 square miles were A-class and 254 square miles B-class forests. The numbers show a decrease of 863 square miles, or 26 per cent, of forest area in the district within a span of twenty-six years.[118]

A similar phenomenon was witnessed in Adilabad district as well. The new policy, along with the commercialization of the forests, enriched the state treasury and gave a great impetus to emerging industries in the state. The eastern forest was used to supply sleepers for the state railways, softwood species for use in the match factory started at Mahboobabad in 1928, and beedi leaves for the widespread cottage industry.[119] The timber requirement for the Singareni coal mines at Bellampalli, Mandamarri, and Ramakrishnapur in Adilabad district and Ramagundam in Karimnagar district was largely met from the forests of Adilabad.[120] The total revenue collected from forest production in the state in 1347F (1938) was Rs 1,611,749,[121] as against Rs 288,337 in 1309F (1900),[122] whereas the Adilabad district forest revenue increased from Rs 130,304 to Rs 327,631 between 1921 and 1935.[123] The Nizam's attempt to enclose the forests was apparently not different from British colonial exploitation in other parts of India. Despite the large amount of extraction from the forest, not a single rupee was spent for the development of adivasis.

Between 1901 and 1914, the forest area of Adilabad district decreased from 4,213 square miles (of which 2,213 square miles were protected and 2,000 square miles were unprotected or open forest) to 2,814.16 square miles (of which 1831.50 square miles were protected and 982.66 square miles were open forest). This underlines the fact that within a span of thirteen years, 1,398.84 square miles of forest were converted into cultivable land.[124] This had further decreased to 1,791.35 square miles by 1936, of which 88.23 square miles were reserved and 1,703.12 square miles were protected forests.[125]

It appears that the Adilabad forest disappeared faster than its counterpart in Chanda. The reason was primarily that a large area of forests in Chanda was under the direct control of adivasi chiefs. In part it was also because the forests in Chanda had been exploited exclusively by the state, whereas the Adilabad forests were also exploited by private contractors who acquired the right to exploit them in public auctions. The decrease in forest area in the districts was attributed to adivasis' practice of podu cultivation and grazing. In fact, the fencing of the forests produced tense conditions in the hills. The new laws and the fencing of the forests made the traditional patterns of forest use and cultivation that had sustained Gond life all but impossible. Their traditional everyday life was criminalized. In other words, Gonds who continued with their normal practices could now be accused of theft and illegal grazing and felling of trees. Despite the stringent punishments, forest thefts and crimes continued to increase throughout the colonial period. The evasion of forest regulations was more conspicuous in southern Chanda district, which was largely inhabited by adivasis. On this the *Forest Administration Report* reported:

The continued increase in the number of reported cases of unauthorised felling and grazing is disquieting. That unauthorised grazing should have increased so largely is the more surprising in that one result of the reduction in the size of copse ... the check of grazing licenses was tightened up during the year, and this may account for the increase under that head, ... there has been no alteration of procedure and no such strengthening of establishment as would account for the increase of illicit fellings reported, and there is some reason to believe that the fines imposed when offences are compounded are too small to be deterrent.[126]

The tight checking and heavy fines did not act as a deterrent; rather, they seemed to increase forest offences by adivasis. An alternative mechanism was evolved in the form of forest villages. However, the forest villages were an utter failure. Many of these forest villages were deserted by adivasis as they were not suitable to their lifestyle, and then they were taken over by caste-Hindus from the plains.[127]

The imperial state-making process that had been introduced in the Chanda territories by the Bhonsles by deploying caste-Hindu peasants in the territory, was developed further by colonial imperialism by deploying a political rationality. The introduction of a rule of property in land and forest regulations helped the colonial state build its edifice in the hills. In this endeavour, the immigration of caste-Hindu peasants was instrumental in establishing new narratives of rule. In particular, land-revenue policies combined with modern agricultural technology played a crucial role in expanding colonial state-making in the forest and hill areas. However, the process was full of tensions, as many of these processes were evaded by the Gond rajas and their people. But eventually they were forced to bear the effects of colonial state power that not only enclosed Gond territories but also their social sphere. Let us now move on to a discussion of the ways in which the adivasi society was enclosed.

NOTES

1. James C. Scott, *The Art of Not Being Governed: An Anarchist History of Upland Southeast Asia* (New Haven: Yale University Press, 2009), p. 3.

2. Richard Jenkins, *Report of the Territories of the Rajah of Nagpur* (Nagpur: Government Press, 1925 [1827]), p. 38.

3. C. B. Lucie Smith, *Report on Land Revenue Settlement of the Chanda District, Central Provinces* (Nagpur: Chief Commissioner's Press, 1870), p. 70.

4. W. V. Grigson, *The Aboriginal Problem in the Central Provinces & Berar* (Nagpur: Government Printing, 1944), pp. 54–62.

5. Christoph von Fürer-Haimendorf, 'Tribal Population of Hyderabad Yesterday and Today', *Census of India 1941*, vol. XXI: *H.E.H. the Nizam's Dominions (Hyderabad State)*, Part I: *Report* (Hyderabad-Deccan: Government Central Press, 1945), pp. i–liii.

6. It is said that all the Chanda territory records were destroyed in 1824 by a Brahman dewan by the name of Lingo Punt Dikshit, who became powerful in the district after it was conquered by the British, in order to

erase evidence of his nepotism. See Smith, *Land Revenue Settlement of the Chanda District*, p. 126.

7. Irfan Habib, *An Atlas of the Mughal Empire* (New Delhi: Oxford University Press, 1982), pp. 36, 59–60. Also see p. 15A.

8. Jenkins, *Report of the Territories of the Rajah of Nagpur*, p. 4. The *Ain-i-Akbari* mentions that there was dense forest around Manikdurg and Ramgir (in Adilabad district). See Habib, *An Atlas of the Mughal Empire*, p. 61.

9. Smith, *Land Revenue Settlement of the Chanda District*, p. 133.

10. *Stephen Hislop's Papers Relating to the Aboriginal Tribes of the Central Provinces*, IOR/F/4/755/20541, p. v.

11. Jenkins, *Report of the Territories of the Rajah of Nagpur*, p. 88.

12. Irfan Habib, *The Agrarian System of Mughal India 1556–1707* (New Delhi: Oxford University Press, 1999), pp. 144–59.

13. Setumadhava Rao Pagdi, *Among the Gonds of Adilabad* (Bombay: Popular Book Depot, 1949), p. 28; Kidar Nath Thusu, *Gond Kingdom of Chanda, with Particular Reference to Its Political Structure* (Calcutta: Anthropological Survey of India, 1980), p. 247.

14. Smith, *Land Revenue Settlement of the Chanda District*, pp. 66–7.

15. Smith, *Land Revenue Settlement of the Chanda District*, p. 206.

16. Jenkins, *Report of the Territories of the Rajah of Nagpur*, p. 84.

17. W. H. Sleeman, *Rambles and Recollections of an Indian Official*, 2 vols (London: Archibald Constable and Company, 1893), vol. I, p. 73.

18. Jenkins, *Report of the Territories of the Rajah of Nagpur*, p. 35; also see Smith, *Land Revenue Settlement of the Chanda District*, pp. 123–4.

19. Mahesh Rangarajan, *Fencing the Forest: Conservation and Ecological Change in India's Central Provinces 1860–1914* (New Delhi: Oxford University Press, 1996), p. 41.

20. Smith, *Land Revenue Settlement of the Chanda District*, pp. 126–7.

21. Smith, *Land Revenue Settlement of the Chanda District*, pp. 130–1.

22. Smith, *Land Revenue Settlement of the Chanda District*, p. 36: Jenkins, *Report of the Territories of the Rajah of Nagpur*, p. 10.

23. Jenkins, *Report of the Territories of the Rajah of Nagpur*, p. 10; Smith, *Land Revenue Settlement of the Chanda District*, p. 2.

24. Smith, *Land Revenue Settlement of the Chanda District*, pp. 203–5.

25. Eyre Chatterton, *The Story of Gondwana* (London: Sir Isaac Pitman & Sons, 1916), p. 76.

26. Ajay Skaria, *Hybrid Histories: Forests, Frontiers and Wildness in Western India* (New Delhi: Oxford University Press, 1999), pp. 193–4; see also

David Hardiman, 'Power in the Forest: The Dangs, 1820–1940', in *Subaltern Studies VIII: Essays in Honour of Ranajit Guha*, edited by David Arnold and David Hardiman (New Delhi: Oxford University Press, 1994), p. 110.

27. *The Central Provinces Land Revenue Act 1881 (XVIII of 1881) (as Modified up to the 1st March 1909)* (Calcutta: Superintendent Government Printing, 1909), pp. 11–96.

28. Jenkins, *Report of the Territories of the Rajah of Nagpur*, p. 85.

29. *Central Provinces and Berar: A Review of the Administration of the Province 1921–1922* (Nagpur: Superintendent Government Printing, 1923), pp. 119–26.

30. *Progress Report on Forest Administration in the Central Provinces 1863–64* (Calcutta: Public Works Department, 1865), p. 11.

31. Smith, *Land Revenue Settlement of the Chanda District*, pp. 132–3.

32. *Central Provinces and Berar: A Review of the Administration 1921–1922*, vol. II, p. 123.

33. *Central Provinces and Berar: A Review of the Administration 1921–22*, p. 116.

34. *Chanda District Gazetteer*, 1909, p. 316.

35. *Central Provinces and Berar: A Review of the Administration 1921–22*, p. 123.

36. *Central Provinces and Berar: A Review of the Administration 1921–22*, p. 114.

37. *Chanda District Gazetteer*, 1909, pp. 236–7.

38. Vidarbha, RD, S. No. 4469, File no. 51-A-2/1936, ff. 6–16.

39. Vidarbha, RD, S. No. 4469, File no. 51-A-2/1936, f. 20.

40. Vidarbha, RD, S. no. 4926, File no. 1-65/1939, pp. 1–24; Vidarbha, RD, S. no. 4029, File no. 1-95/1935, f. 20.

41. *Revenue Administration Report of HEH the Nizam's Government, 1914–15* (Hyderabad: Gladstone Press, 1916), p. 47.

42. *Revenue Administration Report of HEH the Nizam's Government, 1914–15*, p. 47.

43. *Revenue Administration Report of HEH the Nizam's Government, 1914–15*, p. 48.

44. *Revenue Administration Report of HEH the Nizam's Government, 1914–15*, p. 48.

45. *Administration Report of the Forest Department of His Highness the Nizam's Dominions for the Year 1315F* (1905–6) (APSA, R-22), p. 2.

46. *Report on the Administration of His Highness the Nizam's Dominions for the Year 1322F* (6 October 1912–5 October 1913) (Hyderabad-Deccan: A. V. Pillai & Sons, at the Gladstone Press, 1915), p. 12.

47. *The Hyderabad Forest Conference 1332F* (1922–3) (Hyderabad-Deccan: Government Central Press, APSA, R-22), p. 2.

48. *Administration Report of the Forest Department of His Highness the Nizam's Dominions for the Year 1319F* (7 October 1909–6 October 1910) (Hyderabad-Deccan: A. V. Pillai & Sons, 1912), p. 3.

49. *Report on the Administration of the Revenue and Allied Department of H.H. the Nizam's Government for 1324F* (1914–15) (Hyderabad-Deccan: Gladstone Press, 1916), pp. v, 53–4.

50. *Report on the Administration of the Revenue and Allied Department of H.H. the Nizam's Government for 1324F*, p. 128; *Gazetteer of Hyderabad,* 1909, p. 188.

51. *Gazetteer of Hyderabad,* 1909, pp. 191–2; *Report of the Royal Commission on Jagir Administration and Reforms, H.E.H the Nizam's Government 1356F* (1945–6) (Bangalore: Bangalore Press, 1947), p. 37: also see V. Ramakrishna Reddy, *Economic History of Hyderabad State: Warangal Subha 1911–1950* (New Delhi: Gian Publication House, 1987), p. 96.

52. Smith, *Land Revenue Settlement of the Chanda District*, p. 2.

53. *Gazetteer of Hyderabad,* 1909, p. 184.

54. Smith, *Land Revenue Settlement of the Chanda District*, p. 5.

55. Jenkins, *Report of the Territories of the Rajah of Nagpur*, p. 7; Smith, *Land Revenue Settlement of the Chanda District*, p. 2.

56. *Gazetteer of Hyderabad,* 1909, pp. 187–8.

57. *Chanda District Gazetteer,* 1909, p. 169.

58. *Chanda District Gazetteer,* 1909, p. 171.

59. *Early European Travellers in the Nagpur Territories: Reprinted from Old Records* (Nagpur: Government Press, 1930), p. 141.

60. Smith, *Land Revenue Settlement of the Chanda District*, p. 85.

61. *Chanda District Gazetteer,* 1909, p. 170.

62. *Progress Report on Forest Administration in the Central Provinces 1867–68 and 1868–69* (Calcutta: Public Works Department Press, 1870), p. 2.

63. *Progress Report on Forest Administration 1867–68 & 1868–69*, p. 7.

64. Vidharbha, RD, Confidential, S. no. 5916, File no. 6/1945, f. 44.

65. *Report on the Nagpur Experimental Farm in the Central Provinces for the Year 1897–98, Ending 31st March, 1898* (Allahabad: Pioneer Press, 1898), p. 1.

66. *Report of the Department of Land Records and Agriculture, Central Provinces, for the Year 1901–02 Ending 31st March 1902* (Nagpur: Secretariat Press, 1903), p. 3.

67. *Report of the Department of Land Records and Agriculture, Central Provinces, for the Year 1911–12* (Nagpur: Government Press, 1912), p. 5.

68. Jenkins, *Report of the Territories of the Rajah of Nagpur*, p. 39.

69. *Report of the Department of Land Records and Agriculture, Central Provinces, for the Year 1914–15* (Nagpur: Government Press, 1915), p. 11.

70. *Report of the Department of Land Records and Agriculture, Central Provinces, for the Year 1915–16* (Nagpur: Government Press, 1916), p. 11.

71. Smith, *Land Revenue Settlement of the Chanda District*, p. 91; *Chanda District Gazetteer*, 1909, p. 163.

72. *Report of the Department of Land Records and Agriculture, Central Provinces, for the Year 1917–18* (Nagpur: Government Press, 1918), p. 4.

73. *Report of the Department of Land Records and Agriculture, 1915–16*, p. 11.

74. *Report on the Working of the Department of Agriculture of the Central Provinces for the Year Ending 31st March 1932 and 31st March 1933* (Nagpur: Government Press, 1933), p. 11.

75. *Report on the Working of the Department of Agriculture of the Central Provinces and Berar for the Year Ending 31st March 1940* (Nagpur: Government Press, 1941), p. 12.

76. Smith, *Land Revenue Settlement of the Chanda District*, p. 79.

77. *Chanda District Gazetteer*, 1909, p. 149.

78. *Census of India 1911*, vol. X: *Central Provinces and Berar*, Part I: *Report* (Calcutta: Superintendent Government Printing, 1912), p. 24; *Census of India 1921*, vol. XI: *Central Provinces and Berar*, Part I: *Report* (Nagpur: Government Press, 1923), p. 27.

79. *Statistical Abstract HEH the Nizam's Dominions, from 1321F–1330F* (1911–21) (Hyderabad-Deccan: Government Central Press, 1925), p. 140.

80. *Agricultural Statistics: Notes and Estimates of Area and Yield of Principal Crops in Hyderabad State from 1935–36 to 1939–40* (Hyderabad-Deccan: Government Central Press, 1942), p. 27.

81. *Report of the Department of Land Records and Agriculture, Central Provinces, for the Year 1913–14* (Nagpur: Government Press, 1915), p. 11.

82. *Report on the Working of the Department of Agriculture of the Central Provinces for the Year 1919–20* (Nagpur: Government Press, 1920), p. 7.

83. *Report of the Department of Land Records and Agriculture, 1917–18*, p. 11.

84. *Report on the Working of the Department of Agriculture, 1919–20*, p. 21.

85. Smith, *Land Revenue Settlement of the Chanda District*, p. 79.

86. Vidarbha, Settlement, S. no. 920, File no. 4-7/1922, f. 6; *Final Report on the Re-settlement of the Three Cis-Wainganga Tahsils of the Chanda District in the Central Provinces* (Nagpur: Government Press, 1924), p. 15.

87. Adilabad district was known as Sirpur Tandur prior to 1905, and the figures given here pertain to Sirpur Tandur. See Maulavi Said Mohdi

Ali, *Report on the History of the Famine H.H. the Nizam's Dominions in 1877–77, 1877–78* (Bombay: Exchange Press, 1879), p. 40.

88. *Report on the Administration of His Highness the Nizam's Dominions for the Year 1308F to 1312F (7th October 1898 to 6 October 1903)* (Hyderabad-Deccan: A. V. Pillai & Sons, Government Printers, 1907), pp. 38–40.

89. *Statistical Abstract of H.E.H. the Nizam's Dominions from 1331F to 1340F* (1922–31) (Hyderabad-Deccan: Government Central Press, 1938), p. 146.

90. W. V. Grigson, *The Challenge of Backwardness* (Hyderabad-Deccan: Government Press, 1947), pp. 24–9.

91. *Report on the Administration of the Central Provinces, 1901–02*, pp. 9–11.

92. Neeladri Bhattacharya, 'Pastoralists in a Colonial World', in *Nature, Culture, Imperialism: Essays on the Environmental History of South Asia*, edited by David Arnold and Ramachandra Guha (New Delhi: Oxford University Press, 1995), p. 73.

93. *The Indian Forest Act, 1878 (VII of 1878). As Modified up to the 1st December, 1902* (Calcutta: Superintendent of Government Printing, 1903), p. 8.

94. David Arnold and Ramachandra Guha (eds), *Nature, Culture, Imperialism: Essays on the Environmental History of South Asia* (New Delhi: Oxford University Press, 1995), p. 10.

95. *Gazetteer of Hyderabad*, 1909, p. 185; Smith, *Land Revenue Settlement of the Chanda District*, p. 5.

96. Smith, *Land Revenue Settlement of the Chanda District*, pp. 1, 5.

97. *Gazetteer of Hyderabad*, 1909, p. 188.

98. Rangarajan describes this debate in an illuminating way; see his *Fencing the Forest*, pp. 48–94.

99. *Progress Report on Forest Administration 1863–64*, p. 35.

100. *Progress Report on Forest Administration 1863–64*, pp. 42–59.

101. *Report on the Administration of the Central Provinces 1901–02*, p. xvi.

102. *Report on the Administration of HEH the Nizam's Dominions for the Year 1331F (6th Oct. 1921 to 5th Oct. 1922)* (Hyderabad-Deccan: Government Central Press, 1925), p. 61.

103. *Report on the Administration of the Nizam's Dominions for the Year 1331F*, p. 61.

104. *Progress Report on Forest Administration 1863–64*, p. 65.

105. *Progress Report on Forest Administration in the Central Provinces 1866–67* (Calcutta: Public Works Department Press, 1867), p. 32.

106. Hardiman, 'Power in the Forest', pp. 112–16.

107. Vidarbha, RD, S. no. 2882, File no. 58-7/1931, f. 2.

108. Vidarbha, RD, S. no. 2882, File no. 58-7/1931, ff. 7–12.

109. *Progress Report on Forest Administration 1863–64*, p. 47; also see *The Indian Forest Act, 1878*, p. 18.

110. Rangarajan shows how the Chanda forest was crucial in building the railways in India. See his *Fencing the Forest*, p. 67.

111. *Chanda District Gazetteer*, 1909, pp. 266–7.

112. *Report on the Forest Administration of the Central Provinces for the Year 1923–24* (Nagpur: Government Press, 1925), pp. viii–x.

113. *Final Report on the Re-settlement of the Siraoncha and Garchiroli Tahsils of the Chanda District in the Central Province during the Years 1922–24* (Nagpur: Government Press, 1926), pp. 1–3.

114. *Progress Report on Forest Administration 1863–64*, p. 13; *Central Provinces and Berar: A Review of the Administration 1934–35* (Nagpur: Superintendent Government Printing, 1936), vol. II, p. 46.

115. *Progress Report on Forest Administration in the Central Provinces for the Year 1865–66* (Calcutta: Public Works Department Press, 1867), p. 26.

116. *Chanda District Gazetteer*, 1909, p. 264.

117. *Chanda District Gazetteer*, 1909, p. 260.

118. *Report on the Forest Administration of the Central Provinces for the Year Ending 31 March 1932* (Nagpur: Government Press, 1933), p. 9.

119. Reddy, *Economic History of Hyderabad State*, p. 26.

120. Reddy, *Economic History of Hyderabad State*, p. 26.

121. *Administration Report of the Forest Department of H.E.H. the Nizam's Dominions for the Year 1348F* (1939) (Hyderabad-Deccan: Government Central Press, 1940), p. 45.

122. *Annual Progress Report of Forest Administration in His Highness the Nizam's Dominions for the Year 1309F* (7 October 1899–6 October 1900) (Hyderabad-Deccan: A. V. Pillai & Sons, Printers to H.H. the Nizam's Government, 1901), p. 1.

123. *Hyderabad District Gazetteers: Adilabad District Tables Volume, 1931–1936* (Hyderabad-Deccan: Government Central Press, 1940), p. 88.

124. *Revenue Administration Report of HEH the Nizam's Government, 1914–15*, p. 128; *Gazetteer of Hyderabad*, p. 188.

125. *Hyderabad District Gazetteers: Adilabad District Tables Volume, 1931–1936*, p. 97.

126. *Report on the Forest Administration of the Central Provinces for the Year 1924–25* (Nagpur: Government Press, 1926), p. 3.

127. *Report on the Forest Administration of the Central Provinces for the Year 1925–26* (Nagpur: Government Press, 1927), p. 34.

4

ENCLOSING ADIVASIS
THE MAKING OF THE COLONIAL PERIPHERY

THE PROCESS OF COLONIAL STATE-MAKING in the hills and forests involved the eviction of adivasis and their reduction to landless agricultural labourers. Some tried to retain their independence by migrating into the remaining forest tracts, which the British and princely rulers now classed as reserved for the sole use of the state. They were banned from utilizing reserved forests in the old ways—through hunting, gathering, shifting agriculture, or grazing livestock. In general, adivasis—whether living in the plains or in the forests—suffered increasing marginalization throughout India under colonial rule.[1] Colonial political rationality was indeed designed to populate the hills with caste-Hindu peasants. The ryotwari, malguzari, and ijara revenue tenures helped caste-Hindu peasants grab large areas of land in the hills through moneylending and by force. The influx of caste-Hindus not only ousted adivasis from their land, but also impacted their social and cultural life.[2]

All of this led to revolts and resistance in this region. The colonial state had been changing its strategies depending on the adivasis' response to its rule. Particularly during the early twentieth century, the strategy of civilizing adivasis by settling them as agriculturists shifted to protectionism, with the reservation of tracts, places, and positions for them. This was, in itself, controversial.[3] The larger process of settling these communities continued right into the twentieth century, and in some cases was never fully carried through. In the process, however, the hill and forest societies became firmly divided from the societies of the plains. Colonial anthropology was crucial in establishing that divide by typifying adivasi society. Most recent studies of the Gonds have failed to capture this aspect of the genealogy of the divide between the plains and the hills. These studies are mainly thick descriptions of the destruction of adivasi society by the colonial state.[4] In this chapter, I shall attempt to explain the ways in which the adivasis were enclosed with the introduction of land enclosures in the region. In turn, this process hardened the divide between the plains and the hills.

MAKING OF THE PERIPHERY

As discussed in the preceding chapter, the process of enclosing the Gonds in modern times began with the Maratha regime and was aggravated during British colonial rule. Most of the rich and irrigated lands of the plains were grabbed by non-adivasi peasants before the British took over the region, particularly in northern Chanda, and the Gonds were pushed towards southern Chanda which was covered by dense forests. This part of Chanda had been substantially opened up by the colonial rulers.[5] The colonial land-revenue system and modern agricultural methods were designed to create demand for land, particularly in the hills and forests. It was this development that evicted a large number of Gonds from their lands and drove them further into the forest. This process is clearly recorded in an Administration Report of the Central Provinces, which says:

> Hindu immigrants first settled themselves permanently in the Nerbudda valley and in the interior, coming at first in small numbers they were peaceably received by the Gonds who readily assigned them lands and leave to cultivate them and were content with trifling return in kind. Gradually their numbers were increased by fresh settlers who in time became a formidable body, and before advancing cultivation the Gond chiefs with their followers retired slowly from the hills and jungles, abandoning their former villages to the Hindu agriculturists.[6]

The Gonds thus would bring waste or forest land under cultivation, and when the land began giving good returns it was taken over or 'grabbed' by the caste-Hindu peasants from the plains. Under British colonial rule, adivasis lost their land mainly through forced surrender and moneylending. In malguzari villages, adivasi holdings were largely in the form of 'tenants at will' and not absolute occupancy.[7] Unlike the traditional practices, the new rules did not allow the tenant to ascertain his occupancy right after a failure of seasons or on return from migration during the bad season.[8] In the old system, land was held by the village community, but in the new system the malguzar was given hereditary proprietorship of the village land. This turned the cultivators from village ryots into the malguzar's tenants. In a strict sense, cultivators now became tenants to the landlords.[9]

When the first settlement was begun in 1869, the cultivators, particularly Gonds, did not realize that it was the perpetual ownership of the land that was being conferred to the Brahmans and other influential malguzars. They realized this only at the end of the settlement, and began asserting the right to their land. But by the time they realized the value of the pattas, everything had already slipped out of their hands.[10] Although there was a rule that land rent could not be increased until the next settlement, the malguzars collected extra rent from the tenants as they chose. There was no comparison between the government demand and the actual collection of the rent.[11] A huge number of Gonds surrendered their land to malguzars due to the pressure of rent or arrears of rent. Such surrendered land was largely handed over to dominant caste-Hindu peasants, particularly to Brahmans, Kumbis, Mahars, and Marwaris. No aboriginal was given any part of the surrendered land. Most of the malguzars, even in the adivasi tracts, were non-adivasis, and many of them were absentees who managed their villages through *muqaddam-gumashta*s (village clerks). For each village or group of villages there would be one muqaddam-gumashta. Most of these were also non-adivasis, and they were paid good remuneration in cash or in the form of land. Initially, adivasis were also appointed as muqaddam-gumashtas, but they were paid very nominally and irregularly. As a result, no adivasi was willing to take up this position. As we have seen in the previous chapter, sometimes the malguzar deliberately persuaded them to leave the position. What is more, adivasi malguzars were generally considerate to their fellow cultivators in collecting rent. The rents used to accumulate for years and finally result in the ousting of the malguzar.[12]

Land rents in Chanda district increased continuously. In the 1869 settlement, soil was classified into four categories including 'always irrigated land'. The rent was fixed based on the past history of the turnover of the land. Accordingly, it was fixed at Rs 7 per acre for always irrigated land, Re 1 and 5 annas for 1st class land, Re 1 and 10 annas for 2nd class land, 8 annas for 3rd class land, and 4 annas for 4th class land.[13] In the 1897 settlements, these rates were increased by 17 per cent in the district.[14] The rents were increased abruptly in the 1922 settlement, particularly in Sironcha and Gadchiroli tahsils which were largely adivasi habitats. In Sironcha tahsil, rents were enhanced to 28 and 25 per cent in malguzari and zamindari villages respectively. Whereas in Gadchiroli tahsil, it was 33 per cent and 25 per cent in malguzari and zamindari villages respectively. The enhancement of the rents was justified with reference to the increase of produce and land value and overall developments in the tahsils.[15]

The abrupt increase of the land rent brought pressure to bear not only on adivasi malguzars but also on adivasi peasants. Most of the caste-Hindu malguzars did not think well of the adivasi mode of cultivation, and wanted to hand over the adivasis' rich lands to dominant peasants, as they felt that the latter would not only produce high yields using modern methods, but would also pay rents on time. Zungria Rajgond of Manora village in Chanda tahsil held rich paddy lands. There was some delay in paying rent. The malguzar forced him to surrender the land in his occupancy by threatening to drag him to court for not paying the rent. The land was given to a peasant from the dominant Teli peasant caste.[16]

In ryotwari villages, the adivasis were largely evicted from their land through moneylending as well as by force. W. V. Grigson reported that 'no aboriginal ... is capable of paying debts with interest. He has never succeeded in understanding the function of interest. He pays and pays and pays, and in spite of it all the *Bania* gets his cattle and house and land.'[17] All grain debts were generally borrowed during the rains and before the next harvest, when prices were highest. The tenant was debited at these high prices. These grain debt valuations, together with any cash borrowed plus prospective interest, calculated till the next harvest period and at rates varying from 25 to 50 per cent in good years and 50 to 100 per cent in bad years, were secured by a bond (*bahikhata*) acknowledgement. Repayments were always made in grain at harvest time, and generally from the harvest floor. Grain was measured out by a special measure known as the *sahukar's koonda* (the moneylender's big pot). Then the grain so delivered was valued not at current rates, which were generally lowest at harvest times, but at rates which were below the prevailing rates by 25 to 30 per cent. Thus the tenant paid an exceptionally exorbitant interest. The debts never ended. The accounts kept on running from year to year and the liabilities were carried forward as legacies from fathers to sons. This ultimately resulted in ousting the Gond ryot from his land.[18] The state intervened in the matter through the Moneylenders Act of 1934, but it legalized moneylending in the province and failed to check the extortion faced by the adivasis.[19]

Irrespective of the revenue tenure (malguzari, ryotwari, or zamindari), adivasis were evicted from their land by the non-adivasi peasants. The eviction of the adivasis was more vigorous from the second decade of the twentieth century. In the malguzari villages of Chanda tahsil, adivasi tenants lost 9,579 acres between 1920 and 1940. Over the same period, the number of adivasi tenants decreased from 2,673 to 2,237. Eviction of the adivasis from their land was more conspicuous in areas where roads and communication had been developed. The adivasis lost their land for non-payment of rents and for accumulated debts. Grigson recorded a striking case of a widow from Palasgaon in Chanda tahsil. Her husband Sitaram Gond owed Rs 62 as arrears of rent. He was very ill, and the malguzar informed him that if he paid even half the amount, he would not take action against him. The tenant, believing him, arranged to pay him Rs 33. The malguzar took the money, but nevertheless had him evicted. He died and the widow became destitute. There were many such cases.[20] A clearer picture of the condition of Gond tenants in plains can be read from Table 4.1.

As shown in Table 4.1, the Kumbi and Brahman tenants were in an advantageous position, as they constituted the highest percentage in the A and B categories of tenants.[21] Clubbed together, Kumbi and Brahman

Table 4.1 Classification of tenants according to caste and status in the three plains tahsils: Warora, Chanda, and Bramhapuri

Castes	A	B	C	D	E	Total	Percentage
Kumbi	469	3,034	8,739	791	1,456	14,489	33
Mahar	70	512	2,927	190	752	4,451	10
Mana	30	588	2,087	188	353	3,246	7
Teli	59	501	1,968	148	312	2,988	7
Gond	10	200	1,842	147	584	2,783	6
Brahmin	557	624	915	30	43	2,169	5
Kohli	55	226	651	75	141	1,148	3
Marar	3	89	541	65	162	860	2
Others	639	1,491	7,252	553	1,543	11,478	26
Total	1,892	7,265	26,922	2,187	5,346	43,612	
Percentage	4	17	62	5	12		

Source: *Final Report on the Re-settlement of the Three Cis-Wainganga Tahsils of the Chanda District in the Central Provinces* (Nagpur: The Government Press, 1924), p. 7.

tenants in the A and B categories constituted 54.2 per cent and 50.3 per cent respectively. In contrast, the Gond tenants constituted 0.5 per cent and 2.7 per cent of the A and B categories respectively. This means that only about 3 per cent of Gond tenants were in the safe zone, while about 97 per cent of them were in the dangerous zone. In particular, Gond tenants in the D and E categories (who constituted 26.2 per cent of the total Gond tenants) were vulnerable to all kinds of exploitation and led a hand-to-mouth existence. The condition of Gond tenants in the C category, who constituted 66 per cent of all Gond tenants, was equally miserable. Irrespective of the category, all Gond tenants were subjected to land eviction.

After they lost their lands in the khalsa areas, the adivasis would resettle either in forest areas or the Gond zamindaris. In fact, the severity of the land problem was relatively less in the zamindaris, as they were covered by huge forest areas and the zamindars generally had a sympathetic approach towards the adivasi tenants. This resulted in the steady growth of adivasi tenants in the zamindaris. In the Ahiri zamindari of Sironcha tahsil, the number of adivasi tenants increased from 2,700 to 6,033 between 1895 and 1939–40. In the same period, the number of non-adivasi tenants in the same zamindari increased from 1,310 to 2,017. In the Gadchiroli zamindaris (other than the Ahiri zamindari), cultivable land occupied by non-adivasis rose from 15,978 acres to 46,863 acres between 1895 and 1939–40. This underlines that non-adivasi migration into the zamindaris was also increasing equally. This influx of non-adivasis into zamindaris pushed the adivasis out from their land. In Ahiri and Dewalmari villages, 323 adivasi tenants lost 1,699 acres of land between 1920 and 1940–1.[22] In 1939–40, the area occupied by adivasis in Chanda district was 244,200 acres, or 21.9 per cent of the total occupied area of 1,114,700 acres. This shows that non-adivasis occupied 870,500 acres or 78.1 per cent of arable land in the district.[23]

The case in Adilabad district was similar. Here, absentee landlords, particularly Velmas, Kumbis, Kapus (Reddy), Brahmans, and Muslims occupied huge tracts of land in forest areas.[24] Fürer-Haimendorf notes that 'absentee landlords … had and have naturally an interest to settle good cultivators in their villages; they encouraged the immigration of non-aboriginals and gradually replaced their Gond tenants, whose agricultural methods are comparatively backward, by more experienced cultivators, capable of paying higher rents'.[25]

The absentee landlords were produced by the state's revenue policy, which pushed the adivasis into the forest. As we have discussed in the preceding chapter, traditional revenue collectors and village heads were transformed into big landlords under the ryotwari and ijara tenures, which forced the adivasis to relinquish their land. Initially these reforms did not affect the simple life of Gonds and Kolams. The intensity of these policies was felt by adivasis around the beginning of the twentieth century, with the coming of traders and craftsmen to marketplaces such as Asifabad and Utnur. The development of roads, railways, and transport systems in the state accelerated the process of adivasi alienation. Between 1921 and 1935, metal roads increased from 32 miles to 235 miles in Adilabad district alone; 334 miles were covered by bus services under the Road Transport Service by 1950.[26] The state had acquired 688 miles of broad-gauge and 1,360 miles of metre-gauge railway lines by the end of 1942. The Kazipet–Ballarshah railway line, which passed through the district, brought enormous changes to the hill tracts.[27] The development of communications between Mancherial and Rajura on the eastern side of the district, and between Nirmal and Adilabad on the western side, gave enough scope to outsiders to infiltrate the district both from the south and from the north.

The larger part of the district was, initially, inhabited almost exclusively by adivasis, and there are reasons to believe that among them, the Kolams are the oldest community.[28] Subsequently, with the Nizam's new forest and revenue policies, upper-caste Hindus and Muslims migrated to this region in a big way. In 1931, the population of newcomers was as follows: Kumbi, 85,290; Komati, 12,766; Velama, 7,530; Brahman, 14,557; Maratha, 29,312, and Muslims, 45,821. There were also other backward castes like Chakali, Mangali, Kummari, Lambada, Yadava, Mala, Madiga, and Vadrangi,[29] but they were brought to serve the dominant castes and work in the fields, since it was felt that adivasi labour did not suit modern cultivation.[30] In the beginning, the upper castes settled in urban centres such as Rajura, Adilabad, Asifabad, and Nirmal, and later, as land in the hill tracts became valuable and attractive, they started moving towards them.

With this phenomenon, Gond prosperity and Gond culture began to decline.[31] The caste nexus between officials and outsiders played an important role in ousting adivasis from their lands. Gonds cultivated mainly light soils on the plateau and on slightly inclined slopes, and shifted their fields every two to three years, abandoning each plot before the soil showed signs of exhaustion. They grew only kharif crops: *sama* (a small millet), *kora* (finger millet), *jawari* (millet), and oil seeds. As in Chanda earlier, adivasis in Adilabad did not realize the danger augured by the in-migration of outsiders. Prior to this change, the Gonds too had had the possibility of obtaining individual pattas, and many Gonds were actually granted patta rights. On the whole, however, adivasis were slow to realize the necessity of acquiring pattas. Later, when the pressure on land became acute and they understood the value of the documents, everything had already slipped out of their hands. Moreover, the upper castes from the plains often succeeded in contesting the validity of even the few existing Gond pattas and brought about changes in revenue records. Though adivasis offered huge bribes (*mamuls*) to patels, patwaris, and tahsildars, the system always worked against the interests of adivasis. Even those Gonds who had been granted patta rights lost their lands in later years to outsiders through dealings with moneylenders.[32]

The adivasis generally borrowed from moneylenders to meet expenses for agriculture or social occasions. Though the official interest rate was 9 to 12 per cent, the actual interest rate worked out to between 20 and 50 per cent, sometimes more than this. The debts increased abruptly, and the adivasi not only handed over part of his land but also promised to render labour to his creditor. This chain continued to their children and grandchildren.[33] The moneylenders, particularly the Komatis and Marwaris, thus extended their activities during the late nineteenth and early twentieth centuries to the frontier areas, and grabbed land through both moneylending and using their connections with revenue officials.[34] As has been said previously, the adivasis generally would acquire waste-land and convert it into good, arable land through their hard work, only to find that it was eventually grabbed either by the moneylenders or by the dominant peasant castes. In this way, non-adivasis grabbed huge arable lands in the region which had once been largely cultivated by adivasis.[35] A Velma landlord of Mandamarri adivasi village in Adilabad district had a few acres in 1900 when he migrated from Karimnagar district. But, by 1940, he had become the owner of 8,000 acres of land.[36]

In 1942, the number of adivasi pattadars was hardly one-fifth of their population. Thus, of a total of 3,300 families in Utnur, there were only 471 pattadars. In Asifabad, which is the heart of the adivasi region, of the total number of 2,400 families, about 900 were pattadars. In Rajura, of 3,170 families, only 678 were pattadars. Most of them were petty cultivators, owning less than 5 to 6 acres.[37] Thus, 80 per cent of the total adivasi population found themselves without a means of livelihood, with precarious existences and with homes liable to dispersal at any moment, subject to the whims, fancies, and petty exactions of menial officials. Some endeavoured to escape from this condition by running away into the forests.

However, as discussed in the preceding chapter, forest areas had already been brought under the colonial administration; even zamindari forests had been leased or bought by the British government. The adivasis' forceful infiltration into forest tracts turned violent as soon as the colonial *junglat* or forest officials hit them back with force.[38] Although the B-class forests of Chanda were declared to be available for culti-vation, they were largely allotted to non-adivasi peasants as they were seen as more profitable. As we have discussed in the preceding chapter, the colonial state and Hyderabad State cleared up vast areas of forests in a short time. The two administrations realized the fast diminishing of forest areas only at the beginning of the twentieth century.[39] The ruining of forests was generally attributed to podu cultivation and graz-ing. With the enactment of the forest regulations, there was a strict ban on podu cultivation.[40] Podu cultivation was viewed by the state as a wasteful mode of cultivation and it sought to discourage it.[41] In the B-class forests, the state was successful in checking podu cultivation, but the practice continued in the reserved (A-class) forests down into the twentieth century.[42]

Even in the B-class forest, the regeneration programme hampered the adivasis' cultivation and cattle grazing. Under this programme, work-ing circles were formed and regeneration was undertaken through both natural regeneration and plantation. These circles were closed for about fifteen years, during which no podu cultivation or grazing was allowed in it.[43] This brought tremendous pressure to bear on the adivasis and resulted in a huge increase in forest offences in the province. In the year 1923–4, 1,174 cases were registered against 3,302 people in the North Chanda division, and 506 cases were registered against 1,191 people in South Chanda division. Most of the cases related to unauthorized grazing and felling and podu cultivation.[44] For many adivasis, podu cul-tivation and minor forest resources were their main source of livelihood, particularly in the summer and at the time of failure of rains. This had been their practice for centuries, but the new forest policy curtailed their free movement in the forest.[45]

Fürer-Haimendorf gives a lengthy description of how, with the new forest laws, adivasis were denied free access to the Adilabad forests. The eviction of the adivasis had begun from the beginning of the demarcation of forests. At the time of the demarcation of reserve forests, many Kolam and Gond villages were disbanded and the inhabitants were compelled to leave their houses in several taluks of the district. Though nominally podu cultivation was allowed to continue in some areas which were formed into enclaves, these were soon exhausted. Adivasis were, on the other hand, prevented from felling trees with the implementation of the new laws. Their traditional economy virtually ended. Consequently, the Kolam and Gond communities migrated to other places to work where the land included hill slopes, and where they were permitted to cultivate in their old style.[46]

The auctioning of forest produce virtually prohibited the Gonds and Kolams from entering the forest. Forest produce such as grass, *mahua*, *chironji* (berries), and bamboo were brought under the public-auction system, and were usually grabbed by outsiders as auctions took place only in towns. It appears that many contractors took grass, chironji, and mahua on lease, not with a view to exporting these articles for sale, but to levy tax from the adivasis. Since adivasi life was structured around the forest, they invariably depended on the forest for survival. This dependence of adivasis on the forest was largely exploited by contractors. For example, the chironji contractor toured the village sometime after the fruit season and charged the adivasis either per house or per tree for the fruit, which he assumed the adivasis and their children had eaten. The charges varied from 2 to 8 annas per house or 4 annas to Re 1 per tree.[47] Sometimes, contractors compelled them to collect chironji without paying them any wages.

Similarly, the mahua flower was auctioned to contractors and adivasis were prohibited from free collection. Gonds fed mahua to their cattle and used it both for distilling liquor and as food when there was scarcity of food. Grass was also auctioned, and contractors acted on the same principles there too. Adivasis used grass for thatching their houses. Export of grass was apparently unprofitable to the contractor, so they toured the villages and collected between 8 annas and 1 rupee per house from adivasis, irrespective of their utilization. Bamboo was auctioned only in some localities, and the contractors collected annual fees from the adivasis for bamboo used for fences, platforms, and cattle-shed walls, as was done in the case of grass. In almost all the hills of Adilabad district, forest lines were so close to the adivasi gudams that the Gonds had no other way to graze their cattle than in the reserves, and grazing fees were collected as a matter of routine. These amounted to Rs 0.25 for cows, Rs 0.87 for buffaloes, and Rs 0.12 for goats in 1942. These rates varied from place to place.[48]

Thus, the adivasis, with the extension of the state into the forests, lost their customary rights over the forest which they had enjoyed for centuries. Their free movement was curtailed, and they were forced to live in one place. They were reduced to a situation of paying even to pluck a leaf. Consequently, they were disgusted with the demands of the forest officials. An annual mamul of Re 1 per house to the *chaukidar* (watchman) was common in the process of collection. These officials also demanded contributions in kind from the adivasis. Every chaukidar, *saredar* (a taluk-level revenue officer), and ranger expected to receive free supplies during their stay in an adivasi village.[49] In this way, the Gonds were trapped between the Revenue and Forest Departments. Often they managed to escape from the plains and settle down in forest land by bribing the revenue officials, but the forest officials would come and oust them, claiming that it was forest land. This tension culminated in a violent revolt in Adilabad in the 1940s.[50] We shall take this up in the next chapter.

The overpopulation of the hills had cut down the movements of the Gonds. In fact, populating the hills was a colonial scheme that turned inaccessible areas into state spaces. This served the colonial state in multiple ways. It enabled extension of the effects of colonial power, modernization of agriculture and the exploitation of agricultural produce, the exploitation of forest and mineral resources, and the transformation of the long-established ways of life of adivasis who were now forced to become docile bodies. To meet this design, the disciplining of wild territories as well as of dissenting peoples was necessary.[51] The colonial state strongly believed that the influx of caste-Hindus into the hills was crucial to realizing this end.[52] The caste-Hindu peasants of the plains were thus encouraged by the colonial state to migrate to the hills. This was done by providing huge concessions on land tax/rent and offering village-level positions. This resulted in a steady increase of non-adivasis in the hills. The density of population per square mile in 1866 in Chanda was 55.4, and this had risen to 82 in 1941.[53] Whereas in Adilabad, the density of population per square mile increased from 42.7 to 113 between 1881 and 1941.[54]

As shown in Table 4.2, there was a steady increase of population in Chanda district. In the first sixteen years (1866–81), the district

Table 4.2 Steady increase of population in the districts

Years	Chanda District			Adilabad District		
	Total Population	Scheduled Tribe Population	Scheduled Tribes as % of the Total Population	Total Population	Scheduled Tribe Population	Scheduled Tribes as % of the Total Population
1866	537,295	176,840	32.9	–	–	
1881	649,146	–		214,674	–	
1891	697,610	175,696	25.1	231,754	63,037	27.2
1901	554,105	141,187	25.4	272,815	50,840	18.6
1911	677,544	138,041	20.3	620,426	65,964	10.6
1921	660,630	131,289	19.8	655,536	89,785	13.6
1931	759,695	157,386	20.7	762,030	104,807	13.7
1941	873,284	170,126	19.4	823,622	125,589	15.2

Source: Compiled from the census reports of the respective years; Grigson, *The Aboriginal Problem*, p. 54; *Hyderabad District Gazetteer: Adilabad District Tables Volume*, p. 13.

population increased by 17.2 per cent. This was basically owing to the
first land settlement in 1869 that created demand for the waste forest land in the district. There was a decrease of 14.2 per cent in the
second decade (1891–1901). This was largely due to severe famines in
the district in 1895–97 and 1899–1900. A large number of people died.
In the 1899–1900 famine alone 3,700 people lost their lives.[55] Many
migrated to other regions. The famine report of these years recorded that
'from Chanda many people immigrated to Berar in search of agricultural
work, but the region was already overcrowded and many returned empty
handed and starving, unable to support themselves or even pay for their
return home.'[56] But after this incident the district population continued
to increase. Particularly from 1921, there was steep increase. This was
largely due to influx from other regions. During the decades of 1921 and
1931, the total population of the district included 40,454 and 51,576
immigrants respectively.[57] The influx of settlers was larger in the forest
and zamindari areas due to the availability of open land. The settlers'
population in the Ahiri zamindari increased by 57 per cent in the first
decade of the twentieth century.[58]

In Adilabad district also, there was a steep increase of population
from the last decade of the nineteenth century. The district population
almost doubled in 1911. This was partly because of the reorganization of
the district boundaries.[59] However, there was an additional increase in
population of 28 per cent in the district, owing to large-scale immigration from both Andhra and Telangana districts. The census report of the
year recorded that 'the conversion of Adilabad into a full district during
the decade would seem to have made it more attractive to settlers, as a
large area was lying uncultivated'.[60] Thus, the creation of the district
attracted settlers in a big way. Thereafter, the population of the district
increased by nearly 100,000 each decade, mostly owing to settlers arriv-
ing from other districts. The inflow of settlers to the district in 1921 and
1931 was 65,282 and 58,114 respectively.[61] Interestingly, there was no
substantial increase in adivasi population in both these districts. On the
contrary, the reorganization of Chanda and Adilabad districts decreased
the percentage of adivasis in the district drastically. Some zamindaris of
Chanda in Partially Excluded Areas were transferred to Durg district in
1907, which resulted in a drastic decrease of the adivasi population in

the district in 1911.[62] Even after this, there was no considerable increase in Chanda district's adivasi population. However, there was a gradual increase of adivasi population in Adilabad district from the second decade of the twentieth century, but this was due to immigration of the Lambada tribe from the Marathwada region. The heavy influx of non-adivasi peasants ultimately evicted the adivasis from their land. While the adivasis were being evicted from their lands, the state stood by. It began intervening in the issue only when the tension between adivasis and non-adivasis resulted in law and order problems in the region.

Although there was some protection of adivasi land in Chanda from 1916 under the Land Alienation Act, it was poorly implemented. In Adilabad, such protections came too late and could not save the toiling peasant from the clutches of the dominant peasants and jagirdars, who were strongly established and maintained a close nexus with the local government authorities. Based on his experience in the adivasi tracts of Adilabad district, Fürer-Haimendorf commented that 'the Land Alienation Act appears to be here little more than a dead letter'.[63] A systematic protectionism was evolved by the colonial state under the Act of 1935.[64] This protectionism was rooted in what Archana Prasad calls 'ecological romanticism'.[65]

ECOLOGICAL ROMANTICISM AND COLONIAL PROTECTIONISM

The creation of the Scheduled Areas or Scheduled Tribes was part of the colonial state's policy of protectionism. As discussed earlier, colonial rule had ruthlessly destroyed the long-established livelihood practices of the adivasis and thrown them into acute poverty and scarcity. The adivasis were banned from utilizing the now 'reserved' forests in the old ways of hunting, gathering, shifting agriculture, or grazing livestock. The migration of the land-hungry dominant peasants and moneylenders into the hills made existing adivasi life impossible. In general, the adivasis suffered increasing marginalization throughout India under colonial rule.[66] This pushed the subordinate castes and classes to adopt more violent methods of resistance to the colonial rulers. This was more apparent in the forest and hill areas. In response, the colonial state adopted a policy of protectionism from the last decades of the nineteenth century in order to pacify the toiling adivasis. As a part of this project, the colonial state created new administrative categories for adivasis. Professional anthropologists, who were greatly inspired by Western Romanticism, were crucial in advocating such adivasi protectionism.[67]

There was also a strong strand of Romanticism in the Orientalist understanding of India that grew out of eighteenth-century Western Romanticism. This outlook was shared by certain colonial officials, Indologists, historians, sociologists, and anthropologists.[68] The Romantic understanding of adivasi society was not confined only to professional anthropologists; many colonial administrators also internalized these values very strongly. Hardiman and Skaria have shown how tribal masculinity was celebrated by colonial administrators and forest officers in western India. These officials equated the egalitarian values (honesty, frankness, communal life) of the adivasis with Rousseau's 'state of nature', seeing the adivasis as innocent and childlike. They depicted them as noble, honest, loyal, and ruggedly independent. Some officials internalized adivasi values and culture to the extent that they took to drinking and hunting along with them. As Skaria says, this celebration is ethnocentric and ethnocentrism is anti-ethnocentric.[69]

Indeed, the underlying intention was to acquire more knowledge of the adivasi world and then to encourage them to adopt more 'civilized' ways of life. The officials, after acquiring acquaintance with the adivasis, gradually directed them towards settled and commercial agriculture and encouraged outsiders (moneylenders, traders, and peasants) to come into the forest so as to incorporate adivasis within the wider civilization, hoping that it would then be easy to control them.[70] Many colonial forest officials were *shikaris* (hunters), and they needed the assistance of forest-dwelling adivasis in their hunting. With this in mind, the forest officials developed a rapport with the adivasis by internalizing adivasi culture and methods in hunting, but this process went hand in hand with the exclusion and subordination of the adivasi, the free adivasi hunter being reduced to a mere labourer serving the interests of British trophy hunters. As Skaria puts it, '[C]olonial celebration of the wild and the forest are best understood as a civilized dalliance with wildness—the dalliance that often goes by the name of primitivism.'[71] But the fact is that this primitivism was premised on domination and mastery. The celebration of primitivism itself alluded to the colonizer's domination over subordinate adivasis, and it served to extend control over them. Eventually, it led to the brutal eviction of adivasis from the forests in a phased manner and also served the forest-conservation agenda of colonial rule.

With the entry of the professional anthropologist from the early twentieth century, the Romantic understanding entered a new phase. Anthropologists went into the adivasi areas with preconceived ideas that adivasis were uncivilized, innocent, and honest, taken advantage of by unscrupulous outsiders. They tried to immerse themselves in the lives of those they studied, even in some case marrying tribal girls to prove their commitment to tribal culture and life.[72] Among them, Verrier Elwin and Fürer-Haimendorf were two stalwarts who worked with the adivasis of central and southern India; the adivasis in these places still have great reverence for them, not realizing the wider implications of their work.[73] Fürer-Haimendorf asserted that adivasi society was exclusive and isolated, so that any intervention was likely to cause devastation of their simple and naturalistic life. He argued that much damage had been done by outsiders, including state bureaucrats, and suggested that enhanced powers be granted to tribal leaders along the lines adopted by the British in areas of indirect rule.[74] Elwin viewed adivasis as creatures of nature whose worldview was entirely at odds with that of civilized people. The solution, as he saw it, was to protect the adivasis by creating national parks for them.[75]

ENCLOSING ADIVASIS

At one point, partly because of the professional anthropologists' advocacy of adivasi protectionism, the government encircled adivasi tracts and excluded them from general administration under the Act of 1935. The encircled tracts were called Partially Excluded Areas or Tribal Agency Areas.[76] The history of the creation of a tribal agency goes back to the early nineteenth century when the East India Company formed separate corps to crush the Bhil and Gond chiefs after the conquest of the Marathas. A separate force called Khandesh Bhils Corps was created in 1825.[77] Similar corps were also formed to check the raiding Gonds in the Narmada Valley and Chanda territories.[78] As discussed in Chapter 2, after the British took over the Gond territories, they separated the hill and forest tracts by keeping them under the Gond zamindars, who were in turn checked by a manager appointed by the colonial administration.[79]

Simultaneously, attempts were also made by the colonial state to separate the adivasi areas from the general administration. This policy was first started when the Rajmahal Hills tract was withdrawn from the jurisdiction of the ordinary courts in 1782. These rules were made into law by Regulation I of 1796. The tract was administered by the collector without any of the regular laws of the British government applicable there. The collector could make his own rules for the conduct of affairs. This regulation was subsequently replaced by Regulation I of 1827.[80] With the introduction of the famous Wilkinson Rules under Regulation 13 of 1833, considerable change was brought into the administration of the adivasi areas. This regulation abolished military collectorship of hill areas and put them under a special officer, designated 'Agent to the Governor-General', after which the adivasi areas were called Agency Areas. The Agent was made responsible for the civil and judicial administration of the Agency Areas.[81]

Almost all the adivasi areas in India were brought under special administration under one or another regulation, excluding them from the general administration. Further, all the Agency Areas were brought under a common rule with the introduction of the Scheduled District Act of 1874. Following this Act, many densely populated adivasi regions received the status of Scheduled Districts, and the adivasis living in those districts were designated Scheduled Tribes. This Act was aimed at providing complete protection to the adivasis, particularly from the land-hungry non-adivasi migrants from the plains and from moneylenders.[82]

Where the adivasis were not covered under this Act, they were protected by separate regulations that dated back to the late nineteenth century. These regulations banned land transfers from adivasis to non-adivasis as in the Agency Areas.[83] A clear and further demarcation of the adivasi areas was laid down in the Government of India Act of 1935, under which the governor could notify any adivasi tract as a Partially Excluded Area. The main difference between the Partially Excluded

Areas and the rest of the province was that the acts passed by the central or provincial legislative assemblies would not apply to the Partially Excluded Areas unless the governor, by notification, so directed; he was empowered to make special regulations for the better administration of the areas. This policy of exclusion of adivasi areas became a political controversy, and there were interesting debates between political leaders and colonial administrators. In 1936, all legislative assemblies opposed this exclusion. The Indian National Congress, in its Faizapur conference, denounced exclusion as another attempt to divide the people of India into different groups. However, there was a change in the attitude of the political leadership of India on exclusion, and the provincial acts were passed by the respective legislative assemblies to that effect.[84] In the Act, the adivasis were designated as Scheduled Tribes.[85] This policy, indeed, was aimed at providing self-governance to the adivasis. But the colonial state was always suspicious of the adivasis' ability to manage their own affairs and never allowed self-rule in the forests and hills. The forest and hill areas were meticulously ruled by the Agents of the governors.

The Government of India Act of 1935 provided a model for the new Constitution of independent India. Indeed, there has not been much discussion or debate on the adivasi question after independence. Most of the intellectual baggage that was carried into the Constituent Assembly drew heavily on the colonial model. The Advisory Committee on Fundamental Rights appointed two sub-committees in 1947 to report on the future administration of the Excluded Areas in Assam, and Excluded and Partially Excluded Areas other than Assam. These committees submitted separate interim and joint reports largely recommending the same colonial model of administration of the adivasi areas. The Constituent Assembly accepted these committees' reports without any discussion on them. The adivasis thus came to be designated as Scheduled Tribes and their habitats as Scheduled Areas in postcolonial India too.[86] Importantly, this exclusion of zones typified adivasis perpetually.

Although the Partially Excluded Areas were not inhabited solely by the adivasis, they were stigmatized as half-human and their habitats as primitive zones. As we have seen in the preceding chapters, adivasis and non-adivasis have been living side by side, maintaining a degree of mutual deference that was more socio-political rather than administrative. In other words, the adivasis had historically maintained a difference from the caste-Hindus of the plains to escape from state power and subjugation. The new boundary created under colonial rule was essentially intended to bring the adivasis under state power and to subjugate them. The isolation effected by the boundary also served to establish cultural hegemony over the adivasis by encouraging stereotypical representations of their identity..[87]

Indeed, the new boundary was largely symbolic but designed to meet the political ends of colonial rule, because there was no qualitative change between the two regions in many respects, particularly in administrative terms. Importantly, although the Agency was predominantly inhabited by adivasis, it included a considerable non-adivasi population. Chanda district covered an area of 9,312 square miles and comprised a population of 873,284; of this, 4,013 square miles with a population of 115,031 were designated as Partially Excluded Areas according to the 1941 census. These Partially Excluded Areas were entirely Gond zamindaris, and the necessary care was taken to separate khalsa villages from these areas. The four zamindaris which had been transferred to Durg district were retransferred to Chanda, as these zamindaris shared historical similarities with the Chanda zamindaris. The khalsa villages of Gadchiroli tahsil were transferred to Brahmapuri tahsil, which was largely occupied by caste-Hindus and consisted of rich khalsa villages.[88]

Despite this arrangement, the adivasis lived in both Excluded and non-Excluded Areas. Of the total population of 115,031 in the Partially Excluded Areas in the district, the adivasi population was 70,821, and the remaining population was caste-Hindu or non-adivasi.[89] The total adivasi population of the district in 1941 was 170,126. It is clear from the numbers that about 100,000 adivasis lived in the plains area.[90] This new boundary was thus an artificial one that served to exoticize and stigmatize a minority of adivasis. They were judged to be 'primitives' who did not deserve self-rule. This is not to suggest that there was no divide between caste-Hindus and adivasis. As has been said, the adivasis had always maintained a difference from the caste-Hindus of mainland India. But the difference articulated by the adivasis went beyond the colonial divide, being rooted mainly in the concepts of self-rule and self-determinism.

Colonial protectionism was also dubious. The colonial administration advocated protection of the adivasis from outsiders on the one hand, and encouraged outsiders to settle in the adivasi areas on the other. The latter policy had many implications for adivasi society. The colonial state through its census and anthropological projects endeavoured to create adivasis as a separate religious category as well. But this effort was again ruptured by its own policies. In Chanda, the adivasis were, irrespective of their will, enumerated as animists from the 1871 census onwards. However, they were given the liberty from the 1891 census to claim any religion. There was a mixed response from the adivasis to such enumeration. In the 1891 census, 79 per cent of adivasis returned themselves as animists. This proportion was 77 per cent in the 1901 census.[91] In the Partially Excluded Areas of Sironcha and Gadchiroli tahsils, 70 per cent of adivasis were recorded as animists in the 1931 census.[92] In subsequent censuses, because of the pressure of Hindu organizations, all adivasi communities were classified as Hindus.

In fact, colonial rule aggravated the process of Hinduization and Rajputization in the hill tracts. The Raj Gond families in particular had largely internalized Rajput social and religious practices from pre-colonial times.[93] Many Gond rajas, as part of their political strategy, also entered into matrimonial relations with the Rajput rajas. The colonial policy of offering zamindari rights, village headships, and patelships aggravated this process. Even the general Gonds began claiming Rajput status in order to get village patelships or some position in the colonial establishment, as it was an informal colonial policy to accommodate those who had a ruling past in the colonial establishment, particularly after the 1857 revolt.

On the other hand, as discussed earlier, colonial agricultural policies combined with the development of communications filled the hill tracts with large numbers of caste-Hindus. They were encouraged by the colonial state to bring waste and barren land under cultivation on nominal assessments. It was hoped that they would provide an example of better cultivation techniques to the hill peoples.[94] This process was particularly apparent in Adilabad district.[95] This inflow not only brought modern agriculture to the adivasis, but also the Hindi, Marathi, and Telugu languages, and caste-Hindu religious and social practices.[96] In the beginning of the twentieth century, it was reported that Gonds were increasingly adopting Brahmanical practices and worshipping Hindu gods, and that this allowed them to adopt not only a 'civilized' life but also modern forms of cultivation.[97] Following this, there was a debate on how the religion of the adivasis should be classified in the census reports. Verrier Elwin, who had lived for many years among the Gonds and was considered to be a champion of adivasi rights, argued:

> [T]he religion of the Indian aboriginal outside Assam should be regarded as a religion of the Hindu family, with a special relation to the exciting, dangerous, catastrophic, Shaivaite type, but as having a distinct existence of its own. For purposes of the Census, all aboriginals should be classed as Hindus by religion but separate returns of their numbers by race should be provided.[98]

This was also asserted by Grigson, who was an officer on special duty to investigate the conditions of the aboriginal communities in the province. The end result was that the Gonds were placed above the Mahars (an ex-untouchable caste) on the Hindu social ladder.[99]

The colonial state's protectionism, or the new boundary between the plains and hills, was thus designed to produce the effects of state power in the hills and forests of India. To put it in other words, the divide created by the colonial administration and colonial anthropology between caste-Hindus and adivasis, which pivoted on the celebration of cultural primitivism, was not only aimed to bring adivasis into state spaces but also to stigmatize them and deny them self-rule. The educated Gonds saw this development as a threat to their culture and identity. They formed an association called the Gond Mahasabha and opposed the classification of adivasis as Hindus. This movement first started as a cultural movement, but soon turned into a political movement demanding the formation of a separate Gond Raj (Gond self-rule) in postcolonial India.[100] Importantly, as we discussed in Chapter 1, irrespective of their religious denomination in census enumerations, the adivasis practice their own religious traditions by worshipping their own gods and goddesses. Nevertheless, they celebrate some Hindu festivals and gods as part of their own political strategy.

Thus, the adivasis under colonial rule were pushed to the fringes of the society. Although the intention was to make adivasis into productive subjects of a modern state, the reality was that they ended up as marginalized and excluded from this process. The colonial project of enclosing land enclosed the adivasis and stigmatized them as primitive or isolated communities. This notion was in fact first constructed by colonial anthropology. The isolation of the adivasis was a result of long-drawn-out processes of marginalization under great empires in history. An administrative boundary was dubiously created under colonial rule between the plains and hill regions of India, with different standards applying to each. The divide culminated in violent resistance in the region at the end of the colonial rule, particularly in Adilabad. Chanda was free of major violent revolts because the adivasis who lost their land could flee and find resort in the zamindaris, where there were vast forest lands available for cultivation. Above all, they were treated amicably by the Gond zamindari establishment. Let us now move on to a discussion of the Gonds' resistance against the Hyderabad State.

NOTES

1. W. V. Grigson, *The Aboriginal Problem in the Central Provinces and Berar* (Nagpur: Government Printing, 1944), pp. 15–18.
2. Grigson, *The Aboriginal Problem*, pp. 54–62.
3. Grigson, *The Aboriginal Problem*, pp. 465–509.
4. For example, see Sanjukta Das Gupta, *Adivasis and the Raj: Socio-economic Transition of the Hos, 1820–1932* (New Delhi: Orient BlackSwan, 2011); Kidar Nath Thusu, *Gond Kingdom of Chanda, with Particular Reference to Its Political Structure* (Calcutta: Anthropological Survey of India, 1980); Suresh Mishra, *The Gond Kingdom of Deogarh* (New Delhi: Manak Publications, 2011); Nandini Sundar, *Subalterns and Sovereigns: An Anthropological History of Bastar 1854–1996* (New Delhi: Oxford University Press, 1997).
5. C. B. Lucie Smith, *Report on Land Revenue Settlement of the Chanda District, Central Provinces* (Nagpur: Chief Commissioner's Press, 1870), p. 206.
6. *Report on the Administration of the Central Provinces for the Year 1901–1902* (Nagpur: Secretariat Press, 1902), p. 10.
7. Grigson, *The Aboriginal Problem*, p. 55.

8. Christoph von Fürer-Haimendorf, *Tribal Hyderabad: Four Reports* (Hyderabad: Revenue Department, Government of H.E.H. the Nizam, 1945), p. 75.

9. *Central Provinces and Berar: A Review of the Administration of the Province 1921–1922* (Nagpur: Superintendent Government Printing, C.P., 1923), vol. II, p. 110.

10. Smith, *Land Revenue Settlement of the Chanda District*, p. 139.

11. *Central Provinces and Berar: A Review of the Administration 1921–1922*, vol. II, p. 111.

12. Grigson, *The Aboriginal Problem*, pp. 159–61.

13. Smith, *Land Revenue Settlement of the Chanda District*, p. 146.

14. *Chanda District Gazetteer*, 1909, p. 331.

15. Vidarbha, SS, S. no. 920, File no. 4-7/1922, f. 12

16. Grigson, *The Aboriginal Problem*, pp. 57–9.

17. Grigson, *The Aboriginal Problem*, p. 179.

18. Vidarbha, Department of Survey and Settlement, S. no. 920, File no. 4-7/1922, f. 11.

19. Grigson, *The Aboriginal Problem*, p. 203.

20. Grigson, *The Aboriginal Problem*, pp. 58–9.

21. The definitions of the A, B, C, D, and E categories are as follows. A: well-to-do, lending money or grain or owning land as malguzar; B: in substantial cultivating circumstances; free from debt, or with debt considerable in proportion to assets; C: in average circumstances, with ordinary debt, but free from mortgage or special risk of losing the holding; D: in reduced circumstances, having fallen in the world, and become deeply indebted or having mortgaged assets; E: living from hand to mouth, such as Gonds or ryots without bullocks, and of the status of day labourers. See *Final Report on the Re-settlement of the Three Cis-Wainganga Tahsils of the Chanda*, p. 8.

22. Grigson, *The Aboriginal Problem*, pp. 54–5.

23. Grigson, *The Aboriginal Problem*, pp. 461–2.

24. Setu Madhava Rao Pagdi, 'Land Problems of Adilabad Aboriginals', *Indian Journal of Social Work* 9, no. 1 (June 1948–9): 21.

25. Fürer-Haimendorf, *Tribal Hyderabad*, p. 69.

26. V. Ramakrishna Reddy, *Economic History of Hyderabad State: Warangal Subha 1911–1950* (New Delhi: Gian Publication House, 1987), p. 53.

27. *Statistical Abstract of H.E.H. the Nizam's Dominion from 1351F to 1355F* (1941–5) (Hyderabad-Deccan: Government Central Press, 1946), p. 337.

28. Fürer-Haimendorf, *Tribal Hyderabad*, p. 68.

29. *Hyderabad District Gazetteer: Adilabad District Tables Volume, 1931–1936* (Hyderabad-Deccan: Government Central Press, 1940), pp. 34–5.

30. Fürer-Haimendorf, *Tribal Hyderabad*, p. 69.

31. D. E. U. Baker has well brought out this phenomenon, examining how the British goal of economic development in the upper Narmada Valley marginalized a range of adivasi groups in the region. See his *Colonialism in an Indian Hinterland: The Central Provinces, 1820–1920* (New Delhi: Oxford University Press, 1993).

32. Baker, *Colonialism in an Indian Hinterland*, pp. 66–90.

33. Baker, *Colonialism in an Indian Hinterland*, pp. 166, 181; Bhangya Bhukya, *Subjugated Nomads: The Lambadas under the Rule of the Nizams* (New Delhi: Orient BlackSwan, 2010), p. 177.

34. Fürer-Haimendorf, *Tribal Hyderabad*, pp. 82, 95, 112, 157, 165, 203.

35. Setumadhava Rao Pagdi, *Among the Gonds of Adilabad* (Bombay: Popular Book Depot, 1949), p. 115.

36. Pagdi, *Among the Gonds*, p. 110.

37. Pagdi, *Among the* Gonds, p. 115.

38. Vidarbha, PM, S. no. 1478, File no. 5-3/1951, f. 2; Vidarbha, RD, S. no. 2882, File no. 58-7/1931, f. 5.

39. *Report on the Forest Administration of the Central Provinces for the Year 1923–24* (Nagpur: Government Press, 1925), p. 13.

40. Rangarajan shows how the British persuaded the adivasis to stop shifting cultivation in the Central Provinces. For a detailed discussion, see his *Fencing the Forest: Conservation and Ecological Change in India's Central Provinces 1860–1914* (New Delhi: Oxford University Press, 1996), pp. 95–137.

41. *Progress Report on Forest Administration in the Central Provinces 1867–68 and 1868–69* (Calcutta: Public Works Department Press, 1870), p. 7.

42. *Report on the Forest Administration of the Central Provinces for the Year 1926–27* (Nagpur: Central Government Press, 1928), p. 37.

43. *Report on the Forest Administration of the Central Provinces for the Year 1923–24* (Nagpur: Government Press, 1925), p. 13.

44. *Report on the Forest Administration of the Central Provinces for the Year 1924–25* (Nagpur: Government Press, 1926), Appendix, p. xx.

45. Fürer-Haimendorf, *Tribal Hyderabad*, pp. 96–7.

46. Fürer-Haimendorf, *Tribal Hyderabad*, p. 99.

47. Fürer-Haimendorf, *Tribal Hyderabad*, p. 105.

48. Fürer-Haimendorf, *Tribal Hyderabad*, pp. 106–7.

49. Fürer-Haimendorf, *Tribal Hyderabad*, p. 114.

50. Fürer-Haimendorf, *Tribal Hyderabad*, p. 93.

51. Michel Foucault has told us how the creation of docile and disciplined individuals is the main concern of the modern state. See his *Power/ Knowledge: Selected Interviews and Other Writings, 1972–1977*, edited by Colin Gordon (London: Harvester Wheatsheaf, 1980), p. 40.

52. *Stephen Hislop's Papers Relating to the Aboriginal Tribes of the Central Provinces*, IOR/V/27/910/49, f. 12; *Chanda District Gazetteer*, 1909, pp. 66–8.

53. Grigson, *The Aboriginal Problem*, p. 343; Smith, *Land Revenue Settlement of the Chanda District*, p. 36.

54. *Census of India 1901*, vol. XXII: *Hyderabad*, Part I: *Report* (Hyderabad-Deccan: A. V. Pillai & Sons, 1901), p. 26; *Census of India 1941*, vol. XXI: *H.E.H. the Nizam's Dominions (Hyderabad State)*, Part I: *Report* (Hyderabad-Deccan: Government Central Press, 1945), p. 110.

55. *Chanda District Gazetteer*, 1909, pp. 67–8.

56. R. H. Craddock, *Report on the Famine in the Central Provinces in 1899– 1900* (Nagpur: Secretariat Press, 1901), p. 24.

57. *Census of India 1921*, vol. XI: *Central Provinces and Berar*, Part I: *Report* (Nagpur: Government Press, 1923), p. 30; *Census of India 1931*, vol. XII: *Central Provinces and Berar*, Part I (Nagpur: Government Printing C.P., 1933), p. 71.

58. *Census of India 1911*, vol. X: *Central Provinces and Berar*, Part I: *Report* (Calcutta: Superintendent Government Printing, 1912), p. 42.

59. The old Adilabad district was called Sirpur-Tandur and was a subdistrict in Warangal Subha. Nirmal and Narsapur taluks of Nizamabad and Chinnur and Lakshetipet of Karimnagar were merged in Adilabad and formed into a full-fledged district in 1905. See *Gazetteer of Hyderabad*, 1909, p. 187.

60. *Census of India 1911, Hyderabad*, p. 26.

61. *Census of India 1921*, vol. XXI: *Hyderabad State*, Part I (Hyderabad-Deccan: Government Central Press, 1923), p. 35; *Census of India 1931*, vol. XXII: *H.E.H. the Nizam's Dominions (Hyderabad State)*, Part I (Hyderabad-Deccan: Government Central Press, 1933), p. 40.

62. Aundhi, Koracha, Panabaras, and Ambagarh-Chauki zamindaris were transferred from Chanda to Durg district in 1907. Grigson, *The Aboriginal Problem*, p. 54.

63. Fürer-Haimendorf, *Tribal Hyderabad*, p. 72.

64. Grigson, *The Aboriginal Problem*, p. 417.

65. Prasad describes Verrier Elwin's celebration of cultural primitivism as ecological romanticism. We use this phrase in almost the same sense.

See Archana Prasad, *Against Ecological Romanticism: Verrier Elwin and the Making of an Anti-modern Tribal Identity* (New Delhi: Three Essays Collective, 2003), pp. xiii–xxiv.

66. Sundar, *Subalterns and Sovereigns.*
67. Prasad, *Against Ecological Romanticism*, pp. 35–72.
68. Ronald Inden, *Imagining India* (Oxford: Blackwell, 1992), p. 93.
69. Ajay Skaria, *Hybrid Histories: Forests, Frontiers and Wildness in Western India* (New Delhi: Oxford University Press, 1999), p. 199.
70. David Hardiman, 'Power in the Forest: The Dangs, 1820–1940', in *Subaltern Studies VIII: Essays in Honour of Ranajit Guha*, edited by David Arnold and David Hardiman (New Delhi: Oxford University Press, 1994), pp. 108–12; also see Skaria, *Hybrid Histories*, pp. 198–200.
71. Skaria, *Hybrid Histories*, p. 198.
72. Verrier Elwin, *Maria Murder and Suicide* (London, 1943), see Preface.
73. Ramachandra Guha, 'Savaging the Civilised: Verrier Elwin and the Tribal Question in Late Colonial India', *Economic and Political Weekly* 31, no. 35 (1996): 2375–89, see p. 2378.
74. Fürer-Haimendorf, *Tribal Hyderabad*, pp. 33–5.
75. Elwin, *Maria Murder and Suicide*, p. 1.
76. Grigson, *The Aboriginal Problem*, p. 417.
77. David Hardiman, *Missionaries and Their Medicine: A Christian Modernity for Tribal India* (Manchester: Manchester University Press, 2008), p. 25; Hardiman, 'Power in the Forest', p. 107.
78. Board's Collection, IOR/F/755/20541, f. 74; Smith, *Land Revenue Settlement of the Chanda District*, p. 74.
79. Smith, *Land Revenue Settlement of the Chanda District*, pp. 179–83.
80. G. S. Ghurye, *The Scheduled Tribes* (Bombay: Popular Prakashan, 1959), pp. 71–4.
81. Vinita Damodaran, 'Colonial Constructions of the "Tribes" in India: The Case of Chotanagpur', in *Adivasis in Colonial India: Survival, Resistance and Negotiation*, edited by Biswamoy Pati (New Delhi: Orient BlackSwan, 2011), pp. 73–4.
82. Ghurye, *The Scheduled Tribes*, pp. 78–9.
83. W. V. Grigson, *The Challenge of Backwardness* (Hyderabad-Deccan: Government Press, 1947), pp. 84–5.
84. Grigson, *The Challenge of Backwardness*, pp. 79–83.
85. Laura Dudley Jenkins, 'Another "People of India" Project: Colonial and National Anthropology', *Journal of Asian Studies* 62, no. 4 (November 2003): 1143–4.

86. Amit Prakash, 'Decolonisation and Tribal Policy in Jharkhand: Continuities with Colonial Discourse', *Social Scientist* 27, nos 7–8, July–August 1999: 125–7; also see *The Framing of India's Constitution: Select Documents*, vol. III (New Delhi: Indian Institute of Public Administration, 1968), pp. 733–45.
87. *The Framing of India's Constitution*, pp. 735–40.
88. Grigson, *The Aboriginal Problem*, pp. 54, 417.
89. Grigson, *The Aboriginal Problem*, p. 454.
90. Grigson, *The Aboriginal Problem*, p. 54.
91. *Report on the Administration of the Central Provinces, 1901–02*, p. 44.
92. Grigson, *The Aboriginal Problem*, p. 454.
93. Grigson, *The Aboriginal Problem*, p. 67.
94. *Stephen Hislop's Papers*, IOR/V/27/910/49, f. 12; *Chanda District Gazetteer*, 1909, pp. 66–8.
95. Fürer-Haimendorf, *Tribal Hyderabad*, pp. 66–154.
96. Vidarbha, SS, S. no. 920, File no. 4-7/1922, ff. 2–4.
97. *Report on the Administration of the Central Provinces, 1901–02*, p. 44.
98. Grigson, *The Aboriginal Problem*, p. 8.
99. *Stephen Hislop's Papers*, IOR/V/27/910/49, f. 12.
100. Grigson, *The Aboriginal Problem*, pp. 374–5.

5

INSURGENCY AND
DEVELOPMENTALISM
AN UNRESOLVED TANGLE

COLONIAL PROTECTIONISM FAILED TO PUT a check to the dispossession of the Gonds. Over the years, however, the intense disaffection it produced was transmuted into a political consciousness that grew into a full-scale insurgency in Adilabad. The loss of historically established rights over land and forests, ruthless evictions, and exploitation mobilized the Gonds of Adilabad into a political force that resulted in open insurgency against the Hyderabad State in 1940 under the leadership of Kumaram Bhimu. Though this is not often seriously acknowledged in the literature, there is evidence to suggest that the aspiration, articulated from within the worldview of the Gonds, was for a separate and independent Gond Raj. In other words, the Gonds' response to colonial political rationality was more political than socio-economic.[1]

The Government of Hyderabad felt it could neutralize the agitating Gonds by improving their economic and social condition. As a first step, the state deployed anthropologists to study and suggest development schemes for the Gonds. In the course of time, the anthropologists themselves became developers and agents of change and transformation. Their work did provide some relief to the Gonds in terms of land distribution and concessions on forest rights. However, the anthropological schema remained developmental and did not take the issues raised by the insurgency to their logical end. In other words, it did not recognize the insurgency as raising the question of the political rights of the adivasi community.[2]

One aim of this chapter is to relate Bhimu's insurgency to the larger debate on adivasi movements in colonial India. In general—and ironically—the adivasis' response to colonial intervention was ascribed to the category 'pre-political' and described as sporadic, spontaneous, and unorganized by orthodox Marxist scholarship.[3] The paradox here is that these scholars also believe that the celebration of anti-colonial adivasi resistance would set the stage for the creation of a new class consciousness among the adivasis and enable the adivasi areas to become a base for radical politics and movements. Marxist scholarship has also not been able to provide an adequate understanding of adivasi movements, as it fails to make distinctions between autonomous adivasi insurgence and the hegemonic nationalist movement.[4]

As a result, adivasi politics of resistance has been stereotyped as primitivist. Adivasi thought, which is the source of this insurgent consciousness, has not been regarded as a source of the forms of resistance and the contestation of power. It is treated merely as consisting of myth and rumour. Ranajit Guha has thoroughly exposed these elitist approaches of nationalist, Cambridge School, and Marxist scholarship towards the peasant movements of colonial India.[5] However, Guha failed to appreciate the existence of divergent political interests within the peasant community. Importantly, how was adivasi politics different from that of the peasantry of the plains?[6] Alpa Shah charges Guha with maintaining silence on the destructive role of the Church in collaboration with the colonial state. She also shows the importance of cultural histories in suturing ruptured communities, and points out how the secular left has failed to understand those histories.[7] Our attempt here is to examine the ways in which the Gonds tried to recover their lost sovereignty, and in this process how the adivasi communities' cultural values, bonds, myths, and rumours were catalysts in creating an insurgent consciousness. An attempt will also be made to show how the insurgency started by the Gonds had wider support from other adivasi as well as non-adivasi communities. I shall examine how the insurgent consciousness of the adivasis is transformed when it is viewed through a developmental lens. I shall also examine how the adivasi question takes us far beyond the development question.

TOWARDS INSURGENCY

The dispossession of the Gonds was more severe in the Adilabad region than in Chanda. This was partly because Chanda had huge Gond zamindari areas, and the Gonds who lost their land in the khalsa areas could flee to the zamindari regions where there was plenty of cultivable forest land. Also, importantly, since the zamindars were Gonds, the Gond ryots did not find themselves unduly hassled in the zamindaris. In Adilabad, however, the reality was different. Christoph von Fürer-Haimendorf, who toured the Asifabad, Rajura, and Utnur taluks of the district one year after the Gond insurgency, documents the hard realities of Gond life. The removal of the Gond zamindars, maqtadars, and mokhasis had grave consequences for the common Gonds. These Gond rajas/zamindars had had a different position till the middle of the nineteenth century. Though they formally recognized the sovereignty of the Nizam, in actual fact they were not only rulers in their areas but the principal landholders and cultivators. However, the introduction of the ryotwari system dispossessed the Gond rajas/zamindars, which resulted in the common Gonds becoming prey to land-hungry caste-peasants from the plains. Importantly, as the district was surrounded by plains on all sides, it received immigrants from all sides. Dominant caste-peasant Kumbis from Berar, Kapu (Reddy) and Velama from Karimnagar and Warangal, and Kammas from the Andhra region of Madras Presidency came into the district, as there was great pressure on the land in their respective areas. As we have discussed in the preceding chapters, the Nizam's government also welcomed this immigration. All this left the adivasis hard-pressed.[8]

What is more, the implementation of colonial political rationality in Hyderabad State produced a twofold system that involved ruthless exploitation of subaltern communities. The top-level administration was reformist and built on this colonial rationality, whereas the local-level administration deployed the new forms of governance and law only when these operated to their advantage, while acting in coercive and illegal ways when they did not.[9] The lower-level power structure was, as Ranajit Guha has described it, a system of exploitation and subjection under the sarkar, sahukar, and zamindar.[10] The Gonds were the worst victims of the new system. Besides the land eviction and harassment by forest officials, corruption by lower-level non-adivasi officials was rampant in the region. Exactions of money and provisions from Gonds by local officials such as *girdawar*s (taluk-level revenue officers), *patwari*s (village clerks), police patels, tahsil *chaprasi*s (office attendants), and janglat chaukidars was regular. And the adivasi were totally fed up with this.

Fürer-Haimendorf asserts that exaction of money and provisions by local officials was the immediate cause for the Gonds' unrest. It would be interesting to look at a striking case from Deopur village of Asifabad taluk reported by him. All the land in Deopur belonged to a Brahman *vakil* (lawyer) who lived in Asifabad. The village comprised forty Gonds and ten Kolam households. A Gond patel, Mesram Paiku, with some other Gonds cleared a piece of jungle which mainly consisted of dried bamboo on the vakil's patta in order to enlarge their fields. The chaukidar who visited the village saw the felled jungle and told the Gonds that they would have to pay a fine of Rs 2,000. There was bargaining and the chaukidar reduced his demand to Rs 425. The Gonds paid Rs 200 on the spot. It was agreed that the remaining amount would be paid within a week. Two months earlier, on two visits, the same chaukidar had collected Rs 80 mamul, 2 *goni*s (bags) 32 *seer*s (1 *seer* is around 1 kilograms) of *jowar* (sorghum), 10 maunds of cotton, 3 maunds of chillies, 8 seers of chironji, 8 seers of oil seed, 1 wooden cot, 17 baskets, and 20 chickens—in addition to the 5 he had consumed in the village. Finally the villagers approached Fürer-Haimendorf, and he asked them to meet the forest ranger. But before the ranger examined the issue, the chaukidar negotiated with the Gonds, saying that if they withdrew the complaint made against him to the ranger, he would not demand the remaining Rs 225. The Gonds agreed, dreading that he would otherwise harass them with false accusations in the future.[11] Whatever the final outcome of this story, the account underlines the intensity of exactions by local officials.

Before the introduction of forest regulations, the Gonds had moved freely in forest areas. When restrictions were suddenly placed on their movement, and they became victim to exactions of money, they had to embrace arms. Kumaram Bhimu's (see Figure 5.1) own life and his revolt at Jodeghat, some 12 miles west of Asifabad in 1940, is the best example.

We have no documentary evidence with regard to the early life of Bhimu. But oral evidence collected by Sahu and Allam Rajaiah in the 1980s establish that he was born at Sankenpally, about 5 miles from Asifabad. Later his family moved to Sirdhapur. When he was young, Bhimu had killed an outsider named Sidhiqui who had quarrelled with Bhimu's brothers and claimed that their lands belonged to him. He fled to Ballarshah and then to Assam. He worked there in a tea plantation. He soon realized that conditions in the plantation were worse than those

Figure 5.1 Modern depiction of Kumaram Bhimu.
Source: Author's personal collection.

in the gudam and returned. Meanwhile, in Ballarshah, he had learned to read and write. He understood the fact of British exploitation and the relation between the British and the Nizam. After the Sirdhapur incident, Bhimu's family had shifted to Khakanghat where they became *paledhar*s (tenants) under the raja of Pangadi. After five years, the raja ousted them. Then Bhimu organized all the Gonds to move towards the fertile Bhabijery. Inspired by Bhimu, a large number of Gonds and Kolams cleared the forest and settled there. Before Bhimu came to Bhabijery, it was dense reserved forest demarcated as the Dhanora State Forest.[12]

Official sources say that Bhimu came to Bhabijery in 1345F (1934) and became the leader of Gonds who were cultivating the land in patches. He also began his own cultivation, and induced the Gonds to settle there permanently and cultivate the land in spite of the Forest Department's objections, as this region was a reserved forest area. Bhimu had set his sights on some five deserted villages in the region. He had written a letter to the first talukdar of Asifabad, saying that the *parwana* (patta) of the five villages should be given to him. Instead, the Forest Department filed a case against him and his associate in the district court for cultivating forest land. When he was refused rights over these five villages, he began mobilizing Gonds against the forest and revenue officials. This was seen by the state as the main reason for his revolt.[13] It was reported that 'the Gonds are by nature peaceful. But they are easily influenced. They were sadly misled by Bhimu for his own purpose'.[14]

However, the oral literature of the community collected a year after the incident by Fürer-Haimendorf gives us a different account of these events. As the region was part of the reserved-forest area, the Gonds were asked to evacuate, but without being given a fixed date by which they had to leave the region. Thus, the forest guards burned down the huts. Many Kolams went to Rajura taluk, but the Gonds and nine households of Kolams went to Jodeghat, a site east of Bhabijery, and got permission to settle there by offering Rs 500 mamul to a chaukidar. After some time, the chaukidar demanded a further Rs 2,000, saying that the earlier sum was for him and this amount was for the saredars and the ranger. He threatened that if they failed to pay, they would be driven away and their houses burnt down as in Bhabijery. Because of their inability to pay this high amount, they decided to bring the matter to the Nizam's notice. Bhimu and four Gonds went to Hyderabad to meet the ruler, and it is believed that they got permission to cultivate 57 acres at Jodeghat, but the chaukidar still insisted on a payment of Rs 2,000.[15] Fürer-Haimendorf remarks:

> The sum of Rs 2000, fantastic as it may seem, was mentioned to me by several entirely independent informants in widely separated villages; the Chaukidar probably hoped that the Gonds would start bargaining ... and pay a few hundred rupees; but Bhimu was not prepared to do this; he seems to have been a powerful personality with great influence among the Gonds and a moderate amount of education.[16]

It is evident from Fürer-Haimendorf's description that the continued harassment and evictions by forest and revenue officials led the Gonds towards resistance. But the local officials attributed Bhimu's rising against the state simply to self-interest. Bhimu adopted arms only when his pleas to get permission to cultivate the land failed. Just before taking up arms, he even wrote a letter to the divisional forest officer (DFO). Instead of solving the problem amicably, the DFO sent a force to crush the Gonds. He sent several armed forest guards to enforce evacuation. As the party moved towards Jodeghat, they burned several settlements. Some cattle tied in the sheds were trapped and died in the fire.[17]

RECLAIMING SOVEREIGNTY

With this, Bhimu started his direct fight against the state. As delineated by Allam Rajaiah and Sahu, the laudable revolt of Ramji Gond was a continuous source of inspiration for all later revolts in the region. The story of the fighting spirit of Ramji Gond, in particular, was familiar to Kumaram Bhimu through many telling and retellings. Allam Rajaiah says that the experience of freedom and political autonomy in the pre-colonial period was recalled repeatedly during social gatherings. In the traditional political system, the mokhasis, who were under the Gond rajas, were the heads at the gudam level, and were freely accessible to their brethren; there was no interference in their socio-cultural and political life from any external authority. With the imposition of the Nizam's rule, the egalitarian political system and independence of the Gonds was destroyed. It would appear that Kumaram Bhimu sought the restoration of the traditional system with the formation of a separate Gond Raj.[18]

Bhimu declared the twelve villages[19] around Jodeghat as 'Gond Raj' and sent an ultimatum to the authorities saying that henceforth the people in this area would not abide by the laws of the Nizam's state.[20] The idea of Gond Raj, in fact, shook the Hyderabad State. As it was reported in an official correspondence,

> There would have been a hue and cry throughout these parts that the government of the Nizam was no more and that *Gond Raj* was now firmly established. Bhimu would surely have ransacked the country all round. As his written letters testify he would indeed have made himself the *Gond Raja* and begun his executions all round. He would have been a terror all round. He would surely have carried on his marauding expeditions to the headquarters of the district itself and ransacked and ravaged the whole country around.[21]

After declaring Gond Raj, Bhimu framed laws for its functioning. In the new Raj, the gudam heads would act as executives at the village level as well as at the level of the Raj. A *fauj* (army) consisting of young men from all gudams was formed for defence, and the men were armed with guns (*bharmar bandooq* or old-fashioned guns), swords, spears, and *lathi*s (batons).[22] The expenditure for the maintenance of the army was to be met by contributions from all gudams. Different wings of the Raj were established and duties allotted to them. The Ragal Jhanda (red flag) was considered the state flag. The burnt-down village of Jodeghat was reconstructed at the same place.[23] One day, an *amin* (sub-inspector) came to Jodeghat to enquire why the Gonds were not appearing in court. The Gonds and the Kolams gave him a good thrashing. News of this incident spread to the surrounding gudams and several of them started extending their support to Bhimu's movement. This was the first major achievement in the Gond struggle.

As it was clear that action was necessary to check Bhimu before his movement assumed more dangerous proportions, the first talukdar of Adilabad district decided to march to Jodeghat on 10 September 1940 with a 100-member police force, accompanied by the district superintendent of police, the civil surgeon, and the assistant talukdar and tahsildar.[24] This message was passed on to all the gudams. Around 500

Gonds gathered at Jodeghat in response to the *thudum* (Gond drumbeat). Bhimu delivered a long speech and inspired them to fight for the cause of the Gond Raj. Initially, reports indicate, the talukdar invited Bhimu for negotiations, but as the two parties could not come to any consensus, war seemed inevitable. The talukdar had come with a plan to crush the adivasis ruthlessly. Though they had not provoked the police, the talukdar gave orders to fire at the adivasis.[25] According to official sources, ten Gonds, including Bhimu, died on the spot, and their army were brutally crushed within an hour. Thirteen adivasis suffered critical injuries and four of them died in hospital.[26]

After this tragic incident, there were interesting developments. The Gond question immediately attracted the attention of the larger society. The Andhra Mahasabha, formed in 1930 and politically active in the region, had already shown keen interest in the Gonds' issue. They appointed a fact-finding committee to study the issue, consisting of B. Yella Reddy, M. Narasinga Rao (editor of *Rayyat*), B. Ramkishen Rao, and Ravi Narayan Reddy. The committee's findings were published in *Golkonda Patrika* (a Telugu newspaper) in two parts under Yella Reddy's name. Members of the Mahasabha also made a representation to the Nizam's prime minister. In their representation, they said that the number of casualties and injured given by government were misleading and false. The actual number of deaths was 130, and many more were injured. The police had cremated all the dead bodies collectively after the incident in order to hide the facts. They demanded an inquiry against the deputy superintendent of police who was responsible for the incident.[27] In the debate that followed, the main issue was who had fired first—the Gonds or the police. Yella Reddy argued that when the police reached Jodeghat, the Gonds had gathered for a social ceremony. The police arrived and, without issuing any caution, began firing on the unarmed Gonds. The committee tried to make a case for the Gonds. Instead, cases were booked against Yella Reddy and other members of the Mahasabha for anti-state activities and their voices were suppressed. Police officials 'successfully established' that the Gonds had first fired on the police and the latter had fired only to protect themselves.[28] Later, after an inquiry by the district police, it was said that Yella Reddy did not visit Jodeghat at all. Police suspected that he was informed by a local vakil, Pekajee, an Andhra Mahasabha activist, and his lieutenant Sada Siva Gupta, a Komati by caste.[29]

A more systematic study of the incident was in fact undertaken by Kasinath Rao Vaidya (of the Congress), Ramachary (an advocate from Hyderabad), Siraj ul-Hasan (a vakil), Narasinga Rao (the editor of *Rayyat*), Prem Kumar (an Arya Samajist), and Srinivasa Rao (of the Hindu Praja Mandal). They toured Asifabad and submitted a detailed report on the incident to the home secretary. They found that local officials were hiding the facts, and questioned the local officials' action against the Gonds. They noted that according to one official version, the Gonds did not fire because they were told by their leader Bhimu that the police bullets would be rendered harmless on account of his knowledge of magic and charms, and that they would fire on the police after the latter's ammunition was exhausted. They asked the government why it was necessary to take 100 armed constables to execute warrants against a few Gonds. What was the justification for the firing? They also demanded an independent inquiry into the incident.[30] The first talukdar of Asifabad was asked by the home secretary to respond to these allegations. The talukdar gave a detailed reply refuting all the charges. In fact, he described the Jodeghat resistance as a political movement against the state that could not be overlooked.[31]

The Jodeghat resistance also received an overwhelming response from the local non-adivasis. Fürer-Haimendorf notes that during the last days before his death, Bhimu was in touch with a Brahman vakil in Asifabad who encouraged him in his stand.[32] Bhimu himself stayed in Jodeghat, but his messengers went at night to the vakil's house where they were promised money and support; the vakil told them, however, that should they have to die, they must not mention his name. It is further stated that some merchants of Asifabad promised the Gonds sufficient grain and other necessities to see them through their difficulties.[33]

Although the Gonds thus received wider support from non-adivasis, there were different interest groups among their supporters. These groups can be broadly divided into two: political and religious. The first group was mainly represented by the Andhra Mahasabha and other political groups who were broadly Indian nationalist in their ideology. This group tried to induce the insurgent Gonds to join their party and spread their political base in the forest and hill areas. The second group, which was represented by the Arya Samaj and the Hindu Praja Mandal, was aggressively pursuing a religious agenda directed against the Muslim government in the forest areas. Local Komatis and Marwaris were particularly instrumental in this activism.[34] It was during this period that there was serious debate over the enumeration of adivasis as animists. Especially from the 1921 census, all tribes in the state, irrespective of their religious claims, were enumerated under the category of 'animist'. This reduced the size of the enumerated Hindu population. The Arya Samaj strongly opposed this move and demanded that the government enumerate adivasis as Hindus. These developments led the Arya Samaj to spread its activities in the forest areas. Finally, in the 1941 census, the adivasis were enumerated as Hindus, and after this they lost their separate religious identity in national data. In fact, the Arya Samaj was very active in this district because it bordered the Marathwada region, where Arya Samaj and Rashtriya Swayamsevak Sangh (RSS) activities were strong. Nagpur was home to the RSS and a centre of activity during this period.[35] In this political setting, earlier exploiters appeared as champions of Gond rights. G. S. Gupta, a Marwari Arya Samaj activist, wrote a lengthy article in two parts in *Golkonda Patrika* explaining the plight of the Gonds under the Nizam's rule and how this was being exploited by Christian missionaries. However, he remained silent about the exploitation of the Gonds by caste-Hindu peasants and moneylenders.[36]

Although the intervention of non-adivasis in Gond affairs was politically and religiously motivated, these interventions helped the Gonds in their resistance against the state. Yet the manner in which non-adivasis dealt with the Gond issue undermined and destroyed the autonomous politics of the Gonds. After the Jodeghat incident, arrests continued for some days. About thirty-one Gonds were arrested, some of them sentenced to imprisonment. The local vakils, particularly Ramchander Rao Paika, helped the Gonds to deal with the court cases. Ramchander Rao wrote to the higher authorities on behalf of the Gonds. The Gonds did not know what he was writing in these representations. It is interesting to look at the representations he drafted. One of them reads thus:

> Kumram Bhimu and Kumram Raghu, residents of Joday-ghat [Jodeghat] persuaded us that they would get for us exception for free grazing and free

clearing of trees and induced us to join them.... While we were there, you and the other officials, etc, came to Joday-ghat and you ordered that those who should go should go away. Some went away and we were also ready to go away but Bhimu and Raghu threatened us saying that if you go outside his 'magic circle' you will all die. They also said that they would see that the bullets of the police did not harm them. He will catch those bullets with his hands and devour them. Being afraid we remained.... This was our fault.[37]

Further, he also coached the Gonds about their behaviour in court and the language to be used to impress higher officials and judges. This strategy worked effectively and impressed upon the higher officials and judges that the Gonds were innocent. Abdul Sattar, first talukdar of Asifabad, in his letter to the director general of revenue, wrote:

I went today to the court to record my evidence before the Sessions Judge. As soon as I sat down all the prisoners in the case fell at my feet and gave the enclosed application to me. Some were weeping and some were entreating. All of them without a single exception seemed to be deeply repentant. The Sessions Judge himself was deeply impressed by this scene though he tried not to show it. But everyone could see that he was impressed deeply.... They all expressed their feelings of gratitude to [the] Government before the Session Judge and said that they were not at all criminals but were peaceful citizens who were caught in the clutches of Bhimu and his men by promises of lands and free grazing etc.... I hope the Government would be pleased to consider the application of these poor deluded, misguided jungle tribes with mercy.[38]

Thus the Gonds, under the direction of the vakil Ramchander Rao, acted before the officials and judges as simple-minded, law-abiding citizens who had been misled. This strategy worked as far as obtaining their release was concerned. Abdul Sattar's letter in particular impressed the government, which pardoned all the accused in the case and released them from jail.[39] However, strategies such as these undermined the insurgent spirit of the adivasis. The Jodeghat resistance, which was a rejection of outside authority, was in this process reduced to a struggle for land and grazing rights by simple tribals. Even Fürer-Haimendorf, who worked extensively with the Gonds, failed to appreciate the political ideology of resistance in Bhimu's actions. According to him, Bhimu's main demand was freedom from *dumpa patti* (plough tax) and grazing fees.[40]

We would argue that the Jodeghat movement was an illustrious one, deeply rooted in aspirations of Gond sovereignty, and designed to attain total emancipation from the rule of outsiders, particularly from the Nizam's state. Bhimu's idea of the formation of a separate Gond Raj may be found in many places in the official and confidential reports of the Nizam's government. In fact, the file on the Jodeghat resistance was named 'Political Agitation: Asifabad Gonds' Rising'. This shows that the Nizam's government treated the resistance as a political movement, not just as a movement for dumpa patti. The larger aspirations for a Gond Raj can also be discerned in the folk songs of Gonds and Kolams recorded in the works of Sahu and Allam Rajaiah. There is no doubt that Bhimu was very clear about the injustice of the land and forest enclosure process, and rallied all the Gonds and Kolams who were exploited around his movement. And he clearly used traditional instruments to mobilize people. A more detailed and imaginative investigation into the role and meaning of what is described as magical power, rumour, and belief is necessary if we are to appreciate their meaning and the active agency of the Gonds in the operation of the resistance.

However, Bhimu misjudged the ruthless antagonism of the state force which ultimately took his life. In his vision, the spirit of Gond Raj involved the retention of Gond culture as well as political sovereignty. As illustrated by Guha, the adivasi insurgencies marked a history of political consciousness which acted autonomously and aimed to turn the socio-political order upside down.[41] It was in this same spirit that Gond leaders submitted a memorandum to the States Reorganisation Commission in the 1950s, demanding the formation of a separate state for adivasis carved out of the adivasi areas of Chhattisgarh and contiguous districts of the Rewa and Vidarbha regions, generally known as Dandakaranya.[42] It is sad that even Fürer-Haimendorf, with all his sympathy for the Gonds, was unable to appreciate the deeply political nature of Bhimu's movement. I quote him:

> I believe, however, that far too much has been made of his reputation as a religious leader; the idea that he intended to found a 'Gond Raj' or had any such far reaching plans seems to me entirely erroneous; his and his co-villagers' aims were always strictly limited—namely their undisturbed cultivation of land in Jhoreghat. The fact that hundreds of other Gonds rallied to his

cause, is a symptom of their bitterness against the forest subordinates, and in this way they hoped they might rid themselves of their burdens.[43]

This is to say that the Gond demand was not one for political autonomy. All Fürer-Haimendorf could discern in these complex developments was a critique of corrupt subordinate officials, and a demand for land and for rights to use the forest. He was not able to understand the vision or aspiration for sovereignty, or appreciate its significance. This position was common to colonial anthropologists in general. What is significant is that this anthropological consensus has formed the basis for the design of all 'adivasi development' efforts in independent India too. We will term this 'anthropological developmentalism'.

ANTHROPOLOGICAL DEVELOPMENTALISM

From the 1930s, the colonial state conceived of the adivasi question as a developmental issue. The advocacy of the anthropologist was instrumental in establishing such a notion. Anthropology was developed as a faculty in most Indian universities,[44] and produced a good number of anthropologists who were not only engaged in applied anthropological research but also acted as administrators of adivasi areas that were separate from the general administration. Not only European, but also Indian anthropologists played an equal role in setting up the All-India Tribal Welfare Bureau, which was constituted of both administrators and anthropologists, and which acted as an apex body on development issues related to adivasis.[45]

In fact, the colonial state used anthropologists to realize three imperatives: first, to extend their reach into the hill and forest regions; second, to clear the air in adivasi areas before it expanded its power; third, to transform the already conquered adivasis into willing and docile subjects. This strategy of the colonial state can also be surmised from the following account by Fürer-Haimendorf:

> One day in January 1944 a messenger sent by Grigson from Hyderabad brought me an impressive looking, sealed letter which contained a telegram from Philip Mills, Adviser to the Governor of Assam for Tribal Areas and States. His telegram offered me an appointment by the government of India as Special officer on the North-East Frontier, and a subsequent letter made it

clear that I would be assigned to the Balipara Frontier Tract, where I was to 'establish friendly relations with the unadministered hill-tribes, collect data on general conditions and tribal customs, and ultimately explore the upper reaches of the Subansiri River'.[46]

Like Christian missionaries, the anthropologists and their studies were part of the colonial mission of civilizing the adivasis. Indeed, anthropologists were crucial in setting up the colonial state in hills and forests. They worked as researchers and administrators, and often thought of themselves as emancipators of adivasis. They were projected as the face of colonial development in the hill and forest areas.

Adivasi development projects were generally designed on the premise that the adivasis were only half human and stood at the bottom of the civilizational ladder, and further that 'civilized' people were far better equipped to make productive use of adivasi terrains. Caste-Hindu society was generally the yardstick for such an understanding. Fürer-Haimendorf and Grigson were architects of adivasi policy both in Hyderabad State and in the Central Provinces. For both, Verrier Elwin was a philosophical guru. Elwin was trained originally in English literature and then in theology at Oxford. His love for English Romantic literature was to influence his approach to adivasis, which can also be described as romantic in the ordinary sense of the term. Elwin came to India in the 1920s as a missionary, but later broke with his mission and settled in a Gond village where he carried out social and educational work. He eventually married a Gond tribal woman. He worked extensively with the adivasis of the Central Provinces and Bastar and wrote a series of monographs on the Khonds, Baigas, Marias, and Agarias.[47]

Fürer-Haimendorf was sent by the British to Hyderabad State in the early 1940s to advise the Nizam in his handling of the rebellious Gond adivasis of Adilabad. His career as an anthropologist was helped considerably by his appointment as adviser to the Nizam for tribal and backward classes, and as professor of anthropology at Hyderabad's Osmania University. He and his wife often travelled to the tribal areas where they stayed for long periods, developing a rapport with the people. These periods of research produced four reports on the socio-economic conditions of, respectively, the Hill Reddis, Gonds, Koyas, and Chenchus.[48] W. V. Grigson, who came to India in 1920, was an administrator-cum-anthropologist. He worked in the Central Provinces and Hyderabad State in different high positions, but was mostly involved in framing adivasi policy. In his administrative capacity, he toured extensively in the Central Provinces and Hyderabad State and produced influential works. He is famous for his *Notes on the Aboriginal Problem in the Mandla Districts* (1940), *The Maria Gonds of Baster* (1938), *The Aboriginal Problem in the Central Provinces and Berar* (1944), and *The Challenge of Backwardness* (1947).[49]

The striking similarity between these anthropologists was their ecological Romanticism. They were more deeply interested in 'primitive' forest groups as against 'advanced' ones. As mentioned in the preceding chapter, they considered the adivasis as simple and beautiful forest creatures who needed to be handled with care and protected, their lifestyles preserved. It was against this background that Fürer-Haimendorf, when he first came to India in 1936, had chosen to work on the Konyak Nagas of the north-east frontier who were considered to be the most primitive forest group in India. His second choice was the Chenchus of the Nallamalla Hills in Hyderabad State, who were also a food-gathering and hunting people. While making his choice of studying in Hyderabad, he said that 'I had only vaguely heard about the Chenchus, but if I was to study the aboriginal tribes of the Nizam's Dominion, it seemed reasonable to begin with the most primitive and least known of them all'.[50] His third choice was the Konda Reddis of the Bison Hills (Paloncha forests of Hyderabad State), who were another 'primitive' forest group. What was particularly appealing to Fürer-Haimendorf about the Konda Reddis was that they were completely cut off from the wider world—the only way to reach their habitat was by boat! He also chose to study other forest groups such as the Apa Tanis of Assam and Sherpas of Nepal. For our account, it is important to note that he was asked to work with the Gonds because they were raising arms against the Nizam's government.[51]

The literature produced by these stalwarts was the main source for framing a development policy in relation to adivasis. This literature assumed and consolidated a teleology in which adivasi bodies, habitats, lifestyles, social and political practices, and podu cultivation were all termed simple or backward, and in need of being developed to bring them on a par with caste-Hindus. Among the many things obscured here is the rich agricultural history of this region under the Gond rajas, and the imperatives under which the adivasis practised podu cultivation. We should also note that adivasi areas were regarded as *kala pani* country (backward and unhealthy areas). Malaria was widespread all over the Central Provinces, but yaws (an infectious tropical disease resembling syphilis in its early stages, marked by red skin eruptions and ulcerating lesions) was specific to the Chanda region.[52] Adivasis were typically associated with hoe, podu, or dhya cultivation which involved purely rain-grown crops and was practised on light soils and in rotation on the flat hilltops. This mode of cultivation was depicted as the opposite of the caste-Hindu mode of cultivation in the plains.[53] It was also said that an adivasi was equipped

> only with poor household-possessions such as a hoe, digging-stick, hatchet, one or two knives and sickles. These are all he requires for the raising of hill-crops, the collection of jungle produce and making baskets. He dresses in a narrow *langoti*, drawn between the legs and tucked into his belt in front and behind, while his wife wears a saari and a few cheap ornaments.[54]

The Gond 'type', Fürer-Haimendorf wrote, was characterized

> by a broad and rather flat face, high cheek-bones, a small, short nose which widens rapidly from a narrow depressed ridge, a weak and not very full mouth, and a small pointed chin. Faces of this type with their broad cheek-bones and the weak lower jaw may be described as heart-shaped, though in the plumpness of youth they often appear round and tend to give even adults a certain childlike look.[55]

Adivasis were also generally described as a population who drank large quantities of home-brewed liquor for festivals, marriages, and worship. Drunkenness was invariably attributed as the cause for all their problems and underdevelopment.[56] This picture of adivasi society was fundamental to all colonial and postcolonial adivasi development projects and policies.

A closer look at Fürer-Haimendorf's report on his experience with the Gonds of Adilabad would help us to understand the ways in which anthropological developmentalism was shaped and deployed in India. As has been mentioned above, Fürer-Haimendorf had a special interest in Hyderabad, and made Marlavai village in Adilabad district his home in India.[57] He reached Marlavai along with his wife in mid-December 1941, about one year after the Jodeghat incident. Although the insurgency had been successfully suppressed, the Gonds continued to breach forest laws. On his arrival, he noted that the Gonds were contesting patta lands being assigned to non-adivasis, resisting the payment of mamuls to subordinate forest and revenue officials, and approaching courts with their grievances. He based his camp in Marlavai village, located in a remote forest area about 30 kilometres from Utnur. He literally lived there for three years, but continued to make frequent visits even after that. Lachu Patel of Marlavai was his guide, and it was with his help that he established mastery over the Gonds.[58] We get a sense of this relationship when we realize that the graves of Fürer-Haimendorf, his wife Betty, and Lachu Patel were raised in Gondi style side by side in Marlavai. Fürer-Haimendorf named his son after Lachu Patel, as he had died on the day of his son's birth. A statue of Fürer-Haimendorf welcomes us at the entrance of Marlavai (see Figure 5.2). His son, Nicholas Lachu Patel, visits Marlavai regularly to pay homage to his parents.[59]

Fürer-Haimendorf focused mainly on education, providing relief work, and bringing in administrative reforms.[60] Initially he was engaged in studying and observing Gond traditions and practices. He submitted four reports to the Nizam's government, with concrete suggestions about the development of adivasis.[61] He also acted as mediator between the Gonds and the government by passing on their representations to the concerned officials. Because of Grigson, who was the revenue minister in the Nizam's government at the time, Fürer-Haimendorf got greater support from the government.[62] He regarded education not only as essential to the liberation of the Gonds from their primitive lifestyle, but also as necessary to protect themselves from land-hungry caste-Hindus. In his autobiography he observes:

> Much of their inability to deal with government officials and the illegal transfer of their land was due to their illiteracy and consequent ignorance of government laws and rules. As long as they could not read even the simplest receipt or document they were at the mercy of more wily outsiders and venal minor government employees. Hence the removal of illiteracy was the obvious first step towards an improvement of the Gonds' position.[63]

Figure 5.2 Statues of Fürer-Haimendorf and his wife, Betty, in Marlavai, being celebrated by the local Gonds
Source: Collected from Chokotnakabur website.

Marlavai was the base for all his activities. He developed a Gond education scheme and formally started a training school in Marlavai in 1943 with the help of the government. He gathered those he regarded as more intelligent and trained them in writing and reading in the Gondi language as well as in Marathi, and, later on, in Urdu. This scheme was taken over by the government and was key in developing education among the Gonds. The most significant feature of the scheme was the selection and training of adivasi men to work as teachers in adivasi areas.[64] Emphasis was placed on both adult and regular education by setting up special schools in these areas. To meet this goal, textbooks were written in Gondi and the subject matter was drawn mainly from their own environment and their mythological stories.[65]

Apart from reading and writing, Gonds were also trained in the rules and functioning of the Revenue and Forest Departments. This enabled their employment as forest guards and village officers. It appears that another objective of teaching revenue and forest rules was to make the Gonds obey them. Some crafts, modern agriculture, and other subjects of everyday importance formed other parts of the education scheme. The government took this work seriously and spent considerably on Gond education schemes. The total amount sanctioned to the Gond Education Scheme, Adilabad, in 1353F (1942–3) was Rs 45,267. This was increased to Rs 134,104 in 1359F (1948–9).[66] Most of the money went into publishing textbooks and paying stipends to trainees and teachers. Under this scheme, sixty-nine schools were established with seventy-six teachers spreading over 35 per cent of the adivasi villages. Among the trainees at the Marlavai Centre, 76 per cent were appointed as teachers, 16 per cent were employed as clerks, and about 8 per cent were not absorbed anywhere. This training centre was abolished in July 1965, contending it was not functioning well.[67] The total literacy rate of Gonds in the state in 1961 was 2.65 per cent only. Of the total Gond literates, only forty persons had completed matriculation and the rest studied up to the primary level or had no qualification.[68] It would appear that neither the Marlavai school nor the Gond education centre had brought any significant change to Gond life. In my recent field trip to Marlavai (June 2014), I found that the school established by Fürer-Haimendorf had been converted into a residential school in 1956 and upgraded to class 10. But very few Gond children graduated from the school. Those who did pass the 10th grade have settled down as teachers or forest jawans. A few students were studying in colleges in Utnur and Adilabad. I am told that very few have graduated with degrees.

Another very important activity undertaken by Fürer-Haimendorf was land distribution. Through his influence, a Special Tribes Officer, who would look after overall development activities, was appointed to Adilabad in 1943. Subsequently, Fürer-Haimendorf himself was appointed as Aboriginal and Backward Tribes Adviser to the Nizam's government. An agency called Social Service was established within the Revenue Department to look after the development activities of the adivasis. The employees of this agency were trained by Fürer-Haimendorf at Osmania University. All development activities were undertaken under the head, 'rehabilitation'.[69] Finally, Fürer-Haimendorf succeeded in separating 'notified' adivasi areas from the general administration and placing them under a special officer from 1946 onwards.[70] This allowed the government to map the adivasi areas easily and implement development schemes. The allotment of land to adivasis in Adilabad began in 1944. Moazzam Hussain, Special Tribes Officer, played a crucial role in executing this project. A total of 130,000 acres of land was distributed in the district between 1944 and 1948 on *laoni patta* (colonization rules). Of these, 47,000 acres were excised from the Daboli block in Utnur taluk, and 23,000 and 30,000 acres were excised from Tirani and Manikgarh blocks in Asifabad and Rajura taluks respectively. It was said that in 1944 there had been only 600 adivasis holding land with pattadar rights, and that after the distribution of land by the government this number rose to 11,198. With this, about 50 per cent of the total population of adivasis held lands with patta rights.[71]

To those who were given land, thakkavi (crop) loans were also granted for purchasing bullocks. In 1946, 324 bullocks were purchased and distributed to adivasis at a cost of Rs 47,000. However, recoveries were very poor due to poor conditions of agriculture. The land distributed to adivasis was forest wasteland, and the yield was low. To teach modern agriculture to adivasis, an agriculture farm was set up in 1946 at Marlavai consisting of 28 acres. New crops and hybrid seeds of various crops were introduced to adivasis by an agriculture demonstrator. The farm had produced what they described as 'remarkably fine juari from improved seed', but adivasis seemed uninterested. To liberate adivasis from the moneylender, Fürer-Haimendorf proposed the introduction of cooperative societies. Under this scheme, seventy-eight grain banks and three rural banks (in Marlavai, Manikpur, and Keslapur) were started. The members of these banks contributed a share and the government gave an equal contribution. The total amount was lent to members. On the same lines, to avoid their being cheated by the sahukars, cooperative stores were started in 1949. These would buy the adivasis' produce—mainly minor forest produce—and market it.[72]

Medical aid was also provided to Gonds. The Public Health Department was involved in providing healthcare to the Gonds. The department was mainly engaged in preventive measures in the form of vaccination, particularly to eradicate smallpox and other epidemics. Malaria and yaws were controlled by spraying huts and cattle sheds to destroy mosquitoes. Thiosarmine injections were also administered periodically to cure yaws.[73] Government efforts bore little fruit, since the adivasis would disappear when they saw the doctors. What is more, doctors were reluctant to serve in forest areas which were considered to be unhealthy. Gonds were trained in some elementary anti-malaria control, but here again, the effort was not successful. The Health Department organized a health exhibition at Keslapur during the *jatara* (religious celebration). Few Gonds visited it. Importantly, all the posters and placards were written in either English or Urdu, and Gonds did not understand them as they did not read these languages.[74] It has been established in recent studies that epidemics such as malaria and cholera were widespread during colonial rule. Colonial rule made Indian bodies susceptible to viral and bacterial diseases, as under the new conditions they were deprived of the nutritious food they used to consume.[75]

To reach out to the adivasis even more, the state converted Keslapur Jatara into a Gond darbar in which the state heard and resolved Gonds' grievances. Keslapur village is 28 miles from Adilabad town. Gonds of the region assemble at Keslapur annually on the new moon of the Telugu month of Pushya (January) to worship Naga Shesha. On this day, all the revenue, forest, and police officials and village patels would come to Keslapur and organize a darbar with the Gonds to hear their concerns, and Gonds would also submit their presentations to the officials. Distribution of loans, land pattas, and positions would take place on this day. In one of these darbars, it is recorded that Grigson distributed forty-two sanads of appointment to new Gond patels.[76]

Under the Multi-purpose Tribal Block, various development schemes were initiated to improve agriculture, irrigation, land reclamation, soil conservation, health and rural sanitation, social education, communications, rural arts and crafts, cooperatives, and rural housing.[77] The development initiatives were no doubt started with enthusiasm to improve the standard of Gond life. However, they did not bring any significant change in adivasis' lives. Even what was achieved under Fürer-Haimendorf's guidance did not survive long. In his later works, Fürer-Haimendorf recounts:

> Many of the Gonds and Kolams who had been settled and provided with patta in the 1940s were once again deprived of their land. When in 1976

I began an intensive restudy of the Gonds of Utnur, I found a scene completely transformed by the presence of innumerable settlers, most of them emigrants from Maharashtra.... It is not quite clear what triggered this invasion, but local Gonds as well as officials tell of the long columns of bullock carts on which the immigrants carried household goods and grain stores, and of the herds of cattle which they brought with them. It seems that this movement of non-tribals into the tribal areas of Utnur reached its climax between 1965 and 1975, but even at the time of writing, i.e. 1980, it has not completely stopped.[78]

Thus, despite the energy and commitment with which it was pursued, the anthropological approach failed to resolve what governments thought of as 'the adivasi question'. I would add that this was mainly because at root, anthropological developmentalism was driven by its answerability to the state—be it the Nizam's state or the colonial state, or even the post-independence Indian state. It did not recognize the adivasi resistance as political, and did not respect the political rights of the adivasis. Adivasis were given land, but they were not given power to protect their land from the caste-Hindu peasants. As we have mentioned earlier, the dispossession of adivasis has continued even in postcolonial India, because adivasi development policies in independent India have been based on the philosophy of colonial anthropological developmentalism. Jawaharlal Nehru, the first prime minister of India, who is generally seen as the architect of 'Tribal Policy' in India (popularly termed 'Panchasheela'), was hugely influenced by Elwin's ecological Romanticism. While writing the foreword to Elwin's *A Philosophy for NEFA* (1957), Nehru proclaimed:

Verrier Elwin has done me the honour of saying that he is a missionary of my views on tribal affairs. As a matter of fact, I have learnt much from him, for he is both an expert on this subject with great experience and a friend of the tribal folk. I have little experience of tribal life and my own views, vague as they were, have developed under the impact of certain circumstances and of Verrier Elwin's own writings. It would, therefore, be more correct to say that I have learnt from him rather than that I have influenced him in any way.[79]

Nehru was clearly heavily indebted to Elwin, who was considered a champion of the adivasi cause. Elwin was also adviser on tribal affairs to the North-East Frontier Agency between 1954 and 1964 and worked hand in hand with Nehru.

It is said that the primary aim of Nehru's adivasi policy was that adivasis should be allowed to develop along the lines of their own genius, and external imposition should be avoided; that attempts should be made to protect their tradition and culture; that their rights in land and forests should be respected; that they should be allowed to administer themselves and that they should not be over-administered. The ultimate aim of any tribal-development project was to achieve quality of human character.[80] This policy came as a middle path against the two then existing dominant theories—the theory of isolation and the theory of assimilation. The first had its roots in Verrier Elwin's ecological Romanticism, whereas the second was rooted in G. S. Ghurye's Hindu nationalism.[81] However, in practice, this policy of integration was paradoxical and became willy-nilly converted into forced assimilation. This is evident from Nehru's inaugural address at the Third Tribal Welfare Conference held at Jagdalpur in March 1955. To quote him:

> After the achievement of Independence, the basic problem of India, taken as a whole, is one of integration and consolidation. Political integration is now complete but that is not enough. We must bring about changes much more basic and intimate than mere political integration.... All we can do is to nurture it and create conditions where it finds congenial soil. So, the greatest problem of India today is not so much political as psychological integration and consolidation.[82]

For Nehru, the adivasi question was a sociological, psychological, and developmental issue rather than a political one. From the beginning he held this position on the adivasis of India. He made this clear when intervening in the debate in the Constituent Assembly on the interim report of the Committee on Fundamental Rights. He said that adivasis were backward, through no fault of theirs. Protecting them from their rapacious neighbours and bringing advancement in their life would be the policy of any government of India.[83]

Outside the Constituent Assembly, there was a rather interesting debate in 1947 on the integration of adivasis between the adivasi leaders and Nehru. Nehru summoned Jaipal Singh, Ram Dayal Munda, and other adivasi leaders to Delhi. There was also serious debate over the issue of the secession of adivasis from the Indian union. Nehru and Patel were clear that they could not think of an India without tribes. Singh, who had trained at Cambridge, charged Nehru with failing to involve adivasis in the making of the Constitution. The Constitution ensured only welfare and development to adivasis, but not political rights. All that was promised to adivasis was laid down in the Directive Principles of State Policy, which is a non-justiciable part of the Constitution.[84]

The Directive Principles of State Policy assured the development of the adivasis. It is often difficult to distinguish the developmentalism that ensued from what goes by the name of welfarism or charity as a principle of the liberal democratic state. In other words, one has to read whatever the Indian state 'offered' to the adivasis as charity, not rights. It is only from the 1990s that the Indian government began to adopt a rights-based approach to development initiatives. A series of acts were passed by the government ensuring the rights of adivasis.[85] But by the time the acts were passed, everything had already slipped out of the adivasis' hands. Adivasi areas are no more in the control of adivasis themselves. Everything in the so-called Scheduled Areas is determined by caste-Hindus. This is partly because decision-making in the Indian democracy is done in a top–down manner, not in bottom–up mode. And those at the top do not have an insider's interests, an insider's feel, or an insider's investments in these rights. Although the self-determinism of adivasis is applauded inside and outside the Indian Constitution, in reality, adivasis hardly find a place in this schema. An important factor is that adivasi society is largely based on participatory democracy, but this was successfully replaced with representative democracy. The result was that those who emerged as adivasi leaders were mediocre people who were acceptable to the Indian government.[86] These practices have often resulted in unrest in adivasi areas. The Indravelli incident which took place in the forests of Adilabad district is one such unrest, which we shall dwell on further in the Postscript.

To conclude, the Gonds' resistance in Adilabad district first started with the movement against eviction from land and forest rights, suppression and exploitation, but gradually culminated in a political movement. The introduction of a political rationality by the colonial state became detrimental to the long-established autonomous life of the Gonds. The forest and hill tracts were gradually opened up for the exclusive use of both the state and non-adivasis. Land alienation, eviction, and exploitation by the state and non-adivasis pushed the Gonds into taking up arms against the state. The Nizam's government realized the danger of the resistance and crushed it effectively with its development agendas. A few non-adivasis came to the Gonds' rescue, but their role was dubious as they were not only exploiters of the Gonds but endeavoured to use the adivasi insurgent consciousness for their own political ends.

The Gond experience helps us to understand forms of adivasi struggle in new ways. Most studies stereotype adivasi struggles as sporadic, spontaneous, violent, unorganized, and apolitical. But the Gonds embraced arms only when all their modest attempts to convince the government of their long-established rights failed. One has to see the Gond insurgency as a counter-politics, and their violence as counter-violence, not violence. The intellectual history of the Gonds provides an ideological integrity to their politics, which was crucial in creating an insurgent consciousness among them. Their resistance was strongly rooted in the realization of Gond political sovereignty. It was an attempt to recover the lost sovereignty of their community, or, to put it simply, their 'freedom'.

The Hyderabad State responded to adivasi insurgency with a programme of anthropological developmentalism. In this endeavour, it deployed anthropologists to deal with the insurgent adivasis. The anthropologists came out with a number of studies on adivasis, which saw their sedentarization, backwardness, and poverty as inherent in the character of adivasi society. Sometimes they attributed the problem to the adivasis' social practices and drunkenness. To put it in other words, anthropologists perceived the adivasi question as a developmental issue, psychologized many political problems, and sought to equip the adivasis with modern instruments and ways of life. However, this did not take the adivasi question to its logical end, as the adivasi question is essentially political. Anthropological developmentalism could successfully downplay this fact for a while, but it resulted in the unrest that Indian forests and hills continue to witness to this day.

NOTES

1. Letter from Director General of Police to Home Member dated 14 September 1940, APSA, HD, Confidential File no. 15/PA/1349F (1940), f. 231.

2. Christoph von Fürer-Haimendorf, *Life among Indian Tribes: The Autobiography of an Anthropologist* (New Delhi: Oxford University Press, 1990), pp. 1–23.

3. For example, see A. R. Desai (ed.), *Peasant Struggles in India* (Delhi): Oxford University Press, 1979).

4. D. N. Dhanagare, 'Subaltern Consciousness and Populism: Two Approaches in the Study of Social Movements in India', *Social Scientist* 16, no. 11 (November 1988): 18–35.

5. Ranajit Guha, 'On Some Aspects of the Historiography of Colonial India', in *Subaltern Studies I: Writings on South Asian History and Society*, edited by Ranajit Guha (New Delhi: Oxford University Press, 1994), pp. 1–8.

6. Ranajit Guha, *Elementary Aspects of Peasant Insurgency in Colonial India* (New Delhi: Oxford University Press, 1983), pp. 167–219.

7. Alpa Shah, 'Religion and the Secular Left: Subaltern Studies, Birsa Munda and Maoists', available at: http://aotcpress.com/author/alpa-shah/ (accessed 13 January 2014), p. 3.

8. Christoph von Fürer-Haimendorf, *Tribal Hyderabad: Four Reports* (Hyderabad: Revenue Department, Government of H.E.H. the Nizam, 1945) p. 65.

9. Bhangya Bhukya, *Subjugated Nomads: The Lambadas under the Rule of the Nizams* (New Delhi: Orient BlackSwan, 2010), p. 238.

10. Guha, *Elementary Aspects of Peasant Insurgency*, p. 8.

11. Fürer-Haimendorf, *Tribal Hyderabad*, pp. 116–18.

12. Sahu and Allam Rajaiah, *Komaram Bhim* (Telugu) (Hyderabad: Revolutionary Writers Association, 1993), pp. 20–60; Fürer-Haimendorf, *Tribal Hyderabad*, p. 123.

13. Letter from First Talukdar of Asifabad to Director General of Revenue dated 26 December 1349F, APSA, HD, Confidential File no. 15/PA/1349F (1940), f. 124.

14. Letter from First Talukdar of Asifabad to Director General of Revenue, 26 December 1349F, f. 125.

15. Fürer-Haimendorf, *Tribal Hyderabad*, p. 123.

16. Fürer-Haimendorf, *Tribal Hyderabad*, p. 124.

17. Fürer-Haimendorf, *Tribal Hyderabad*, p. 125.

18. Sahu and Rajaiah, *Komaram Bhim*, p. iii.

19. The twelve villages were Jodeghat, Pafnapur, Bhabijhery, Murikiloka, Nassapur, Kallegam, Chelbaradi, Toikan Movadam, Bhiman Gondi, Ankusapur, Demiguda, and Gogin Movadamz. Sahu and Rajaiah, *Kumaram Bhim*, p. 169.

20. Fürer-Haimendorf, *Tribal Hyderabad*, p. 125.

21. Letter from First Talukdar of Asafabad to the Secretary to Government, Judicial, Police and General Dept., dated 6 February 1350F, APSA, HD, Confidential File no. 15/PA/1349F (1940), f. 133.

22. I am told by Laxmana Rao of Modi that the Gond chiefs used to possess a considerable number of guns, and when Bhimu organized a fauj against the Nizam, they voluntarily offered the weapons to him.

23. Letter from First Talukdar of Asafabad to the Secretary to Government, Judicial, Police and General Dept., dated 6 February 1350F., APSA, HD, Confidential File no. 15/PA/1349F (1940), ff. 135–8; also see Sahu and Rajaiah, *Komaram Bhim*, pp. 179–88.

24. Letter from Director General of Police to Home Member dated 14 September 1940, APSA, HD, Confidential File no. 15/PA/1349F (1940), ff. 229–30.

25. Fact Finding Report by Kasinathrao Vaidya and others submitted to the Nizam's Government dated 11 October 1940, APSA, HD, Confidential File no. 15/PA/1349F (1940), ff. 102–4.

26. Letter from Director General of Police to Home Member dated 14 September 1940, APSA, HD, Confidential File no. 15/PA/1349F (1940), ff. 230–1.

27. APSA, HD, Confidential File no. 15/PA/1349F (1940), f. 195.

28. APSA, HD, Confidential File no. 15/PA/1349F (1940), ff. 13–15.

29. APSA, HD, Confidential File no. 15/PA/1349F (1940), f. 119.

30. APSA, HD, Confidential File no. 15/PA/1349F (1940), ff. 115–17.

31. APSA, HD, Confidential File no. 15/PA/1349F (1940), ff. 129–39.

32. The vakil's name was Ramchander Rao Paika. Atram Laxmana Rao shared this information with me during my fieldwork in Adilabad on 24 January 2015.

33. Fürer-Haimendorf, *Tribal Hyderabad*, p. 126.

34. APSA, HD, Confidential File no. 15/PA/1349F (1940), ff. 108–10.

35. Bhukya, *Subjugated Nomads*, p. 223.

36. G. S. Gupta, ' Gonduwari Avedana', *Golkonda Patrika*, 3 July 1941 and 7 July 1941.

37. APSA, HD, Confidential File no. 15/PA/1349F (1940), f. 145.

38. APSA, HD, Confidential File no. 15/PA/1349F (1940), f. 142.

39. APSA, HD, Confidential File no. 15/PA/1349F (1940), f. 25.

40. Fürer-Haimendorf, *Tribal Hyderabad*, p. 125.

41. Guha, *Elementary Aspects of Peasant Insurgency*, pp. 266–7.

42. K. S. Singh (ed.), *Tribal Movements in India* (New Delhi: Manohar, 1982–3), vol. 2, p. xi.

43. Fürer-Haimendorf, *Tribal Hyderabad*, p. 125.

44. Anthropology was taught in Calcutta, Patna, Benares, Lucknow, Madras, Bombay, Mysore, and at Osmania University by the late 1930s. See W. V. Grigson, *The Challenge of Backwardness* (Hyderabad-Deccan: Government Press, 1947), p. 87.

45. Grigson, *The Challenge of Backwardness*, pp. 88–90.

46. Fürer-Haimendorf, *Life among Indian Tribes*, p. 93.

47. Verrier Elwin, *Maria Murder and Suicide* (London, 1943), see Preface.

48. Fürer-Haimendorf, *Tribal Hyderabad*, see Foreword.

49. Grigson, *The Challenge of Backwardness*, see Preface.

50. Fürer-Haimendorf, *Life among Indian Tribes*, pp. 5–6, 24.

51. Fürer-Haimendorf, *Life among Indian Tribes*, p. 40.

52. Grigson, *The Aboriginal Problem*, pp. 300–5.

53. Christoph von Fürer-Haimendorf, *The Raj Gonds of Adilabad: A Peasant Culture of the Deccan* (London: Macmillan, 1948), p. 83.

54. Fürer-Haimendorf, *The Raj Gonds of Adilabad*, p. 34.

55. Fürer-Haimendorf, *The Raj Gonds of Adilabad*, p. 40.

56. Grigson, *The Aboriginal Problem*, p. 313.

57. This may be because Hyderabad provided him shelter during the war period, as he was not allowed in the British Empire having unintentionally become a German subject when Hitler occupied Austria during World War II. He happened to meet Sir Theodore Tasker, then the revenue and home minister in the Nizam's government, at an Anthropological Congress in Copenhagen, and Tasker invited him to Hyderabad. Fürer-Haimendorf sheltered in Hyderabad till he could prove himself to be a harmless ex-Austrian. See Fürer-Haimendorf, *Life among Indian Tribes*, p. 22.

58. Gupta, 'Gonduwari Avedana', 3 July 1941; also see Fürer-Haimendorf, *Life among Indian Tribes*, pp. 69–72.

59. In my recent (June 2014) field trip I found people still remembering Fürer-Haimendorf's help in getting land and settling disputes with forest jawans. I saw pictures of Fürer-Haimendorf hung on the walls of many houses in the adivasi areas of Adilabad.

60. Fürer-Haimendorf, *Tribal Hyderabad*, p. xii.

61. A list of suggestions were included at the end of the reports; see Fürer-Haimendorf, *Tribal Hyderabad*, pp. 141–54.

62. Fürer-Haimendorf, *Tribal Hyderabad*, p. 74.

63. Fürer-Haimendorf, *Tribal Hyderabad*, p. 81.

64. Fürer-Haimendorf, *Tribal Hyderabad*, pp. 89–92.

160   THE ROOTS OF THE PERIPHERY

65. A total of seven textbooks were published, namely *Gondi Reading Chart for Adults No 1, 2 and 3; Gondi Primer, First Reader for Adults; First Reader for Children*; and *The Myth of Manke*. See *Social Service among the Tribes and Backward Class in Hyderabad* (Hyderabad: Government Press, 1951), p. 29.

66. *Social Service among the Tribes and Backward Class in Hyderabad*, pp. 28–36.

67. *Census of India 1961*, vol. II: *Andhra Pradesh*, Part V B(I): *Ethnographic Notes, A Monograph on Gonds* (Hyderabad: Director of Census Operation, A.P.), p. 32.

68. *Census of India 1961, A Monograph on Gonds*, p. 13.

69. Fürer-Haimendorf, *Life among Indian Tribes*, pp. 26–7; Grigson, *The Challenge of Backwardness*, p. 40.

70. The areas notified as Scheduled Tribal Areas include the whole of Utnur taluk, 72 villages in Adilabad taluk, 74 villages in Kinwat taluk, 46 villages in Both taluk, 87 villages in Asifabad taluk, 18 villages in Lakshetipet taluk, 58 villages in Rajura taluk, and 29 villages in Sirpur taluk. See Fürer-Haimendorf, *Life among Indian Tribes*, p. 126.

71. *Social Service among the Tribes and Backward Class in Hyderabad*, p. 29.

72. *Social Service among the Tribes and Backward Class in Hyderabad*, pp. 30–2; Grigson, *The Challenge of Backwardness*, p. 45.

73. *Social Service among the Tribes and Backward Class in Hyderabad*, p. 33.

74. Grigson, *The Challenge of Backwardness*, pp. 41–5.

75. For a much broader debate, see David Hardiman, *Missionaries and Their Medicine: A Christian Modernity for Tribal India* (Manchester: Manchester University Press, 2008).

76. *Social Service among the Tribes and Backward Class in Hyderabad*, p. 34: also see Grigson, *The Challenge of Backwardness*, p. 41.

77. *Census of India 1961, A Monograph on Gonds*, p. 33.

78. Christoph von Fürer-Haimendorf, *Tribes of India: The Struggle for Survival* (New Delhi: Oxford University Press, 1989), p. 58.

79. K. S. Singh (ed.), *Jawaharlal Nehru, Tribes and Tribal Policy* (Calcutta: Anthropological Survey of India, 1989), p. 136.

80. Singh, *Jawaharlal Nehru, Tribes and Tribal Policy*, pp. 3–4.

81. Ghurye argued for assimilation of the adivasis into the mainstream society. He held that the adivasis of India were Hindus for the simple reason that they were born on Indian soil, worshipped Hindu gods, and spoke the same regional languages as caste-Hindus. He also strongly opposed the enumeration of tribals in the census under the separate category of 'animists'. He described them as 'backward Hindus'. See G. S. Ghurye, *The Scheduled Tribes* (Bombay: Popular Prakashan, 1959), pp. 7–12.

82. Singh, *Jawaharlal Nehru, Tribes and Tribal Policy*, p. 133.

83. Singh, *Jawaharlal Nehru, Tribes and Tribal Policy*, p. 56.

84. Shiv Visvanathan, 'The Tribal World and the Imagination of the Future', Verrier Elwin Memorial Lecture, Vadodara, 11 April 2006, published by the Bhasha Research Centre, Baroda, pp. 1–13.

85. The Government recently enacted the Panchayats (Extension to Scheduled Areas) Act of 1996, the Forest Right Act of 2006, the Right to Education Act of 2009, National Food Security Act of 2013, and so on.

86. Apoorv Kurup, 'Tribal Law in India: How Decentralised Administration Is Extinguishing Tribal Rights and Why Autonomous Tribal Governments Are Better', *Indigenous Law Journal* 7, no. 1 (2008): 87–126.

POSTSCRIPT
INSURGENCY REVISITED

ON 20 APRIL 1981, ACCORDING to the government, thirteen insurgent Gonds were killed in a massacre in Indravelli village 35 kilometres from Adilabad district.[1] On this day, the Girijana Rythu Coolie Sangam (Tribal Farmers and Labourers Union) of Adilabad district had planned to organize a public meeting. The government denied permission, saying that on the same day non-adivasis had also planned a meeting in the village, and this would lead to tension between the groups and cause a law and order issue. The non-adivasis were also told by the police to cancel their meeting and they did so. However, the Sangam continued with its preparations for the meeting. The Girijana Rythu Coolie Sangam was a civil platform of the Communist Party of India (Marxist–Leninist) (CPI[ML]) (the People's War Group [PWG] led by Kondapalli Seetharamaiah), and had been set up to work among and organize adivasis.

This was also the day for the *angadi* (weekly market) in the village, where adivasis came to buy their weekly provisions. Despite the police ban on the meeting and imposition of Section 144 (of the Criminal Procedure Code [CrPC]) in the village, about 5,000 Gonds turned up for the meeting. It is said that a scuffle between the police and the Gonds turned violent when a Gond woman snatched a bayonet from a police-man and stabbed him to death. This led the police to fire indiscrimi-nately at the Gond crowd. A large number of Gonds were killed. The number of deaths is still being disputed. T. Anjaiah (Reddy), then the chief minister of Andhra Pradesh, and Prabhakar Reddy, home minister of the state, attributed the incident to provocation by the Kondapalli Seetharamaiah Naxalite group. The government also described the inci-dent as a confrontation between adivasis and non-adivasis, and not as one against the government or state.[2]

Fact-finding reports by human right forums such as the Andhra Pradesh Civil Liberties Committee (APCLC) and the People's Union for Democratic Rights (PUDR), New Delhi, visited Indravelli and exposed the actual facts of the incident. According to these reports, police high-handedness towards the adivasis turned into violence and a massacre. Gonds and other adivasis had headed for Indravelli, starting out early in the morning on foot and in vehicles from villages of Adilabad and from Chandrapur district. But they were stopped on the outskirts, chased with lathis, beaten up, and sent back. Many Gonds were not aware of the imposition of Section 144 CrPC, and could not understand why they were not being allowed to enter the village. So despite the police barriers, the Gonds continued to enter the village. Police began by firing tear gas, but soon began firing at the Gonds without any warning. Some policemen took up positions on the tops of trees and fired, while others indiscriminately fired at the crowd from open trucks. The firing contin-ued for several minutes till the people ran away. About 100 people died, and of those who survived many had serious injuries. Bodies continued to be recovered for almost for one week from tanks, wells, rivulets, and bushes where they had been dumped. The police carried away the dead and the wounded in trucks. Importantly, the bodies were not handed over to the families but were burnt in a mass cremation by the police. This was seriously against Gond tradition. Gonds bury their dead. The Gonds continued to be harassed and arrested for several months.[3] Of course, harassment by police, revenue, and janglat officials is a regular affair in Gond life.

The Indravelli insurgency brings Bhimu's Jodeghat insurgency to memory. The way the incident was handled by the Andhra Pradesh government was not very different from the Nizam's government's handling of the Jodeghat issue. In many senses, it was a continuation of an established pattern of government response to Gond resistance. Although the land question was salient in the Indravelli resistance, it was Bhimu's spirit of self-rule that provided it with ideological inspiration. We will return to this aspect later on. Let us first discuss how the failure of anthropological developmentalism paved the road for the Indravelli resistance.

The merger of Hyderabad State with the Indian union in September 1948 after what was called a 'police action', and the subsequent merger of the Telangana region of this state with the newly formed state of Andhra Pradesh in 1956, worsened the condition of the Gonds. Adilabad district falls in the Telangana region. Telangana witnessed a difficult time between 1946 and 1956. First there was the impact of the communist-inspired armed struggle, police action by the Indian state, the region's merger with the Indian union, and finally its separation from Hyderabad State and merger into Andhra Pradesh. This, to some extent, disturbed the process of anthropological developmentalism initiated by Fürer-Haimendorf. In fact, these developments, in particular the assignment of Telangana to Andhra Pradesh, opened up the adivasi areas in general for what can only be called naked exploitation, extraction, and eviction of adivasis.

After the formation of Andhra Pradesh, a large number of land-hungry non-adivasis began migrating to Adilabad from the Andhra districts, from Karimnagar and Warangal districts of Telangana, and from Chandrapur and Yeotmal districts in Maharashtra since the so-called 'protective acts' were almost inactive in the region.[4] As mentioned above, the turbulent conditions prevailing turned advantageous for the caste-Hindus who were seeking land. Although the Tribal Land Alienation Act existed in Telangana, it had never been implemented. In addition, confusion prevailed about whether or not this act was in force after the merger of Telangana with Andhra Pradesh. After the formation of the new state, the governor re-promulgated the Scheduled Areas Land Transfer Act of 1917 as the Andhra Pradesh Scheduled Area Land Transfer Regulation I of 1959, but it was originally made applicable to the Andhra Agency area, and only later extended to the Telangana

Agency by Regulation II of 1963. This meant there was no legal protection for adivasi land from 1946 right up to 1963. Taking advantage of the situation, dominant peasant castes and other castes/communities such as Velmas, Reddys, Kammas, Kumbis, Lambadas, Marwaris, Komatis, and Muslims grabbed huge tracts of land in the Adilabad forests and hills.[5] In fact, Gonds have a different conflict with the Lambadas, a nomadic tribe who settled down in the region as agriculturists from the middle of the nineteenth century. The Lambadas were assigned Scheduled Tribe status in 1976. Earlier they had been listed as Denotified Tribes. This made it possible for Lambadas from neighbouring areas, particularly from the Maratha region, to migrate into the district. The Lambadas, who were historically caravan traders and foodgrain transporters and were relatively more 'advanced', began buying Gond land and cornering the lion's share in government development initiatives. A considerable amount of Gond land was transferred to the Lambadas through sale and moneylending, as there was no protection against such transfer of lands—from tribe to tribe—under the Scheduled Area Land Transfer Act.[6]

As mentioned previously, the existence of the Scheduled Area Land Transfer Act in the region itself was in question. This became a boon to many dominant-caste peasants who bought huge tracts of lands and settled down as absentee landlords. Michael Yorke, who visited the Adilabad Agency in 1976–8, gives a detailed account of how the district, once largely inhabited by Gonds, fell into the hands of Velma and Reddy peasants. Indeed, the Velma immigrants led a chain of land grabbing. Velmas who had grabbed huge tracts in the region before independence had settled in urban centres and functioned as absentee landlords. They brought other Velmas to the district and planted them in the villages. These Velmas settled down as local landlords, grabbing Gond lands by force and using their connections with the absentee Velma landlords and government officials. They brought other service castes into the villages and gradually ousted Gonds from their hamlets. In 1929, Tilani village of Asifabad was a small tribal hamlet in the forest. By 1976, it had been transformed into a purely caste-Hindu village with 580 households. The local landlord (*chinna dora* or small landlord) operated in an area dominated by the political control of their distant cousins (*pedda dora* or big landlord), and their control was limited to the villages in which they lived. The pedda dora still had control over Gond hamlets and visited these occasionally. As the caste-Hindus took over their land, the adivasis moved deeper into the forests.[7] This exemplifies a pre-independence phenomenon in the forests and hills where non-adivasis evicted adivasis from their land and the adivasis moved deeper into the forest after losing their land.

A village study by M. Kodanda Ram shows how immigration in forest and hill villages increased abnormally in the early decades of the new state of Andhra Pradesh. In 1961, the total population of Jainoor, a remote hamlet in Utnur taluk, was 270 (of which 225 were adivasis and 45 were non-adivasis). This rose to 2,145 (of whom 485 were adivasis and 1,660 were non-adivasis) by 1991. By the 1980s, this village had been transformed into a trading centre, facilitating non-adivasi activities.[8] Exploitation of the adivasis by sahukars and moneylenders became more ruthless than before. Like the colonial state, the postcolonial state also encouraged non-adivasis to settle in the forest and hills areas in order to bring forest land under cultivation. Andhra peasants occupied the most valuable black-soil lands along the riverbanks of the Godavari, ousting the Gonds from lands that they had lived in and cultivated for as long as anyone could remember.[9]

Adivasis were thus prey to dominant caste-peasants till the 1969 adivasi revolt of Srikakulam district, which was mainly supported by Naxalite groups. This revolt shook the government. After the revolt, the government promulgated the Andhra Pradesh Scheduled Area Land Transfer (Amendment) Regulation I of 1970, which strictly banned land transfer from adivasis to non-adivasis in the notified areas or Agency Areas. The significance of this regulation is that it lays the burden of proof of the deed on the non-adivasi. However, it failed to protect adivasi lands as the adivasis had no power to implement the act; they could only demand its implementation.[10] Importantly, the Andhra Pradesh government passed an order in 1972 declaring all occupation of forest land subsequent to 1964 illegal. This applied to both adivasis and non-adivasis. With this order, all the lands held by non-adivasis in Agency Areas before 1964 became legally possessed land. In addition, Chenna Reddy, the then chief minister of Andhra Pradesh, issued a government order in 1979 exempting up to 5 acres of wet land and 10 acres of dry land owned by lower-caste non-adivasi owners from the regulation. These new rules of the government went gravely against the adivasis.[11] The implementation of this regulation was also in question. Only a very low percentage of Land Transfer Regulation (LTR) cases had gone in favour of adivasis, as they could not manage to produce the paperwork for the claimed lands. By 1988, there were 5,001 LTR cases in Adilabad district, of which 2,858 were settled in favour of adivasis and 2,243 cases remained pending for several years without any final judgement, simply to favour non-adivasis.[12]

The dominant caste-Hindus established complete control over the region, not only by grabbing huge tracts of land but also through taking over contracts for liquor supply, tendu leaves, and other minor forest resources. They also emerged as politically powerful in the forest areas. Some of them even managed to become presidents of tribal development blocks.[13] The exploitation by liquor and tendu-leaf contractors was limitless. Although Girijana cooperative societies existed in the district, they hardly functioned. Adivasis continued to depend on the exchange of goods with the sahukars who visited their hamlets on bullock carts or sometimes on foot. There are many stories about these exchanges. Among the more exotic stories is that of the exchange of a basket of tamarind for a packet of cigarettes.[14]

Lucrative government contracts for development initiatives were also snatched up by dominant caste-Hindu contractors. Particularly after 1970, the Indian government focused on the development of backward rural areas. A special agency called the Integrated Tribal Development Agency (ITDA) was set up to develop adivasi areas through block-development offices. The Planning Commission of India allotted Rs 455.3 million in 1976 for adivasi development in Adilabad district. The overall expenditure in the district for adivasi development between 1974 and 1977 was Rs 741.2 million. The estimated expenditure for the district for 1977–8 alone was Rs 2,788 million.[15] However, the *Economic and Political Weekly* correspondent who visited Adilabad district after the Indravelli resistance reported that 'in more than a dozen villages visited by this correspondent there was little evidence of the lakhs of rupees spent on "development" programmes for tribal uplift'.[16] As discussed in the last chapter, this is partly because of the top–down approach.

Above all, the dominant caste-Hindus who generally took up contracts for all development programmes in the Agency Areas spent very little and retained a large share for themselves. This inevitably happened in collaboration with government officials, who were again often caste-Hindus.

Extraction of money by forest and revenue officials worsened in the districts after independence. On the other hand, development initiatives such as the joint forest-management policy that aimed to involve adivasis in forest development turned against the adivasis when the Forest Department took away land that adivasis were cultivating in the reserved forest. From the late 1970s, with the help of Naxalite groups, adivasis cleared land in the reserved forest and brought it under cultivation. In 1979, the Forest Department ousted adivasis from these lands, saying that the lands were earmarked for regeneration or plantation under the joint forestry scheme. This drove adivasis further towards insurgency.[17]

The Indravelli incident was rooted in an insurgent consciousness that was clearly influenced by CPI(ML) or Naxalite politics. After the Srikakulam revolt of 1969, the Naxalite movement gradually spread in Adilabad and Chandrapur districts, particularly from 1974. The Chandra Pulla Reddy group initially organized the Gonds in Adilabad, but these organizations were suppressed during the Emergency (1975–7). Later, Naxalite activities gained momentum in the district with the spread of the Radical Youth League and Radical Students Union of the PWG led by Kondapalli Seetharamaiah. There is a story about how this group spread in Gond villages. Dasari Lakshmikantham, an activist of the Kondapalli Seetharamaiah group, entered Gond villages in 1972 as a tobacco seller. He sometimes travelled on a bicycle, sometimes on foot. Beside selling tobacco, he educated the Gonds on their rights over the forest and land and their exploitation by non-adivasis. Soon he gained the confidence of the Gonds and was called Porkala Dora (Lord of the Bushes) by them. He organized the Gonds mainly against the moneylenders.[18] Above all, he was crucial in moulding Gond aspirations into the framework of the Naxalite movement. He led the Gond march to Wankede. Wankede is a border village on the eastern side of Adilabad, famous for its weekly market which is visited by all sahukars from Adilabad and Chandrapur districts. Porkala Dora organized a march with 100 bullock carts to Wankede on market day with a plan to attack the sahukars, destroy all the promissory notes submitted by the Gonds, and get back Gond items deposited with them as security for the loans. But the police got wind of this plan and pounced on the Gonds, saying that they had come to the market to attack the shops of the sahukars. Porkala Dora and many others were arrested and put in jail.[19]

From 1977, the PWG became more active in the district with the formation of the Girijana Rythu Coolie Sangam. Under this banner, Gonds were organized in a big way. Initially, the movement was confined to Asifabad and Lakshetipet taluks, but it later spread to Sirpur, Utnur, Khanapur, and Chennur taluks of Adilabad district and Sironcha and Gadchiroli taluks of Chandrapur district. Under the banner of the Sangam, movements were waged against the tendu-leaf contractors, forest contractors, moneylenders, and dominant caste-Hindu land grabbers. Government officials, particularly the Girijana cooperative society, were also targeted by the agitating Gonds. There was severe suppression of the Gonds by the state and about 600 Gonds were arrested in various cases. Police camps were set up in twelve villages and armed forces were increased in twelve other police stations.[20]

Despite the severe suppression, Gonds occupied lands in the forest and reclaimed land from dominant caste-peasants. Land occupation by Gonds began in Adilabad when Gonds in Pipaldari village (Utnur taluk) occupied 100 acres of land, clearing a forest earmarked for regeneration or plantation. Inspired by this action, the Gonds of Thummagudam occupied 500 acres of forest land. The Gonds of Marriguda, Veligi, Kapuguda, Naugaom, and Linuguda of Asifabad taluk occupied about 150 acres of land held by landlords. Many Gond villages followed this trend. Raids on sahukars' houses to loot provisions and destroy debt papers were also part of the Sangam activities. By the end of the 1980s, the total land occupied by Gonds, according to the Revenue Department, was 15,000 acres; according to the Forest Department, 30,000 acres; and according to the Girijana Rythu Coolie Sangam, 80,000 acres. The movement that began with these land occupations gradually culminated in the Indravelli incident.[21]

The sovereign past of the Gond community and their historical attempts to recover it has been the foundation for all their modern politics. The spirit of self-rule or the idea of a Gond Raj put forward by Bhimu was told and retold among the Gonds by the cultural wing of the PWG. Songs, poetry, and short essays on Bhimu were produced by the PWG. Their cultural wing performed programmes at night in the villages. The Radical Student Union (RSU), the student wing of the PWG, took the politics of insurgency to the Gonds under a programme called 'Return to the Village'. They revolutionized adivasi politics besides educating them on day-to-day issues.[22] It is recorded in *Srujana*, the monthly magazine and mouthpiece of PWG politics, that 'the Party helped Gonds to realise the legacy of Kumaram Bhimu's revolt. The Gonds' revolt of Bhabijeri, Jodenghat, Gondgudam, and Maywada between 1940 and 1945 against despotic Nizam rule and exploitation was recalled and brought alive in the minds of Gonds through a several cultural programs'.[23]

K. Balagopal, a human-rights activist, makes an interesting observation about Gond politics in post-independence India. He writes that 'Shifting cultivation and mahua—archetypal themes in journalistic discussions of the "tribal problem"—are no longer issues of much moment with them. Shifting cultivation is confined to the hilly slopes deep inside the forest, and the mahua is an occasional tree that stands out in lonely splendour on the deforested plains.'[24] This shows that shifting cultivation and minor forest-resource collection were not central in the Indravelli insurgency. This is not to suggest that adivasi insurgencies in colonial India were centred on shifting cultivation and mahua flowers or brew. They were never a central issue at any given time; the question of self-rule was a cardinal concern in all adivasi resistances and insurgencies.

After the Indravelli incident, the government began paying serious attention to the development of adivasis in order to stop them supporting Naxalites. It adopted a two-pronged attitude—the levying of cess and addressing the adivasi land and forest question on the one hand, and suppressing the influence of Naxalite supporters and sympathizers on the other hand. The ITDA office which had been operating from Adilabad since its inception was moved to Utnur, which is located in the heart of the adivasi area of Adilabad district.

However, after the Indravelli incident, educated Gond youth played a crucial role in re-establishing their land rights. They formed an organization called the Raj Gond Students' Union (RGSU) under the leadership of Thodasam Chandu, a medical graduate. They organized a major meeting in 1983 in Utnur and in many other villages. They traced the patta and *pahani* (paper deeds) details of lands grabbed from them by non-adivasis and educated their brethren on these issues. When the adivasis began asserting their land rights with the help of their educated youth, the non-adivasis tried to suppress the youth with the help of the police, accusing them of being Maoists. Due to this accusation, students studying in tribal-welfare hostels in towns were not allowed to visit their houses. Their houses were raided and their parents were harassed and tortured for information. Their organization, the RGSU, was regarded as connected with the RSU, the student wing of the Maoist PWG. To escape from this, they changed their organization's name to the Gondwana Sangarshana Samiti (GSS) in 1984. They identified 200,000 acres of grabbed land in the Adilabad district agency and demanded that the authorities settle that land. They were successful in some of the cases, but, as state functionaries always sided with non-adivasis, they could not recover all the lands lost by their parents and forefathers.

The GSS also took up the forest question. *Intipatti, mekapatti, pandiripatti, nagali patti, kancha patti,* and all kinds of forest taxes were being collected by forest jawans, although all these had been abolished by the government after independence. The GSS campaigned against these taxes and asked adivasis to stop paying them. The forest jawans generally visited the adivasi gudams once a year and collected chickens, goats, and grain from the adivasis. On the instructions of the GSS, the adivasis stopped paying these forest 'taxes'. The jawans drove away 1,000 goats from one gudam, and cases were booked against the adivasis on the ground that goat-grazing in forests was harmful to the forest. A legal fight was taken up by the GSS and ultimately they and their goats were released. This case made the adivasis aware that forest taxes had been abolished long ago, and there was no need to pay the jawans.

After this, the GSS took up the issue of adivasi self-rule in the villages. They revived their old *raisabha*s (village councils) which were founded on the philosophy of participatory democracy that ensures the participation of every member in the deliberation of the council. These sabhas still existed here and there, but were confined to cultural and religious matters only. The sabhas now asserted their lost political power and began acting as village councils, discharging all duties at the village level. All the decisions of the village were taken by the council. In a sense, the Gonds began running a parallel government in the villages. This was not tolerated by either the Maoists or the government, since neither liked the adivasis acting autonomously. The Maoists used adivasi areas as their guerrilla zone, but failed to build a class struggle as an adivasi movement.[25] Although the government attempted to suppress this development, the practice became prevalent in the Fifth Schedule areas where there was no village council, as in the Sixth Schedule areas. The new Panchayati Raj Act was introduced in 1993. Initially the Act did not promise village councils in Agency Areas. But the GSS took up a legal fight and stopped elections in the Fifth Schedule areas. At last the Act was modified in 1996 (as the PESA Act) and extended to Fifth Schedule areas.

With this, village sabhas were established, but they replaced participatory democracy with representative democracy that downplayed the adivasi spirit of self-rule. In many cases, non-adivasis became the deciding factor in the elections of the village sabhas. The decision of the sabha is largely influenced by non-adivasis, since their population now constitutes more than 60 per cent in the Scheduled Areas. Adivasis have no option but to accept the rule of the Indian government. In the process, adivasis who were once independent cultivators were forced to become mere agricultural labourers.[26]

Thus, the failure of anthropological developmentalism resulted in the outbreak of a violent revolt in independent India. In a nutshell, the problem with the anthropological construction of adivasis is that it treats adivasi societies as ecological or cultural groupings viewed through an evolutionist lens, never as a political society, or as having a political identity. That is to say, the bone of contention between the state and adivasi society or a self-governing society is not poverty, but politics—a politics of self-governance and a politics of self-determinism. Naxalite parties successfully blended adivasi grievances and aspirations within their politics and endeavoured to organize a peasant revolution. In this endeavour, Naxalites used the adivasis' sovereign past and their intellectual history to revolutionize them. Although the Naxalite movement took a different direction, the adivasis continued to raise their voice for self-rule.

Importantly, the way the postcolonial state has treated the adivasis is inhuman, sometimes worse than the colonial state. The state has always treated the adivasi question as a Naxalite problem and tried to handle it with armed force, but has never tried to listen to the voice of the adivasis, the voice for self-rule. The tallest memorial monument to the Indravelli incident and its commemoration every year on 20 April is still a matter of antagonistic concern to both the adivasis and the state.

NOTES

1. There was a dispute over the number of deaths. The state government claimed that only 13 Gonds were killed in the incident, but the CPI(ML) claimed that there were 60 deaths. Some newspapers reported that the toll was about 100.
2. *Vishalandhra* (daily newspaper), 21 April 1981, p. 1; also see *Vishalandhra* of 24 April 1981, which carried an editorial write-up.
3. The APCLC fact-finding report has been published in Christoph von Fürer-Haimendorf, *Tribes of India: The Struggle for Survival* (New Delhi: Oxford University Press, 1989), pp. 323–6; the PUDR fact-finding report was published in *Srujana* (a Telugu literary monthly journal), no. 15/116, May–June 1981, pp. 88–97.
4. B. Janardhan Rao and T. Yadagiri Rao, 'Land Transfers, Restoration in Tribal Andhra Pradesh: Justice Delayed and Denied', in *Scheduled Tribes and Social Justice* (Secunderabad: A.P. Judicial Academy, 1996), pp. 340–60; also see Michael Yorke, 'The Situation of the Gonds of Asifabad and Lakshetipet Taluks, Adilabad District', in Christoph von Fürer-Haimendorf, *Tribes of India: The Struggle for Survival* (New Delhi: Oxford University Press, 1989), pp. 203–49.
5. M. Raghuram, 'Carnage at Indravelli: A Report', *Economic and Political Weekly* 16, no. 24 (13 June 1981): 1047–50; Jaswanth Rao, 'Tribal Struggle against Land Alienation', *Economic and Political Weekly* 33, no. 31 (17– 23 January 1998): 81.
6. Fürer-Haimendorf, *Tribes of India*, p. 62.
7. Yorke, 'The Situation of the Gonds', p. 207.
8. M. Kodanda Ram, 'Retrogression in the Tribal Belt: Bhurnur in Adilabad District', *Kakatiya University Journal of Social Sciences* 3, no. 1 (January–June 2007): 1–18, see p. 15.
9. Rao and Rao, 'Land Transfers, Restoration in Tribal Andhra Pradesh', p. 348.

10. Rao, 'Tribal Struggle against Land Alienation', p. 81.

11. 'Another Massacre of Tribals' Special Report, *Economic and Political Weekly* 16, no. 18 (2 May 1981): 796–7.

12. Rao and Rao, 'Land Transfers, Restoration in Tribal Andhra Pradesh', p. 350.

13. Yorke, 'The Situation of the Gonds', pp. 235–42.

14. V. G., 'Tendu Leaf Labourers in Telangana: Working Conditions and Struggle', *Economic and Political Weekly* 19, no. 46 (17 November 1984): 1941–3; also see K. B., 'Indravelli 1985', *Economic and Political Weekly* 20, no. 21 (25 May 1985): 906–7.

15. Yorke, 'The Situation of the Gonds', p. 231.

16. Raghuram, 'Carnage at Indravelli', p. 1050.

17. *Srujana*, May–June 1981, pp. 92–5.

18. Raghuram, 'Carnage at Indravelli', p. 1049.

19. *Srujana*, May–June 1981, p. 75.

20. Discussion with Professor Murali Manohar Rao of Kakatiya University, member of the Fact-Finding Committee of the PUDR on the Indravelli incident, 14 January 2015; also see his full report in *Srujana*, May–June 1981, pp. 88–97.

21. C. Sivaramkrishna Rao, K. Murali Manohar, K. Seetaram Rao, and B. Janardhan Rao, 'Report of the Project on Political Economy of Tribal Development in Andhra Pradesh', Unpublished report, Indian Council of Social Science Research, New Delhi, 1988, pp. 157–60; *Srujana*, May–June 1981, pp. 75–92. The correspondent of the *Economic and Political Weekly* reported that the total land occupied by Gonds and other poor peasants at the time of the Indravelli incident was 80,000 acres. See 'Another Massacre of Tribals', p. 797.

22. A four-page pamphlet published by RSU and the Radical Youth Union on 23 April 1981 explains how the sovereign past of the Gonds was helpful in radicalizing the Gonds. Indeed, there was a discussion in the Indian Parliament on this pamphlet. For the full text, see *Ragal Janda Intha Arupematani Adugu, Girijanula Rakthamtho Thadisenani Cheppali*, Girijana Rythu Coolie Sangam, 23 April 1981.

23. *Srujana*, May–June 1981, p. 74.

24. K. B., 'Indravelli 1985', p. 906.

25. For a detailed argument on this aspect, see Alpa Shah and Feyzi Ismail, 'Class Struggle, the Maoists and the Indigenous Question in Nepal and India', *Economic and Political Weekly* 50, no. 35 (29 August 2015).

26. Interview with Dr Thodasam Chandu in Adilabad town, 6 October 2008.

EPILOGUE

THE IDEA OF 'PERIPHERY' IN India is shaped and underwritten by narratives of wildness, empire-building, insurgency, migration, protectionism, and development. The Gonds, who had led a relatively autonomous life in the fringes of mainland India, were pushed to forest and hill areas by the empire-building and caste practices involved in statecraft. Their habitats were represented as peripheries by the imperial powers. However, the fact is that the fringe or periphery has been made and unmade throughout history through continuous struggles between the mainland or plains and the hill and forest areas. This book argues primarily that this periphery was produced in the encounter between the state and a stateless yet self-governing society. The material advancement of statist societies was the crucial contributing factor in the subjugation of self-governing societies which were materially less advanced. In response, the self-governing people evaded state subjugation and taxation by migrating further into deep forests and other non-state spaces.

Migration is generally a protest against the expansion of state territories. This is a phenomenon that may be observed also in early Indian history. Romila Thapar argues that 'the major form of peasant protest against oppressive taxes was not revolt but migration to new lands outside the control of the state to which the peasants belonged'.[1] By the early twentieth century, such evasion had been reduced to a minimum, since the colonial state had successfully sedentarized many communities. However, some communities in India continue to war against the state to retain their own spaces of self-rule, however small those may be.[2] Also, the peripheries witnessed subjugation when there were strong empires, and enjoyed autonomy and freedom with weaker empires and states. Thus, the relation between statist society and non-state societies varied from regime to regime. And in every case, it has been a designed and tactical political act.

As we have seen in the preceding chapters, the Gonds fought against many expanding empires in India. Even after state-making processes confined them to the Vindhya–Satpura hills in the centre of the Indian peninsula, they continued to contest alien authority and tried to preserve themselves as a self-ruling community in their respective territories. In other words—and this should be evident from this book—the adivasis of India are fundamentally political societies. The quest for self-governance led the Gonds to form their own states, often overcoming internal contests for power. The crest of the Chanda raja in which a griffin is seen overpowering an elephant metaphorically exemplifies their victory over empire, as the elephant represents the bigger empire and the lion with the head and wings of an eagle represents a smaller, self-ruled society.[3] Self-rule has been central to adivasi society and politics. Although the Chanda kingdom remained a largely independent periphery of the Mughal Empire, the Marathas conquered it in the middle of the eighteenth century and brought it completely under their control. However, the Gonds continued to evade imperial authority even as the Marathas populated Chanda country with caste-Hindu peasants, and often introduced new modes of agriculture. The Gonds then migrated to those areas where local Gond chiefs were politically strong, and which formed the periphery of British colonial rule.

This process of the making and unmaking of the periphery was induced again when the region was brought under complete British suzerainty around the middle of the nineteenth century. The Gond rajas fiercely resisted British expansion into the forests and hills. Realizing the impossibility of subduing the Gond rajas, the British drew them into the colonial establishment through treaties and agreements, and slowly made the Gond rajas in later periods powerless. Colonial rule successfully levelled the multiple sovereign powers that existed in pre-colonial India and made it possible to establish the colonial state as sovereign. It also channelled Gond subjugation through their chiefs and rajas. Importantly, by the end of colonial rule, Gond resistance to the state had almost ceased. Territories whose independence was recognized and had hitherto been termed peripheries were reconfigured under colonialism as zones of refugees, of uncivilized, primitive, violent, and rugged people. The land and people of the periphery were brought under an imperial civilizational mission by deploying a colonial political rationality and colonial modernity, and by encouraging caste-Hindu migration into the forest and hills. This forced the adivasis to flee further into the forests and hills. The colonial state thus endeavoured to civilize agriculture, administration, and people in the peripheries. However, this agenda was not carried out fully as the Gonds evaded it in many respects.

Sometimes even the Gonds adopted violent strategies—what Scott calls self-barbarization or self-primitivization—to evade the colonial state.[4] We do know, for example, that the Gonds drew on their traditional practices to check state expansion into the hills. If a ritual called for human sacrifice—as, for instance, the beginning of a hunt or a war or a raid—the sacrificial offering was often an intruder from the plains. This practice continued down into the nineteenth century and disappeared only with the intense persuasive effort of the colonial state. However, the practice—as myth and as metaphor—continued to haunt colonial administrators and plains people when they moved around in the forests and hills.[5]

A similar practice of headhunting was prevalent among the Nagas of north-east India and continued until the end of colonial rule. The Nagas hunt for enemies, take their heads, and hang them on the outskirts of their villages. Headhunting was considered heroic in Naga society. This feared practice also kept the colonial state at bay. It dared not enter certain Naga areas. Fürer-Haimendorf also writes about this in his autobiography:

> The system of sacred chiefs, particularly, seemed to be of considerable interest. Mills, who had been to the Konyak country agreed with me but pointed out that about half of the Konyak villages lay in unadministered territory

where headhunting was still rampant, and that I would not be permitted to enter that territory but would have to confine myself to the villages in the British territory. This left me still with a fairly large area for my research, and I was quite happy to promise Mills that I would not cross the border into the unadministered region.[6]

These practices, however, were eventually checked by the state, and the entire hill and forest area was brought under the state control. As we have seen in this book, it is difficult to draw a geographical and political boundary between the two societies, particularly from the British colonial period. There has also been cross-pollination of ideas and market interdependency between the two. But the divide continues to be imagined in the everyday experience of both caste-Hindus and the adivasis, often in terms of the opposition between civilized and uncivilized. The idea that adivasis love to live in isolation and to lead a rugged life is still dominant in the 'civilized', caste-Hindu world in India. This is partly because the history of India has been written from the vantage point of mainland India. Who writes history is then critically important. It reminds us of the well-known African proverb: 'Until the lion has a historian of his own, the tale of the hunt will always glorify the hunter.'

The fact is that the paradox between the two societies allows us to write neither a separate comprehensive history of mainland India nor a history of adivasi India. The history of mainland India and adivasi India are intertwined; one cannot understand the history of the periphery without understanding history of mainland India, and vice versa. Then, as Scott says, we have to read the history of the mainland and periphery one against the other to better understand them.[7] This study should have made it evident that adivasis did not live in complete isolation, nor did they coexist with the plains people of mainland India. It is also true that dominant Brahmanical values crept in, especially among the ruling groups. But we should note that long-established Gond political culture remains the foundation for such changes and adaptation. The Gond community in general was free of these values, although Gond rajas married Rajput women and employed non-Gonds in their statecraft. However, the dividing line between the *kaliparaj* (black people) and *ujliparaj* (white people) that was established with the advent of Aryans in India continued to hold.[8] But Gond interaction with caste-Hindu society did not substantially alter their social and cultural practices in other ways. One has to see these processes as politically designed strategies, rather than cultural assimilation or coexistence. In other words, the Gonds' socioeconomic and political relations with mainland India were politically designed programmes; they cannot be read as coexistence or assimilation. Rather, the relations between the two have been complex and full of tension, as evident from this study.

Adivasi life was largely one of resistance to domination by the state and the people of the plains. Their relative autonomy, resistance, and history of insurgency have been crucial in shaping their present-day life, which is therefore as modern as modern caste-Hindu civilization. The only difference is that adivasi civilization is historically founded on a philosophy of autonomy and freedom or self-rule, whereas the mainland Indian civilization of the plains is founded on caste, taxation, and subjugation. The fact that the memory of adivasi autonomy, self-rule, and periphery is now only folklore (and not history) marks the fact of that dominance. However, the folklore of autonomy or periphery is crucial for the articulation of their identity as aboriginal/adivasi in modern times. In other words, the agency to challenge state spaces comes from the folklore of the periphery or wildness or ruggedness. This is to say that autonomy can be reimagined to realize those lost non-state spaces in a limited way, or to create a space for self-determinism within the modern state. Let me end by quoting Jaipal Singh Munda's response to Jawaharlal Nehru during the Constituent Assembly debates:

> There is little you are offering us. The constitution is yours. The borders are yours. The sovereignty is yours. The flag is yours. What is ours? What is it that is both tribal and Indian in the constitution? What is the shared legacy, the common weave? You have defined rights, the isms, the industry, the science, let something be ours.[9]

NOTES

1. Romila Thapar, *From Lineage to State: Social Formations in the Mid-first Millennium B.C. in the Ganga Valley* (New Delhi: Oxford University Press, 1984), p. 163.
2. Alpa Shah illuminates how the Mundas have been asserting their political spaces in recent times in Jharkhand. See her "'Keeping the State

Away": Politics and the State in India's Jharkhand', *Journal of the Royal Anthropological Institute* 13, no. 1 (March 2007): 129–45.

3. I draw this conclusion from my discussion with Dr Shyamrao Koreti, a Gond professor in the Department of History, Nagpur University, Maharashtra, India.

4. James C. Scott, *The Art of Not Being Governed: An Anarchist History of Upland Southeast Asia.* (New Haven: Yale University Press, 2009), p. x.

5. Eyre Chatterton, *The Story of Gondwana* (London: Sir Isaac Pitman & Sons, 1916), pp. 123–8; also see Crispin Bates, 'Human Sacrifice in Colonial Central India: Myth, Agency and Representation', in *Beyond Representation: Colonial and Post-Colonial Construction of Indian Identity,* edited by Crispin Bates (New Delhi: Oxford University Press, 2006), pp. 19–54.

6. Christoph von Fürer-Haimendorf, *Life among Indian Tribes: The Autobiography of an Anthropologist* (New Delhi: Oxford University Press, 1990), p. 13.

7. Scott, *The Art of Not Being Governed*, p. 27.

8. Ajay Skaria, *Hybrid Histories: Forests, Frontiers and Wildness in Western India* (New Delhi: Oxford University Press, 1999), p. 40.

9. Quoted in Shiv Visvanathan, 'The Tribal World and the Imagination of the Future', Verrier Elwin Memorial Lecture, Vadodara, 11 April 2006, published by Bhasha Research Centre, Baroda, p. 8.

GLOSSARY

adivasi	aboriginal
amin	sub-inspector
angadi	weekly market
anna	sixteenth part of a rupee
assami	a peasant at a light rent
bahikhata	debt bond
Bania	trader
banjar	another term for *ijara*
barra baluti	a village system consisting of twelve service castes
bewar	shifting cultivation
bhari dhan	type of rice which takes a longer time to mature
bharmar bandooq	old-fashioned guns
bhumka	one who charms away tigers from people and cattle
boree	check dam
cauth	a tax collected from foreign territory by Maratha rulers
chaprasi	office attendant

chaturvarna	pertaining to the four *varnas*
chaukidar	watchman
chenna	pulses
chinna dora	local landlord
chironji	berries
darbar	public appearance of a raja or king
Dassera	a major Hindu festival
Deshmukh/Deshpande	traditional revenue collectors at the village level, also landlords
dewan	prime minister
dhya/khamori/ podu	shifting cultivation
diwani	government land
dumpa patti	plough tax
farman	government order or decree
fauj	army
firangi	cannon
gaddi	throne
Gaitas/Bhumias	traditional Gond village heads
gata	traditional Gond rice cultivation system without replanting
girdawar	a taluk-level revenue officer
Gond Raj	Gond self-rule
Goni	Bag
gudam	hamlet
halka dhan	type of rice which takes a shorter time to mature
haveli	surroundings
hazari	possessor of a thousand horses
ijara	land tenure system to bring forest/wasteland under cultivation
jagir	estate
jamdhar	a kind of dagger
jammi	*Prosopis cineraria* (tree)
janglat	forest official
jangli	forest people; wild
jatara	religious celebration

jowar	Sorghum
kala pani	backward and unhealthy areas
kaliparaj	black people
kamdar	servant
khalsa	government land or village
kharab	sandy
kharif	crop season (June–November)
killadar	keeper of the fort
koonda	big pot
laoni patta	land rights given on the basis of colonization rules
lathi	baton
mahal	a revenue unit of a group of villages
malguzar	owner of a malguzari village
malguzari	revenue tenure where the village is a unit of assessment
mamul	bribe
man	gifts paid by Gonds to their rajas
mansabdar	a military rank
maqta	land-cultivation rights with a fixed rent
maqtadar	head of *maqta* (estate)
maund	unit of weight, roughly 30 lb
mleccha/milakkha	indigenous tribes
mokhasi	Gond chief
muqaddam-gumashta	village clerk
naib	deputy tahsildar
nayaka	village chief
pahani/ parwana	paper deed
paledhar	tenant
Pardhan	Gond storyteller
pargana	a territorial division above village
patel	village head
patta	paper deed to land
pattadar	holder of paper deed to land
patwari	village clerk
pedda dora	big landlord

pen	god
Persa Pen	the great God of the Gonds
podu	shifting cultivation
Porkala Dora	Lord of the Bushes
Ragal Jhanda	red flag
raisabha	village council
regar	black soil
ryot	peasant
ryotwari	land revenue tenure under the British
sahukar	trader or moneylender
sanad	government order
saredar	a taluk-level revenue officer
sarkar	a revenue division in Mughal India
sarpech	ornament worn on the front of a turban
saz	ornament
seer	approximately 1 kilogram
shastra	religious text
swadeshi	aboriginal
tahsil	an administrative subdivision of a district
takoli	tribute paid by a subordinate chief to the paramount power
taluk	an administrative division of a district
talukdar	the head of a taluk (district division)
tarvel	Gond warrior
teeka	a *tilak*-like mark
thakkavi	crop loans
thudum	Gond drumbeat
tilak	vermillion applied on the forehead by Hindus
ujliparaj	white people
vakil	advocate or lawyer
vanavasi	forest dweller
wardi	sandy soil or light coloured soil
watan	revenue collection right
watandar	revenue collector at the village level
zamindari	land or estate given to a landlord

BIBLIOGRAPHY

MANUSCRIPT SOURCES

India Office Library, London, United Kingdom

India Political Collection
Board's Collections
Hislop's Papers
Jenkins Private Papers

Vidarbha Archives, Nagpur, Maharashtra, India

Political and Military Department
Revenue Department
Survey and Settlement
Nagpur Residency Records

Andhra Pradesh State Archives, Hyderabad, Telangana, India

Home Department Files
Revenue Department Files

CENSUS REPORTS

Census of India 1891, vol. XI: *The Central Provinces and Feudatories*, Part I: *Report*. Calcutta: Superintendent of Government Printing, 1893.

Census of India 1911, vol. X: *Central Provinces and Berar*, Part I: *Report*. Calcutta: Superintendent Government Printing, 1912.

Census of India 1921, vol. XI: *Central Provinces and Berar*, Part I: *Report*. Nagpur: Government Press, 1923.

Census of India 1931, vol. XII: *Central Provinces and Berar*, Part I. Nagpur: Government Printing C.P., 1933.

Census of India 1901, vol. XXII: *Hyderabad*, Part I: *Report*. Hyderabad-Deccan: A. V. Pillai & Sons, 1901.

Census of India 1921, vol. XXI: *Hyderabad State*, Part I. Hyderabad-Deccan: Government Central Press, 1923.

Census of India 1931, vol. XXII: *H.E.H. the Nizam's Dominions (Hyderabad State)*, Part I. Hyderabad-Deccan: Government Central Press, 1933.

Census of India 1941, vol. XXI: *H.E.H. the Nizam's Dominions (Hyderabad State)*, Part I: *Report*. Hyderabad-Deccan: Government Central Press, 1945.

Census of India 1961, vol. II: *Andhra Pradesh*, Part V B(I): *Ethnographic Notes: A Monograph on Gonds*. Hyderabad: Director of Census Operation, A.P.

GAZETTEERS

Andhra Pradesh District Gazetteers, Adilabad. Hyderabad: Government Central Press, 1976.

Central Provinces District Gazetteers, Chanda District. Allahabad: Pioneer Press, 1909.

Gazetteer of the Central Provinces of India, by Charles Grant. 1870.

Hyderabad District Gazetteers: Adilabad District Tables Volume, 1931–1936. Hyderabad-Deccan: Government Central Press, 1940.

Imperial Gazetteer of India, Provincial Series, Hyderabad. Calcutta: Superintendent of Government Printing, 1909.

Maharashtra State Gazetteers: Chandrapur District. Bombay: Government of Maharashtra, 1973.

PUBLISHED GOVERNMENT REPORTS

Administration Report of the Forest Department of H.E.H. the Nizam's Dominions for the Year 1348F (1939). Hyderabad-Deccan: Government Central Press, 1940.

Administration Report of the Forest Department of His Highness the Nizam's Dominions for the Year 1319F (7 October 1909–6 October 1910). Hyderabad-Deccan: A. V. Pillai & Sons, 1912.

Administration Report of the Forest Department of His Highness the Nizam's Dominions for the Year 1315F (1905–6). Andhra Pradesh State Archives, R-22.

Agricultural Statistics: Notes and Estimates of Area and Yield of Principal Crops in Hyderabad State from 1935–36 to 1939–40. Hyderabad-Deccan: Government Central Press, 1942.

Ali, Maulavi Said Mohdi. *Report on the History of the Famine H. H. the Nizam's Dominions in 1877–77, 1877–78.* Bombay: Exchange Press, 1879.

Annual Progress Report of Forest Administration in His Highness the Nizam's Dominions for the Year 1309F (7 October 1899–6 October 1900). Hyderabad-Deccan: A. V. Pillai & Sons, 1901.

Central Provinces and Berar: A Review of the Administration of the Province 1921–1922. Nagpur: Superintendent Government Printing, 1923.

Central Provinces and Berar: A Review of the Administration of the Province 1934–35, vol. II. Nagpur: Superintendent Government Printing, 1936.

The Central Provinces Court of Wards Manual. Nagpur: Secretariat Press, 1902.

The Central Provinces Land Revenue Act 1881 (XVIII of 1881) (as Modified up to the 1st March 1909). Calcutta: Superintendent Government Printing, 1909.

Craddock, R. H. *Report on the Famine in the Central Provinces in 1899–1900.* Nagpur: Secretariat Press, 1901.

Early European Travellers in the Nagpur Territories: Reprinted from Old Records. Nagpur: Government Press, 1930.

Final Report on the Land Revenue Settlement of the Chanda District in the Central Provinces, Effected during the Years 1897–1906. IOR/W/1429, British Library, London.

Final Report on the Re-settlement of the Siraoncha and Garchiroli Tahsils of the Chanda District in the Central Province during the Years 1922–24. Nagpur: Government Press, 1926.

Final Report on the Re-settlement of the Three Cis-Wainganga Tahsils of the Chanda District in the Central Provinces. Nagpur: Government Press, 1924.

The Framing of India's Constitution: Select Documents, vol. III. New Delhi: Indian Institute of Public Administration, 1968.

The Hyderabad Forest Conference 1332F (1922–3). Hyderabad-Deccan: Government Central Press. Andhra Pradesh State Archives, R-22.

The Indian Forest Act, 1878 (VII of 1878). As Modified up to the 1st December, 1902. Calcutta: Superintendent of Government Printing, 1903.

Progress Report on Forest Administration in the Central Provinces 1863–64. Calcutta: Public Works Department Press, 1865.

Progress Report on Forest Administration in the Central Provinces for the Year 1865–66. Calcutta: Public Works Department Press, 1867.

Progress Report on Forest Administration in the Central Provinces 1866–67. Calcutta: Public Works Department Press, 1867.

Progress Report on Forest Administration in the Central Provinces 1867–68 & 1868–69. Calcutta: Public Works Department Press, 1870.

Rajkumar College Raipur Annual Report, 1936–37. Calcutta: Catholic Orphan Press, n.d.

Report of the Department of Land Records and Agriculture, Central Provinces, for the Year 1901–02 Ending 31st March 1902. Nagpur: Secretariat Press, 1903.

Report of the Department of Land Records and Agriculture, Central Provinces, for the Year 1911–12. Nagpur: Government Press, 1912.

Report of the Department of Land Records and Agriculture, Central Provinces, for the Year 1913–14. Nagpur: Government Press, 1915.

Report of the Department of Land Records and Agriculture, Central Provinces, for the Year 1914–15. Nagpur: Government Press, 1915.

Report of the Department of Land Records and Agriculture, Central Provinces, for the Year 1915–16. Nagpur: Government Press, 1916.

Report of the Department of Land Records and Agriculture, Central Provinces, for the Year 1917–18. Nagpur: Government Press, 1918.

Report of the Ethnological Committee on Papers Laid before Them and upon Examination of Specimens of Aboriginal Tribes Brought to the Jubblepore Exhibition of 1866–67. Nagpur: Chief Commissioner's Office Press, 1868.

Report of the Royal Commission on Jagir Administration and Reforms H.E.H the Nizam's Government 1356F (1945–6). Bangalore: Bangalore Press, 1947.

Report on the Administration of the Central Provinces for the Year 1900–1901. Nagpur: Secretariat Press, 1901.

Report on the Administration of the Central Provinces for the Year 1901–1902. Nagpur: Secretariat Press, 1902.

Report on the Administration of H.E.H. the Nizam's Dominions for the Year 1331F (6th Oct. 1921 to 5th Oct. 1922). Hyderabad-Deccan: Government Central Press, 1925.

Report on the Administration of His Highness the Nizam's Dominions for the Year 1294F (1884–1885). Bombay: Times of India Press, 1886.

Report on the Administration of His Highness the Nizam's Dominions for the Year 1308F to 1312F (7th October 1898 to 6 October 1903). Hyderabad-Deccan: A. V. Pillai & Sons, Government Printers, 1907.

Report on the Administration of His Highness the Nizam's Dominions for the Year 1322F (6 October 1912–5 October 1913). Hyderabad-Deccan: A. V. Pillai & Sons, at the Gladstone Press, 1915.

Report on the Administration of the Revenue and Allied Department of H.H. the Nizam's Government for 1324F (1914–15). Hyderabad-Deccan: Gladstone Press, 1916.

Report on the Forest Administration of the Central Provinces for the Year 1923–24. Nagpur: Government Press, 1925.

Report on the Forest Administration of the Central Provinces for the Year 1924–25. Nagpur: Government Press, 1926.

Report on the Forest Administration of the Central Provinces for the Year 1925–26. Nagpur: Government Press, 1927.

Report on the Forest Administration of the Central Provinces for the Year 1926–27. Nagpur: Central Government Press, 1928.

Report on the Forest Administration of the Central Provinces for the Year Ending 31 March 1932. Nagpur: Government Press, 1933.

Report on the Nagpur Experimental Farm in the Central Provinces for the Year 1897–98, Ending 31st March, 1898. Allahabad: Pioneer Press, 1898.

Report on the Working of the Department of Agriculture of the Central Provinces for the Year 1919–20. Nagpur: Government Press, 1920.

Report on the Working of the Department of Agriculture of the Central Provinces for the Year Ending 31 March 1932 and 31 March 1933. Nagpur: Government Press, 1933.

Report on the Working of the Department of Agriculture of the Central Provinces and Berar for the Year Ending 31 March 1940. Nagpur: Government Press, 1941.

Revenue Administration Report of HEH the Nizam's Government, 1914–15. Hyderabad: Gladstone Press, 1916.

Selection from the Nagpur Residency Records, 1799–1806, vol. I, compiled by H. N. Sinha. Nagpur: Government Printing, M.P., 1950.

Smith, C. B. Lucie. *Report on Land Revenue Settlement of the Chanda District, Central Provinces.* Nagpur: Chief Commissioner's Press, 1870.

Statistical Abstract HEH the Nizam's Dominions, from 1321F–1330F (1911–21). Hyderabad-Deccan, Government Central Press, 1925.

Statistical Abstract of H.E.H. the Nizam's Dominion from 1331F to 1340F (1922–31). Hyderabad-Deccan: Government Central Press, 1938.

Statistical Abstract of H.E.H. the Nizam's Dominion from 1351F to 1355F (1941–5). Hyderabad-Deccan: Government Central Press, 1946.

Stephen Hislop's Papers Relating to the Aboriginal Tribes of the Central Provinces. IOR/F/4/755/20541, British Library, London.

Social Service among the Tribes and Backward Class in Hyderabad. Hyderabad: Government Press, 1951.

SECONDARY SOURCES

Aberigh-Mackay, G. R. *The Chiefs of Central India*, vol. 1. Calcutta: Thacker, Spink, and Co., 1878.

Abul Faz, Allami. *The Ain-i-Akbari*, translated by H. S. Jarrett, vol. 2. Calcutta: Baptist Mission Press, 1891.

'Another Massacre of Tribals'. *Economic and Political Weekly*, Special Report, 16, no. 18 (2 May 1981): 796–7.

Arnold, David, and Ramachandra Guha, eds. *Nature, Culture, Imperialism: Essays on the Environmental History of South Asia*. New Delhi: Oxford University Press, 1995.

Baker, D. E. U. *Colonialism in an Indian Hinterland: The Central Provinces, 1820–1920*. New Delhi: Oxford University Press, 1993.

Bates, Crispin. 'Human Sacrifice in Colonial Central India: Myth, Agency and Representation'. In *Beyond Representation: Colonial and Post-Colonial Constructions of Indian Identity*, edited by Crispin Bates, pp. 19–54. New Delhi: Oxford University Press, 2006.

Bayly, Susan. *Caste Society and Politics in India: From the Eighteenth Century to the Modern Age*. Cambridge: Cambridge University Press, 1999.

Béteille, André. *Caste, Class and Power: Changing Patterns of Stratification in a Tanjore Village*. New Delhi: Oxford University Press, 1971.

———. 'The Concept of Tribe with Special Reference to India'. *European Journal of Sociology* 27, no. 2 (1986): 297–318.

———. 'The Concept of Tribe with Special Reference to India'. In *Indian Tribes and the Mainstream*, edited by Sukant K. Chaudhury and S. M. Patnaik, pp. 21–44. Lucknow: Rawat Publications, 2008.

———. 'The Idea of Indigenous People'. *Current Anthropology* 39, no. 2 (April 1988): 187–92.

———. 'On the Concept of the Tribe'. *International Social Science Journal* 34, no. 41 (1980): 825–45.

———. 'Tribe and Peasantry'. In *Six Essays in Comparative Sociology*, pp. 60–81. New Delhi: Oxford University Press, 1974.

Bhattacharya, Neeladri. 'Pastoralists in a Colonial World'. In *Nature, Culture, Imperialism: Essays on the Environmental History of South Asia*, edited by David Arnold and Ramachandra Guha, pp. 49–85. New Delhi: Oxford University Press, 1995.

Bhukya, Bhangya. 'The Mapping of the Adivasi Social: Colonial Anthropology and Adivasis'. *Economic and Political Weekly* 43, no. 39 (27 September 2008): 103–9.

———. *Subjugated Nomads: The Lambadas under the Rule of the Nizams*. New Delhi: Orient BlackSwan, 2010.

Bhutia, Lhendup G. 'The Eternal Harappan Script Tease'. *Open* (8 December 2014): 40–5.

Briggs, Lieutenant-General. 'Two Lectures on the Aboriginal Race of India, as Distinguished from the Sanskritic or Hindu Race'. *Journal of the Royal Asiatic Society of Great Britain and Ireland* 13 (1857): 275–309.

Buchanan, Francis. *A Journey from Madras through the Countries of Mysore, Canara and Malabar*, 3 vols. London: printed by Fort Cadell and W. Davies, and Black Parry and Kingsbury, 1807.

Casimir, Michael J., and Aparna Rao. 'The Historical Framework of Nomadism in South Asia: A Brief Overview'. In *Nomadism in South Asia*, edited by Aparna Rao and Michael J. Casimir, pp. 43–72. New Delhi: Oxford University Press, 2003.

Chatterton, Eyre. *The Story of Gondwana*. London: Sir Isaac Pitman & Sons, 1916.

Damodaran, Vinita, 'Colonial Constructions of the "Tribes" in India: The Case of Chotanagpur'. In *Adivasis in Colonial India: Survival, Resistance and Negotiation*, edited by Biswamoy Pati, pp. 55–87. New Delhi: Orient BlackSwan, 2011.

Das Gupta, Sanjukta. *Adivasis and the Raj: Socio-economic Transition of the Hos, 1820–1932*. New Delhi: Orient BlackSwan, 2011.

Dhanagare, D. N. 'Subaltern Consciousness and Populism: Two Approaches in the Study of Social Movements in India'. *Social Scientist* 16, no. 11 (November 1988): 18–35.

Dirks, Nicholas B. *Castes of Mind: Colonialism and the Making of Modern India*. New Delhi: Permanent Black, 2002.

———. *The Hollow Crown: Ethnohistory of an Indian Kingdom*. Ann Arbor: University of Michigan Press, 1993.

Diviti, Anjana Devi. *Sammakka Saralamma Jatara Sahitya Samskritika Amshalu* (Telugu). Karimnagar: Anilasai Prachuranlu, 2006.

Doniger, Wendy, and Bardwell Smith, eds. *Laws of Manu*. New Delhi: Penguin Books, 1991.

Dove, Michael R., Hjorleifur Jonsson, and Michael Aung-Thwin. 'Debate: The Art of Not Being Governed: An Anarchist History of Upland Southeast Asia by James C Scott'. *Bijdragen tot de taal- Land- en Volkenkunde* [*Journal of the Humanities and Social Sciences of Southeast Asia*] 167, no. 1 (2011): 86–99.

Eaton, Richard M. *The New Cambridge History of India, A Social History of the Deccan, 1300–1761: Eight Indian Lives*. New York: Cambridge University Press, 2005.

Elwin, Verrier. *Folk-Songs of Chhattisgarh*. Madras: Oxford University Press, 1946.

———. *Maria Murder and Suicide*. London, 1943.

Ferishta, Mahomed Kasim. *History of the Rise of the Mahomedan Power in India till the Year A.D. 1612*, translated by John Briggs, 4 vols. New Delhi: Oriental Book Reprint Corporation, 1981 [1829].

Forsyth, J. *The Highlands of Central India*. Dehra Dun: Natraj, 1994 [1871].

The Freedom Struggle in Hyderabad: A Connected Account, 1857–1885, vol. 2. Hyderabad, 1956.

Ghurye, G. S., *The Scheduled Tribes*. Bombay: Popular Prakashan, 1959.

Grigson, W. V. *The Aboriginal Problem in the Central Provinces and Berar*. Nagpur: Government Printing, 1944.

———. *The Challenge of Backwardness*. Hyderabad-Deccan: Government Press, 1947.

Guha, Ramachandra. 'Savaging the Civilised: Verrier Elwin and the Tribal Question in Late Colonial India'. *Economic and Political Weekly* 31, no. 35 (1996): 2375–89.

Guha, Ranajit. *Elementary Aspects of Peasant Insurgency in Colonial India*. New Delhi: Oxford University Press, 1983.

———. 'On Some Aspects of the Historiography of Colonial India'. In *Subaltern Studies I: Writings on South Asian History and Society*, edited by Ranajit Guha, pp. 1–8. New Delhi: Oxford University Press, 1994.

Gupta, G. S. 'Gonduwari Avedana'. *Golkonda Patrika*, 3 July 1941 and 7 July 1941.

Habib, Irfan. *The Agrarian System of Mughal India 1556–1707*. New Delhi: Oxford University Press,1999.

———. *An Atlas of the Mughal Empire*. New Delhi: Oxford University Press, 1982.

Hardiman, David. *The Coming of the Devi: Adivasi Assertion in Western India*. New Delhi: Oxford University Press, 1987.

———. *Feeding the Baniya: Peasants and Usurers in Western India*. New Delhi: Oxford University Press, 1996.

———. *Missionaries and Their Medicine: A Christian Modernity for Tribal India*. Manchester: Manchester University Press, 2008.

———. 'Power in the Forest: The Dangs, 1820–1940'. In *Subaltern Studies VIII: Essays in Honour of Ranajit Guha*, edited by David Arnold and David Hardiman, pp. 89–147. New Delhi: Oxford University Press, 1994.

Inden, Ronald. *Imagining India*. Oxford: Blackwell, 1992.

Jenkins, Richard. *Report on the Territories of the Rajah of Nagpur*. Nagpur: Government Press, 1925 [1827].

Jenkins, Laura Dudley. 'Another "People of India" Project: Colonial and National Anthropology'. *Journal of Asian Studies* 62, no. 4 (November 2003): 1143–70.

Jones, Kenneth W. *Socio-Religious Reform Movements in British India*. Cambridge: Cambridge University Press, 1989.

Kambhampati, Satyanarayana. *A Study of the History and Culture of the Andhras*, vol. 2. New Delhi: People's Publishing House, 1983.

Kangali, M. C. *Decipherment of Indus Script in Gondi* (Hindi). Nagpur, 2002.

———. *A Study of the History and Culture of the Andhras*, vol. 1. Hyderabad: Visalandhra Publishing House, 1999.

K. B. 'Indravelli 1985'. *Economic and Political Weekly* 20, no. 21 (25 May 1985): 906–7.

Kela, Shashank. *A Rogue and Peasant Slave: Adivasi Resistance 1800–2000*. New Delhi: Navayana, 2012.

Khan, Saqi Mustad. *Maasir-i-Alamgiri: A History of the Emperor Aurangzib-Alamgir (Reign 1658–1707 AD)*. Delhi: Oriental Books Reprint Corporation, 1986 [1947].

Kodanda Ram, M. 'Retrogression in the Tribal Belt: Bhurnur in Adilabad District'. *Kakatiya University Journal of Social Sciences* 3, no. 1 (January–June 2007): 1–18.

Kosambi, D. D. *An Introduction to the Study of Indian History*. Bombay: Popular Prakashan, 1956.

Kurup, Apoorv. 'Tribal Law in India: How Decentralised Administration Is Extinguishing Tribal Rights and Why Autonomous Tribal Governments Are Better'. *Indigenous Law Journal* 7, no. 1 (2008): 87–126.

Ludden, David, ed. *Reading Subaltern Studies: Critical History, Contested Meaning and the Globalization of South Asia*. London: Anthem, 2002.

Mayaram, Shail. *Against History, Against State: Counterperspectives from the Margins*. New Delhi: Permanent Black, 2004.

Miri, Mrinal. *Continuity and Change in Tribal Society*. Shimla: Indian Institute of Advanced Study, 1993.

Mishra, Suresh. *The Gond Kingdom of Deogarh*. New Delhi: Manak Publications, 2011.

Narayana Reddy, Madhadi. *Ankama Raju Katha: Kolata Patalu* [Story of Ankama Raju: Stick Play Songs] (Telugu). Hanmakonda: Rainbow Printers, 2001.

Nathan, Dev, ed. *From Tribe to Caste*. Shimla: Indian Institute of Advance Study, 1997.

Pagdi, Setumadhava Rao. *Among the Gonds of Adilabad*. Bombay: Popular Book Depot, 1949.

———. 'Land Problems of Adilabad Aboriginals'. *Indian Journal of Social Work* 9, no. 1 (June 1948–9): 17–29.

Panchbhai, S. C., and M. K. A. Siddiqui, eds. *Acculturation and Social Change in India: An Interdisciplinary Appraisal*. Calcutta: Anthropological Survey of India, 1989.

Parasher, Aloka. *Mlecchas in Early India*. Delhi: Munshiram Manoharlal, 1991.

Pati Biswamoy. 'Introduction'. In *Adivasis in Colonial India: Survival, Resistance and Negotiation*, edited by Biswamoy Pati, pp. 1–27. New Delhi: Orient BlackSwan, 2011.

Perishta, Mahomed Kasim. *History of the Rise of the Mahomedan Power in India*, edited by John Briggs, 4 vols. New Delhi: Oriental Books Reprint Corporation, 1981 [1829].

Prakash, Amit. 'Decolonisation and Tribal Policy in Jharkhand: Continuities with Colonial Discourse'. *Social Scientist* 27, nos 7–8 (July–August 1999): 113–39.

Prasad, Archana. *Against Ecological Romanticism: Verrier Elwin and the Making of an Anti-modern Tribal Identity*. New Delhi: Three Essays Collective, 2003.

Radhakrishna, Meena. 'Of Apes and Ancestors: Evolutionary Science and Colonial Ethnography'. In *Adivasis in Colonial India: Survival, Resistance and Negotiation*, edited by Biswamoy Pati, pp. 31–54. New Delhi: Orient BlackSwan, 2011.

Raghavaiah, V. R. 'Background of Tribal Struggles in India'. In *Peasant Struggle in India*, edited by A. R. Desai, pp. 12–27. New Delhi: Oxford University Press, 1979.

Raghuram, M. 'Carnage at Indravelli: A Report'. *Economic and Political Weekly* 16, no. 24 (1981): 1047–50.

Rangarajan, Mahesh. *Fencing the Forest: Conservation and Ecological Change in India's Central Provinces 1860–1914*. New Delhi: Oxford University Press, 1996.

Rao, B. Janardhan, and T. Yadagiri Rao. 'Land Transfers, Restoration in Tribal Andhra Pradesh: Justice Delayed and Denied'. In *Scheduled Tribes and Social Justice*. Secunderabad: A.P. Judicial Academy, 1996.

Rao, Jaswanth. 'Tribal Struggle against Land Alienation'. *Economic and Political Weekly* 33, no. 31 (17–23 January 1998): 81.

Ratnagar, Shereen. *Being Tribal*. Delhi: Primus Books, 2010.

Reddy, V. Ramakrishna. *Economic History of Hyderabad State: Warangal Subha 1911–1950*. Delhi: Gian Publication House, 1987.

Russell, R. V., and Hiralal. *The Tribes and Castes of the Central Provinces of India*, 4 vols. New Delhi: Asian Educational Services, 1993 [1916].

Saha, Suranjit K. 'Early State Formation in Tribal Areas of East-Central India'. *Economic and Political Weekly* 31, no. 13 (1996): 824–34.

Sahu and Allam Rajaiah, *Komaram Bhim* (Telugu). Hyderabad: Revolutionary Writers Association, 1993.

Said, Edward W. *Orientalism: Western Conceptions of the Orient*. London: Penguin, 1995.

Sardesai, Govind Sakharam. *New History of the Marathas: The Expansion of the Maratha Power 1707–1772*, 2 vols. New Delhi: Munshiram Manoharlal, 1986 [1946–8].

Sarkar, Jadunath. *A Short History of Aurangzib*. Calcutta: Orient Longman, 1979 [1930].

Sastri, B. N. *Andhra Desa Charitra Samskruti from 1518 to 1990* [History and Culture of the Andhra Country from 1518 to 1990] (Telugu). Hyderabad: Musee Publication, 1990.

Sastry, P. V. Parabrahma. *The Kakatiyas of Warangal*. Hyderabad: Government of Andhra Pradesh, 1978.

Scott, James C. *The Art of Not Being Governed: An Anarchist History of Upland Southeast Asia*. New Haven: Yale University Press, 2009.

Shah, Alpa. 'The Dark Side of Indigeneity: Indigenous People, Rights and Development in India'. *History Compass* 5, no. 6 (November 2007): 1806–32.

———. 'Keeping the State Away: Politics and the State in India's Jharkhand'. *Journal of the Royal Anthropological Institute* 13, no. 1 (March 2007): 129–45.

———. 'Religion and the Secular Left: Subaltern Studies, Birsa Munda and Maoists'. Available at http://aotcpress.com/author/alpa-shah/ (last accessed 13 January 2014).

Shah, Alpa, and Feyzi Ismail. 'Class Struggle, the Maoists and the Indigenous Question in Nepal and India'. *Economic and Political Weekly* 50, no. 35 (29 August 2015): 112–23.

Simkins, Ethel. *The Agricultural Geography of the Deccan Plateau of India*. London: George Philip & Sons, 1926.

Singh, Chetan. 'Forests, Pastoralists and Agrarian Society in Mughal India'. In *Nature, Culture, Imperialism: Essays on the Environmental History of South Asia*, edited by David Arnold and Ramachandra Guha, pp. 21–48. New Delhi: Oxford University Press, 1995.

Singh, K. Suresh, ed. *Jawaharlal Nehru, Tribes and Tribal Policy*. Calcutta: Anthropological Survey of India, 1989.

————, ed. *The Mahabharata in the Tribal and Folk Traditions of India*. Shimla: Indian Institute of Advanced Study, 1993.

————, ed. *Tribal Movements in India*, vols 1–2. New Delhi: Manohar, 1982–3.

————, ed. *The Tribal Situation in India*. Shimla: Indian Institute of Advanced Study, 1972.

Skaria, Ajay. *Hybrid Histories: Forests, Frontiers and Wildness in Western India*. New Delhi: Oxford University Press, 1999.

Sleeman, W. H. *Rambles and Recollections of an Indian Official*, 2 vols. London: Archibald Constable and Company, 1893.

Srinivas, M. N. *Social Change in Modern India*. New Delhi: Oriental Longman, 2001 [1966].

Subrahmanyam, Sanjay. 'The View from the Top'. *London Review of Books* 32, no. 23 (2 December 2010): 25–6.

Sundar, Nandini. *Subalterns and Sovereigns: An Anthropological History of Bastar 1854–1996*. New Delhi: Oxford University Press, 1997.

Thapar, Romila. *From Lineage to State: Social Formations in the Mid-first Millennium B.C. in the Ganga Valley*. New Delhi: Oxford University Press, 1984.

Thusu, Kidar Nath. *Gond Kingdom of Chanda, with Particular Reference to Its Political Structure*. Calcutta: Anthropological Survey of India, 1980.

Vadivelu, A. *The Ruling Chiefs, Nobles & Zamindars of India*, vol. 1. Madras: Guardian Press, 1915.

V. G. 'Tendu Leaf Labourers in Telangana: Working Conditions and Struggle'. *Economic and Political Weekly* 19, no. 46 (17 November 1984): 1941–3.

Visvanathan, Shiv. 'The Tribal World and the Imagination of the Future'. Verrier Elwin Memorial Lecture, Vadodara, 11 April 2006. Published by Bhasha Research Centre, Baroda.

von Fürer-Haimendorf, Christoph. *Life among Indian Tribes: The Autobiography of an Anthropologist*. New Delhi: Oxford University Press, 1990.

————. *The Raj Gonds of Adilabad: A Peasant Culture of the Deccan*. London: Macmillan, 1948.

————. *Tribal Hyderabad: Four Reports*. Hyderabad: Revenue Department, Government of H.E.H. the Nizam, 1945.

————. 'Tribal Population of Hyderabad Yesterday and Today'. In *Census of India 1941*, vol. XXI: *H.E.H. the Nizam's Dominions (Hyderabad State)*, Part I: *Report*, pp. i–liii. Hyderabad-Deccan: Government Central Press, 1945.

————, ed. *Tribes of India: The Struggle for Survival*. New Delhi: Oxford University Press, 1989.

von Fürer-Haimendorf, Christoph (in collaboration with Elizabeth von Fürer-Haimendorf). *The Gonds of Andhra Pradesh: Tradition and Change in an Indian Tribe.* New Delhi: Vikas, 1979.

Wills, C. U. *The Raj-Gond Maharajas of the Satpura Hills, The Central Provinces.* Nagpur: Government Press, 1923.

Wink, Andre. *Land and Sovereignty in India: Agrarian Society and Politics under the Eighteenth-Century Maratha Svarajya.* Cambridge: Cambridge University Press, 1986.

Yorke, Michael. 'The Situation of the Gonds of Asifabad and Lakshetipet Taluks, Adilabad District'. In *Tribes of India: The Struggle for Survival,* edited by Christoph von Fürer-Haimendorf, pp. 203–49. New Delhi: Oxford University Press, 1989.

Xaxa, Virginius. *State, Society and Tribes: Issues in Post-Colonial India.* New Delhi: Pearson Longman, 2008.

JOURNALS AND NEWSPAPERS

Golkunda Patrika (Telugu daily)
Pamphlets by Radical Students Union and Radical Youth Union
Pamphlets, Girijana Rythu Coolie Sangam
Srujana (Telugu literary monthly journal)
Vishalandra (Telugu daily newspaper)

UNPUBLISHED DOCUMENTS

Rao, C. Sivaramkrishna, K. Murali Manohar, K. Seetaram Rao, and B. Janardhan Rao. 'Report of the Project on Political Economy of Tribal Development in Andhra Pradesh'. Unpublished report, Indian Council of Social Science Research, New Delhi, 1988.

INTERVIEWS

Atram Laxmana Rao, age 56, Gond political leader and activist from Modi (Adilabad). Interviewed on 25 January 2015.

Dr Gondraje Atram Bir Shah, age 60, brother of the last raja of Chanda, now involved in Gond social activities based at Warora town of Chandrapur. Interviewed on 22 February 2015.

Mesram Somji, age 70, a Pardhan who acts as storyteller to the Gonds and also worked for the last Utnur raja. Retired Tribal Welfare Hostel Warden, Marlavai. Interviewed in Utnur on 14 June 2013.

Mesram Manohar, age 50, a Pardhan college lecturer in Utnur. Interviewed on 15 June 2014 and 18 November 2014.

Prof. Murali Manohar Rao, age 65, Kakatiya University, member of Fact-Finding Committee of PUDR on the Indravelli incident. Interviewed in Hyderabad on 14 January 2015.

Dr Thodasam Chandu, age 52, a Gond doctor from Adilabad town. Interviewed on 6 October 2008.

INDEX

ABOUT THE AUTHOR

Bhangya Bhukya is Associate Professor of History at the University of Hyderabad, India. Previously he has served as Associate Professor at the English and Foreign Languages University, Hyderabad, and as Assistant Professor at Osmania University, Hyderabad.

Dr Bhukya has specialized in modern Indian history from the undergraduate to the master's level, and has in the process developed a strong interest in the history of subaltern and marginalized groups whose history is largely neglected in mainstream history. He did his MA and MPhil from Hyderabad Central University, India, and his PhD from the University of Warwick, UK, on a Ford Foundation International Fellowship.

He was Postdoctoral Fellow at SOAS, University of London, in 2010 on a British Council Visiting Fellowship. His research interests include community histories, the effects of power/knowledge, governmentality, and dominance on subaltern communities, particularly *adivasi*s (indigenous people); the state and nationalism, and identity movements among forest and hill peoples in the nineteenth and twentieth centuries.

Dr Bhukya is also associated with adivasi human rights organizations in Deccan India. Among his recent publications are *Subjugated Nomads: The Lambadas under the Rule of Nizams* (2010) and several articles in leading international social science journals.